Durkheim and After

Durkheim and After

The Durkheimian Tradition, 1893–2020

Philip Smith

polity

First published in 2020 by Polity Press

Polity Press
65 Bridge Street
Cambridge CB2 1UR, UK

Polity Press
101 Station Landing
Suite 300
Medford, MA 02155, USA

ISBN-13: 978-1-5095-1827-2
ISBN-13: 978-1-5095-1828-9 (pb)

All images reproduced courtesy of Davy, Georges. n.d. (c.1911). *Émile Durkheim: choix de textes avec étude du système sociologique*. Paris. Éditions Louis-Michaud.

A catalogue record for this book is available from the British Library.

Library of Congress Cataloging-in-Publication Data
Names: Smith, Philip (Philip Daniel), 1964- author.
Title: Durkheim and after : the Durkheimian tradition, 1893-2020 / Philip Smith.
Description: Cambridge ; Medford, MA : Polity, 2020. | Includes bibliographical references and index. | Summary: "In this book, Philip Smith examines not only Émile Durkheim's founding texts of sociology, but also reveals how he inspired more than a century of theoretical innovations, identifying the key paths, bridges, and dead ends -- as well as the tensions and resolutions -- in what has been a remarkably complex intellectual history"-- Provided by publisher.
Identifiers: LCCN 2019027623 (print) | LCCN 2019027624 (ebook) | ISBN 9781509518272 (hardback) | ISBN 9781509518289 (paperback) | ISBN 9781509518319 (epub)
Subjects: LCSH: Durkheim, Émile, 1858-1917. | Durkheim, Émile, 1858-1917--Influence. | Durkheimian school of sociology. | Sociologists--France--Biography. | Sociology--History.
Classification: LCC HM479.D87 S54 2020 (print) | LCC HM479.D87 (ebook) | DDC 301.092 [B]--dc23
LC record available at https://lccn.loc.gov/2019027623
LC ebook record available at https://lccn.loc.gov/2019027624

Typeset in 10.5 on 12 pt Sabon by
Servis Filmsetting Ltd, Stockport, Cheshire
Printed and bound in Great Britain by TJ International Limited

For further information on Polity, visit our website:
politybooks.com

Contents

Preface and Acknowledgments

There have been many books about Durkheim and his works, especially for the crucial period from about 1893 to 1917. This one is different. It looks at Durkheim and also the long Durkheimian tradition in social thought. It looks at lineages and connections and covers the span of around one hundred and thirty years of published scholarship from 1893 to 2020. It is at once an introduction, a review, a critical commentary, and a narrative about how things unfolded. To date this is the first book-length effort to attempt this task.

We move fast and I offer basic cultural literacy in a relatively short text. I hope that in around two hundred pages this book gives readers a sense of the terrain. About one-third of the material is on Durkheim himself. It covers his main contributions and his life. This is what I hope will be a time-efficient but somewhat detailed introduction. I have tried to be uncontroversial, and also comprehensive by sweeping up his less well-known thoughts. The remaining two-thirds look to the legacy and its relationship to his original ideas. We investigate the work of the students Durkheim inspired directly, and also the rise of structural functionalism, structuralism, systems theory, normative functionalism, and cultural sociology and anthropology. Material is organized with reference to such traditions and also in terms of nations. This does not reflect the sin of "methodological nationalism" but rather the empirical reality that creative intellectual activity has tended to cluster in specific paradigms in specific national contexts in specific epochs. As one door closes another opens, often in another country.

Our concern with all these diverse traditions of Durkheimian work is not whether scholars at one time or another read Durkheim accurately or "got him right" or "really understood him." It is with how they interpreted his legacy, picked up certain ideas and ran with them, played with them, expanded them, perhaps improved upon them. To be clear: this is not a book of Durkheim scholarship that attempts to provide a brilliant new, or more precise, or more sensitive reading of Durkheim, or of anyone else. Nor is it a report about scholarship on Durkheim that provides an encyclopedic history of reception (although there is some of this here). It is rather a text about the more significant uses of Durkheim and his tradition for creative *social explanation and theory building.* The attempt made here is to offer an introduction and overview of a vibrant and significant paradigm as it shaped social thought and empirical work, attracted talented thinkers and researchers, and gave birth to new ideas, theories, and visions of the social world. Other books on the Durkheimian legacy are possible, perhaps looking more to his normative reception, or to the detailed history of Durkheim interpretation, or to his impact on social philosophy. Those are tasks that are left for another author with another skill set. And I hope someone picks them up.

Finally I disclose that I cite myself in this text more than a little. I trained initially in social anthropology in the UK as an undergraduate, and later in sociology in the USA for the doctorate. I currently work in the United States and I am a visible member of the Strong Program that is described in the final chapter. This information may assist interpretation of the narrative that is provided as well as account for the scope of this work in terms of inclusions and omissions. I admit to being somewhat uncomfortable that American cultural sociology emerges as a kind of savior toward the end of the book. My intention has been to provide a truthful account and not a Whig history. I am calling it the way I see it.

Over the years many Durkheim experts have been sounding boards for the thoughts that have gone into this volume. This group includes Jeffrey Alexander, Randall Collins, Marcel Fournier, Alexander Riley, and Ken Thompson. Various scholars have been helpful in email exchanges during the course of writing where I sought advice on particular themes, issues, or national traditions: Perri 6, Aynur Erdogan, Nicole Holzhauser, Dmitry Kurakin, Jason Mast, Stephan Moebius, Anne Rawls, and Helmut Staubmann. I was a visitor at Nuffield College, Oxford University, during the writing of this book. I thank Nuffield for their hospitality and for providing a quiet intellectual space to get the job done. Nadine Amalfi at the Yale Center for Cultural Sociology assisted with manuscript formatting issues. Fiona Sewell was a remarkably perceptive and detailed copy-editor.

At Polity Press George Owers and Julia Davies provided editorial and production support and were receptive to my suggestion that a book such as this would be more useful than "yet another" one on Durkheim.

Chapter 1
Durkheim's Life and the Four Major Books

Situating Durkheim – early life and training –
The Division of Labor – The Rules of Sociological
Method – Suicide – the middle career phase –
L'Année sociologique – The Elementary Forms
of Religious Life – death

Almost every biographer or intellectual historian runs up against the same frustration. The goal of their labors becomes more elusive and complex the further they travel. Even if we look away from the psyche of Émile Durkheim, for which there is not so much information, to focus on the written work, for which we have plenty to go on, we still find this pattern of regress repeated. The more we read, the more we study, the more the hope that we will come to any final understanding and arrive at our destination evaporates. We seem to be pumping a handcar down railroad lines that converge at infinity.

Look at the ink on the page. Without trying particularly hard or even knowing much about him we can see that Durkheim is associated with many styles of social thought, with multiple vocabularies and authorial postures. These have contributed to debate, to a proliferation of interpretations (Jones 1999; Lukes 1973), and they have been considered by scholars at some times as complementary and at others as contradictory. For example, Durkheim was an advocate of the social fact, positivism, social statistics, and the possibility of a rigorous and objective study of society. But he also spoke about intangibles such as normative integration, morality, and anomie, and suggested that society cohered due to a collective conscience – each of these being somewhat ineffable. A less pretentious word would be "fuzzy." So was he a scientist or a humanist? Later in his career Durkheim brought in elements of a new vocabulary that further complicate the picture. He insisted on ritual, on classification, and on notions of the sacred and profane as the keys to understanding social process. This move brings in a further topic for debate as well as a third set of tools. Some say Durkheim had an epistemological break and that as his career progressed he became a radically different "cultural" theorist. Others insist that there are just shifts in emphasis and point out that the same concepts, problems, and vocabularies can be found – more or less – throughout his work. What is clear is that he remained committed to empirical inquiry. Sociology needed to observe regularities and patterns in the world rather than being a merely theoretical discipline. Yet by the same token Durkheim hated empiricism. The sociologist had to go beyond just describing things. We need to dig beneath the surface to uncover hidden laws, to theorize connections and discover general principles of social organization.

Durkheim can, of course, be positioned as heir to more specific intellectual legacies as well as in terms of axiomatic generalities. While all commentators admit there are multiple influences, many cannot resist boiling these down to just one or two that are, in their reading, truly essential. Candidates include earlier scholars like Comte, Saint-Simon, Rousseau, Kant, Renouvier; or historically embedded intellectual traditions such as French reactionary Catholicism and German Romanticism. The ancestor or lineage that is picked very much depends on whether Durkheim is read as a positivist, an idealist, a critical realist, or a realist, as religious or secular, as a moralist or as a scientist. It also varies according to which book is taken to capture his essence.

We can also attempt to define Durkheim in ways less closely related to the world of pure ideas and the ivory tower sociological enterprise. Here too there are multiple positions to be taken. Consider the case of his politics. For many critical theorists Durkheim is a conservative whose work failed to come to terms with power and injustice. As we will see, this is a complaint that has continued to dog his tradition to this day. However, Durkheim can also be identified as a person who wrote on socialism, who objected to the social impacts of inherited wealth, who saw that contracts could be unfair when there were inequalities between the participants, and who argued that state power needed to be subordinated to the social will. He advocated roles for occupational groups and centralized bargaining in an effort to head off the worst excesses of capitalism. His was a vision of something rather like the Swedish system that was taken as a model of best practice by many critical sociologists with a normative commitment to social democracy.

It is equally significant that Durkheim came out in public support of Alfred Dreyfus (1859–1935), a military officer from a Jewish background who was unfairly convicted of treason in 1895 and condemned to life imprisonment. The Dreyfus Affair split France and was a crucial litmus test of social attitudes at the time. Progressives and liberals pressed vigorously for a pardon and exoneration. On the other side there was a concerted establishment effort to keep Dreyfus in jail, to save face and to cover up of the identity of the real perpetrator. A wider debate attached to the Dreyfus specifics. This concerned the extent to which France was an essentially Catholic nation or one founded upon ideas regarding equal citizenship and human rights. At some risk to his career Durkheim stood up for justice and universalism.

In thinking about Durkheim's multiplicity and complexity we might also refer to a variability of intellectual style, a dimension that has autonomy from the content of the ideas themselves. He can be seen as a deep thinker with a great propensity for abstraction and a consequent extended deployment of image and metaphor. For example, at times he writes somewhat metaphysically and inspirationally, and in a mode not unlike that of his rival the philosopher Henri Bergson, when he speaks of solidarity or the role of currents in the collective conscience. Yet there is also a scholar who can move pedantically and at a painfully slow speed, a kind of high-powered, brute-force chess automaton who tries to arrive at a precise definition or to refute opponents step by step. Another iteration of his authorial persona was that of a punchy, no-nonsense intellectual. For example, there is a Durkheim who thought statistics could resolve things or cut through the chatter: we should follow the trail of social facts. Then there is the polemicist who stands up for sociology against psychology, and the anxious neat-freak social engineer who wants to order and organize society before it is too late. As we will see, the "real Durkheim" is in a sense all of these. It depends a little on where you look and quite a bit upon which interpretative lens you reach for.

About this Chapter, About this Book

Where to start? This chapter is about the big highlights. Here is a slightly facetious analogy. When people go on safari they like to see the "big five" – elephant, buffalo, rhino, lion, and leopard, or some such combination of charismatic megafauna. The search for these is a priority that structures a wider experience in which the tourist might encounter other animals – warthogs, antelope, anteaters, and the like. If they chance upon these it is a bonus, but it is the "big five" that gets them onto that long-haul flight. In this book we follow a similar logic and put first things first. At the end of the day Durkheim is best known to most people as the author of four monographs that changed the path of social science. The full titles for each are *The Division of Labor in Society*, *The Rules of Sociological Method*, *Suicide: A Study in Sociology*, and *The Elementary Forms of Religious Life*. However these books are so well known they are almost universally referred to in scholarship by abbreviated titles as follows: *Division of Labor*, *Rules*, *Suicide*, and *Elementary Forms*.

And so our very long initial chapter starts with these, but with a substantial cautionary note. As we will see later in detail, Durkheim wrote a number of lesser but still highly significant and somewhat lengthy works. Even if his "big four" had never been written, these mid-size contributions and extended essays would have made Durkheim at the very least a significant, highly creative mid-weight player in the history of social theory. This often forgotten output covers a bewildering variety of topics: education, professions, and punishment, to name but three. The plurality does not stop with these books and assembled lectures. He wrote a large number of reviews and introductions in his team's journal, the *Année sociologique*, as well as letters and reports. Intellectual significance does not always covary with length. Sometimes a very short item will provide a major clue to his creative thinking on a big topic – be it totemism or socialism or individualism, or some other "ism," or for that matter "ology."

Because this scattered output is so interesting, dense, and creative, it needs to be understood, also. Shortcuts are risky. It can be more than a little frustrating to try to become a Durkheim scholar because there are just so many such references that need to be read – and our lives being the way they are, these can easily become so many things we should have read but never found time for. It is especially perilous to see the long tail as insignificant for the main game, as it contains fresh ideas and intellectual moves that cast Durkheim's "big four" in a new light. For example, his writings on property have been generally neglected but, when examined, are a way to connect *The Division of Labor* to *The Elementary Forms*. Thankfully a minor industry of expert Durkheim scholarship has existed for quite a while, engaged in just such a task of information retrieval and intellectual reconstruction that pays attention to small details in quiet corners. It has helped generate not only a fuller picture of the man and thinker, but also a sense of dynamic activity and prodigious intellectual engagement.

Durkheim died in 1917. This may seem a long time ago. But think of it this way. The year of his death is only twenty-eight years before the first use of the atomic bomb and *less than* fifty years before The Beatles were at their zenith. We are now *more than* 50 years from *Sgt. Pepper* and moving away fast, but many people still feel the album belongs in our epoch, not in some distant age. This kind of timeline reminds us that Durkheim can be thought of as "recent." In this regard he has had the luck to have two excellent biographers in Steven Lukes (1973) and Marcel Fournier (2013). They have fixed much of the phenomenological experience of immediacy and proximity. Their books combined give us around 1,500 pages of vivid information. Recent decades have also seen the emergence of a cluster of Durkheim scholars, many of them publishing detailed essays in the journal they founded in the 1990s: *Durkheimian Studies/Études Durkheimiennes*. Figures such as W. S. F. Pickering, William Watts Miller, Robert Alun Jones, Philippe Besnard, Massimo Borlandi, Mike Gane, Kenneth Thompson, Alexander Gofman, and Alexander Riley, among many others, have made it their task to engage in detailed reconstruction of Durkheim's thinking, the recovery of lost or forgotten letters and archives, the editing and translation of nearly forgotten texts, the retranslation of well-known ones, and the elaboration of detailed chronologies (see chapter 5 for information on this group). The result of this activity has been a far more comprehensive and three-dimensional account than we had in the initial decades after Durkheim's death. It has put in the foreground several insights that should be remembered in this chapter and the next. Collectively they temper the impression we can easily form of an isolated genius working by candlelight, cut off from the world and obsessed with his four major books to the point where they define who he was. This kind of recent scholarship has demonstrated the following:

• Durkheim was at the center of a team. He taught, encouraged, commissioned, edited, and organized at the expense of his own personal research time. Team members mostly underperformed after his death and without his leadership. However, the group helped him develop his thinking, especially on religion, and the research network or paradigm was for a while an effective way to leverage his influence.

- It is now clearer than ever that Durkheim's work amounted to much more than just four major monographs. We alluded to this above. Specialist Durkheim scholars have pointed to his lectures as major accomplishments, to his multiple book reviews as a substantial intellectual achievement, and to the breadth and diversity of his scholarship (for example, his thoughts on pragmatism, socialism, or education). Much of this is not readily apparent to an undergraduate on a survey course or to a fast, strategic reader.

- Durkheim's major book projects had long gestation periods. We can trace the evolution of his ideas for each of these with a detailed intra-corpus reading. Work on what would become the *Division of Labor* (published 1893) started in 1884; *Suicide* (1897) in a course taught in 1889–90; the *Elementary Forms* (1912) in a course from 1894–5, another from 1900–1, yet another in 1906–7, and in various essays in the *Année sociologique*. This commitment to long-term labor militates against the vision of Durkheim as an opportunist publishing willy-nilly in a quest for visibility and prestige, or as a person struck by inspiration and hence jumping into new topics by whim.

- Many of Durkheim's ideas evolved via real or virtual engagement with other thinkers of his time on the major contemporary topics, such as Tarde on imitation and suicide, or Frazer, Tylor, van Gennep, and Marett on totemism and religion, or James on pragmatism. Many of these debates are now historical footnotes. Yet Durkheim never became bogged down in the task of refutation to the point where his work was only of its time. Rather these figures offered a resource for thinking through to a more timeless general position.

- Durkheim was burdened with administrative responsibilities. As he became more intellectually influential he became more institutionally central. This helps explain a general decline in productivity (by his incredible standards) after 1900. During this later period Durkheim mostly wrote reviews and extended essays, lectures, revisions, and so forth. The gap between *Suicide* (1897) and the *Elementary Forms* (1912) is explained by this bureaucratic leadership role, by work on the *Année sociologique* and, of course, by Durkheim's need to read and think deeply about religion.

So much has been accomplished by the specialist Durkheim scholars. Having said this, it is important to remember that their work is generally about understanding Durkheim, his works, his life, and his time. The priority is on intellectual history and on getting the story as accurate and as comprehensive as possible. For these specialists, knowledge about Durkheim is an object of interest *sui generis*. Why did he write this text at this time? What does he mean by this word in this book and by the same word in that book? How did he revise this footnote? Why did he make such and such an editorial decision? The next two chapters have a different task. They offer a quick survey and do not need the level of detail that looks at various drafts of the same work. We do not delve into private archives or take much interest in letters. Nor do we need to speculate on the relationship of biography to scholarship. We can get by with generalities because our primary interest is neither in getting Durkheim "right," nor in finding origins, nor in evaluating between contending, narrowly differing interpretations of certain ideas. We are also not particularly interested in the philosophical, abstract aspects of Durkheim's legacy. The emphasis here is on what he had to offer for a century or more of empirical inquiry and generalizable social theory concerning the operation of the social world. That said, I try to offer an efficient snapshot of Durkheim's life and his social and intellectual contexts so that the basics are in place – but quickly so.

Early Life

David Émile Durkheim was born on April 15, 1858, in Épinal, Lorraine. Although a small town of around 10,000 people it was also the capital of its *département*, so not a true backwater. This area of France has historically been a border zone with German-speaking lands to the north and east. The German victory in the Franco-Prussian War (1870–1) and their invasion of France when he was twelve years old would have been very much the major political event of Durkheim's childhood. Much has been made of Durkheim's Jewish background and the influence of this on his thinking. He was the son of a rabbi who was himself the descendant of a very long line of rabbis. It has been speculated that being part of a close-knit and excluded minority shaped Durkheim's later views on the pivotal role of solidarity, morality, and belonging. As Fournier (2005: 45) puts it: "To be Jewish in Épinal was to experience the life of a small, cohesive, marginal group." It has also been suggested that specific as well as general elements in Durkheim's thought are derived from this background. For example, Tiryakian (1979) suggests that memories of the Épinal Jewish community and images of the Ancient Hebrews were reflected in Durkheim's later representation of Aboriginal society.

Cutting against the small-town Jewish trope is the fact that Durkheim's family was in many ways secular and modern for its day. As Fournier (2005: 45) points out, photographs are marked by the absence of beards and the use of modern dress. We see something of this in an image of Durkheim and his schoolmates (see figure 1). The family was progressive in terms of gender roles, with women involved in business activity. They spoke French, not Yiddish or Hebrew, around the house. Of course here again we find early clues that can be connected to later beliefs, this time to Durkheim's advocacy of *laïcité* – a term referring to the need for an actively secular state, and to forms of public interaction and civic institutions devoid of religious influences. If Durkheim came out publicly in support of the Jewish Dreyfus (we mentioned this above), this probably says more about his belief in the ideals of law, democracy, and justice than in primal religious solidarity. Finally we note the most important thing about his family background. Almost certainly the biggest "Jewish" influence was a strong community emphasis on literacy and a disciplined and dedicated orientation toward education more generally. Like many of the Jewish faith at the time around Europe, his was a household that valued learning and application and made these a priority. So Durkheim knuckled down and became a very serious person at a very young age. Although not depressive by nature he seemed to struggle to enjoy himself. Lukes (1973: 40) draws on first-hand accounts from Durkheim's students Georges Davy and Célestin Bouglé when he comments that Durkheim had "an exacting sense of duty and a serious, indeed austere view of life; he could never experience pleasure without a sense of remorse." As we will see he was later said to have a stern or monk-like demeanor. Earnest, driven, intellectual, Durkheim was throughout his career a workaholic. None of his much younger students could match him when it came to putting in long hours or meeting exacting deadlines.

Durkheim was a standout school student who was admitted to the *École normale supérieure* (ENS) in 1879. Far more prestigious than the best-known French universities, the so-called *grandes écoles* are the breeding ground for the intellectual, political, and administrative elites of France's centralized and technocratic society. The ENS itself has long remained the destination of choice for those intending to become thinkers or professors (other *grandes écoles* focus specifically on those destined for different leadership roles – say in politics, public administration, or engineering). Entrance takes place through fiercely competitive exams (indeed Durkheim was not admitted at his first attempt) that reward precocity and élan. The best students

Figure 1 Durkheim and his schoolmates, Épinal, c.1874. Durkheim is standing second from the right with his left arm casually resting on a friend's shoulder.

will typically do things like argue the examiner is asking the wrong question, engage in virtuoso answers that twist the concepts in the question around each other to reveal an unseen paradox, or expose contradiction and false choice between alternatives. We find echoes of this approach in the mature written works of more recent graduates like Derrida, Foucault, and Bourdieu, as they refuse the conventional terms of debate and establish new ones of their own choosing. Durkheim's later writings show he was a master of such techniques as he wrong-footed readers and challenged their common sense.

Perhaps not surprisingly given his serious nature, the young Durkheim was impressed by Arthur Schopenhauer (1788–1860), the German atheist philosopher who took a grim view of life as a realm of pointless suffering. This may have inclined Durkheim toward later studies of suicide and anomie. Yet whereas Schopenhauer suggested a temporary consolation for this-worldly misery could be found in the aesthetic realm, Durkheim much later located a solution to meaningless existence in social ties and collective belonging. During his time at the ENS Durkheim was considered by his peers as serious and stern, as intellectually brilliant, and as a good debater by virtue of both reason and passion. His cohort was, however, very strong and Durkheim although above average was by no means the most promising student at this young age. We get a sense of this earnest young man and the intense interactions he would have had with his peers in an ENS class portrait (see figure 2).

Commentators agree that an important proximate influence at the ENS was the director, historian Numa Denis **Fustel de Coulanges** (1830–89). Fustel de Coulanges's most famous book *The Ancient City*, published in 1864, was considered to display a great mastery of French prose style. It explored the interplay of religion, morality, and law in Ancient Rome and showed how these were interlinked and had evolved in parallel. There are clear intimations here of the functionalist view of connected institutions that Durkheim would later espouse. Moreover the mode of analysis was detailed, empirical, almost ethnographic, and hence marked the "dividing point" between the "systematic comparative study of primitive institutions" that would follow in the twentieth century and approaches characterized by "speculative and dogmatic treatises" from the likes of earlier social philosophers "Turgot, Condorcet, Saint-Simon and Comte" (Evans-Pritchard 1960: 11). Themes of *The Ancient City* were to become core to the work of Durkheim and it is no accident that the *Division of Labor* (discussed below) had extensive discussions

10

Figure 2 Durkheim and the class that entered the ENS in 1879. There is some uncertainty as to the exact year this image was taken. Durkheim is standing on the right of the group. It is telling that even at this age he seems serious and formal when compared to his peers

specifically on Roman law. Durkheim, like Fustel de Coulanges, also argued for the religious origins of social institutions.

When it came to normative issues, Fustel de Coulanges insisted on the separation of scholarly work from politics and on the need for intellectual production to be autonomous from immediate contemporary necessities even if there were points of intersection. This model was in many ways similar to that more famously advocated much later by Max Weber in his vision of science as a vocation. True enough, Durkheim was to address his works toward the problems of France in his day, but with the exception of his pamphlets during World War I, this policy orientation was very indirect. When it came to "real-world" issues he was less interested in advocacy and detail than in pointing to general problems in modernity that needed to be addressed. He would also suggest a direction of travel with solutions recommended on the basis of his scholarly inquiries.

On exit the students of the ENS are ranked. Durkheim graduated seventh in philosophy (frequently mentioned) but second from bottom in the class (less often noted) of 1882. Illness had interfered with his preparation. However, the ENS had performed its leader-training function well in Durkheim's case. It reinforced his patriotic commitment to France and the need for reforms that would generate a truly modern nation with a priority given, as Fournier (2005: 49) puts it, to "democracy, secularism and science." There was no sign of Schopenhauer's fatalistic nihilism. The future intellectual giant had emerged as a young man dedicated in a positive way to centering the Third Republic (1870–1940) on a moral commitment to core civic values. Although not an active political figure, throughout his adult life Durkheim believed strongly in these Republican ideals, in the need for national unity and a collective moral compass. His writings on professional ethics (see next chapter), for example, drive home this point time and time again.

During his years at the ENS and immediately after, Durkheim also completed his intellectual formation with extensive philosophical reading. He shifted toward a distinctive concern with society and societal evolution. Of particular interest was Enlightenment thinking on social stages and typologies, and on collective belonging and the social contract. Hence Durkheim's Latin thesis was on Rousseau and Montesquieu. He also read closely some of the major social thinkers of the nineteenth century who had considered social evolution, such as Saint-Simon, Comte, and Spencer. Such figures clearly primed Durkheim with an awareness of the importance of morality, solidarity, unidirectional change, and complexity in modern social life. However, he was to push back against these luminaries by arguing that their approach was too philosophical and speculative. In mapping out the task he would set for sociology Durkheim repeatedly stressed the need for an empirical discipline that would study the actual social world. All this was to seep through to his concern for social facts and his push for a generalizable body of knowledge and theory.

As in many early careers, there followed a series of teaching appointments here and there that sapped energy and that took the young scholar away from the centers of academic power and creative energy. These positions were not particularly fruitful intellectually as they required Durkheim to teach a standard national curriculum. In France a common model is for major intellectuals to write books and conduct research as part of their teaching. This time-efficient double dipping allows them to put together new material and explore ideas in seminar settings. Durkheim was to enjoy this luxury only later in his career. Initially he was teaching in prestigious high schools. A school inspector commended him in his notes for a serious but organized and clear delivery of material. It was in 1887 that things began to both settle down and look up. Durkheim married Louise Dreyfus. The marriage was to prove stable and companionate. As such it offered the ideal domestic platform for Durkheim's later productivity. The same year he took up a position in Bordeaux, a major provincial city, teaching "social science and pedagogy" (note: sociology was not in the job description). Although Bordeaux was not Paris, Durkheim did not spend his time whining about not being in the center of things. Rather he took advantage of the adequately salaried post and a geographical location free of distractions to put his head down and push his career forward. Importantly the position had enough stature that he was finally able to develop his own lecture courses on topics of personal interest. In Bordeaux there began a very productive ten-year spell that would establish Durkheim's reputation as a major intellectual. The year 1893 saw the publication of *The Division of Labor in Society*, his first truly significant work. We turn to this now and in so doing finally arrive at the years specified in the subtitle of this book. Although Durkheim wrote some items earlier than *The Division of Labor* that are of interest to specialists, it is with this publication that his mature thought emerged and his contribution to the history of social theory really begins.

The Division of Labor in Society

In *The Division of Labor in Society* Durkheim traced the evolution of **social solidarity** and **morality**. The first of these terms refers to a sense of collective identity, belonging, togetherness, fellow-feeling, and strength. The second refers to beliefs about what is right and wrong, valued, proper, and even sacred. The title notwithstanding, the book is mostly about social complexity and its consequences for culture and social regulation. It provides Durkheim's clearest statement on the nature of modernity. He has a broadly positive outlook. Not everything was perfect but modernity could be improved and life could get better. His was a non-complacent but appreciative stance that detected growing freedoms and growing chances for self-actualization. As Frank Parkin (1992: 86) put it: "Against Marx's messianic utopianism, and Weber's counsel of despair, Durkheim holds out the fair prospect of orderly social change and steady moral progress."

In *The Division of Labor* Durkheim surprises readers early on, not once but twice. From the title we are expecting a book about work, the economy, and industrial organization. Yet less than a dozen pages into the first chapter he writes:

> We are thus led to consider the division of labor in a new light. In this instance, the economic services that it can render are picayune compared to the moral effect that it produces, and its true function is to create in two or more persons a feeling of solidarity. In whatever manner the result is obtained, its aim is to cause coherence among friends and to stamp them with its seal. (1947: 56)

So the book is about intangible things like emotion, morality, and solidarity. By the end of that first chapter Durkheim has moved on yet again and suggests we should spend a lot of time looking at punishment and the history of legal evolution. This, he argues, is because they make visible the collective morality in which he is interested: "Our method has now been fully outlined. Since law reproduces the principal forms of social solidarity, we have only to classify the different types of law to find therefrom the different types of social solidarity which correspond to it" (1947: 68).

Durkheim next observes that crimes are a shock and offend against the **collective conscience**. The term refers variously to shared morality, solidarity, and a sense of societal identity. Lukes (1973: 4) points out it has been tricky to translate. The French term *conscience* "is ambiguous, embracing the meanings of the two English words

14

'conscience' and 'consciousness'. It fuses moral sensibility and the cognitive apprehension or awareness." In the preface to his translation of *The Division of Labor*, the one we are using here for our quotations, George Simpson also notes the difficulty of the term. Explaining why he translates the French *conscience* as the English "conscience" he helpfully writes "a conscience for Durkheim is pre-eminently the organ of sentiments and representations; it is not the rational organ that the term 'consciousness' would imply . . . Moreover, the moral character of the sentiments and representations in a conscience would seem to render my translation more in the spirit, as well as the letter, of the original" (Simpson in Durkheim 1947: ix). It is customary to agree with this choice while noting that a residuum of "awareness" or "self-awareness" or even "reflexivity" rests somewhere deep inside the term.

To return to the *Division of Labor*: Durkheim argues that if crime causes damage, then punishment is a way of healing the harm to collective sentiment caused by the criminal act. The social response to crime is emotive and moralistic. Crime "brings together upright consciences and concentrates them" (1947: 102). It results in moods of outrage and indignation and so "punishment consists of a passionate reaction" (1947: 85). In sum, Durkheim argues punishment is only superficially about changing the culprit or enacting deterrence. The real purpose is to unite society and stitch together the damaged moral fabric.

> The case is the same with punishment. Although it proceeds from a quite mechanical reaction, from movements which are passionate and in great part non-reflective, it does play a useful role. Only this role is not where we ordinarily look for it. It does not serve, or else only serves quite secondarily, in correcting the culpable or in intimidating possible followers. From this point of view its efficacy is justly doubtful and, in any case, mediocre. Its true function is to maintain social cohesion intact, while maintaining all its vitality in the common conscience. (1947: 108)

Note the use of the word "function" in the last sentence of the quote above. Durkheim's discussion of punishment is considered a gold-standard illustration of his functionalist theoretical armature. This interprets social life according to the role that parts play in sustaining the whole. We return to this theme below. While Durkheim argues that the root cause of the desire to punish and the social functions of punishment are everywhere the same, he also makes contrasts between simple societies and those in modernity. The former have harsh, spontaneous punishments that are visibly emotive and involve community participation. Vengeance is central to this **repressive law**. In modern societies the urge to punish is the same, but it is buffered by collective, specialized institutions, is less immediate and less cruel. There we find **restitutive law** with its focus on rights, on contract, on returning things to normal, and on bringing the individual back into society. Heated emotions still exist but they are somewhat controlled and cooled off. Something fundamental has changed in our culture and society with the movement to modernity.

By this point in Durkheim's book we seem to have wandered a good distance from the "division of labor" that was in its title. But Durkheim has in fact been working backward from indicator to concept to origin to get to his explanatory target. For Durkheim, laws and punishments were visible markers (indicators) of hidden moral forces, these being a non-material social fact that could only be observed indirectly. If punishment changes then so has morality (the concept). Hence we can draw lessons from the study of law and punishment for understanding wider social, cultural, and moral change. And why did the nature of collective morality itself change? For Durkheim – finally we get there – the explanation (the origin) lay in the complexity that comes with the growing division of labor over history.

Durkheim asserts as the book goes on that in primitive societies people tend to do similar tasks to each other. There is little division of labor. This leads to an intense but undifferentiated sense of collective identity where people tend to think alike, value conformity, and even look alike (all of these now disputed or discredited claims, of course). There are "states of conscience which are common to all the members of the same society" (1947: 109). This is called by him **mechanical solidarity**. The term has long confused students as they associate modernity, not tribal life, with "machinery." The meaning, however, is more akin to "automatic" or "direct." In modern society, by contrast, people perform many functions. There is a greater respect for difference and individuality, as without this value pattern we would not be able to have a complex, mutually interdependent society. Values of tolerance come to the fore. This is a situation of **"organic solidarity"** (the metaphorical reference here is to differentiated organs in the body with different functions, the heart, lungs, etc.). The balance of repressive and restitutive law in a society lets us see the difference for ourselves.

With this shift from mechanical to organic solidarity there is also an increase in **dynamic density**. This refers to the number and

16

frequency of interactions in a society, to mental stimulation, and to the size of groups. The emergence of organic solidarity permits a shift to a society with more dynamic density. The concept of dynamic density tends to be forgotten even by Durkheim scholars. It aligns with the materialist and positivistic interpretations of Durkheim more than does the image of a collective conscience, which has a clearer connection to cultural sociology. For example, there seems to be a deterministic undertow when he writes:

> From the time that the number of individuals among whom social relations are established begins to increase, they can maintain themselves only by greater specialization, harder work, and intensification of their faculties. From this general stimulation, there inevitably results a much higher degree of culture . . . [People] move because they must move, and what determines the speed of this march is the more or less strong pressure which they exercise upon one another, according to their number. (1947: 337)

Durkheim eventually claims that the mutual dependency and higher dynamic density of interaction today make society potentially stronger even if it might initially appear more fragmented. This argument allows him to claim in the *Division of Labor* and elsewhere that expanding individual autonomy under modernity is not incompatible with a growing sense of social belonging, with rights, with a net expansion of the solidaristic collective conscience, and with the rule of contract. Or at least in theory: Durkheim's vision was in fact of a modern world that has sometimes failed to live up to its potential and that was in crisis. There was too much anomie, poor organization, and dysfunction.

Book 3 of *The Division of Labor* tries to diagnose all this through a somewhat uneven treatment of "abnormal" forms of the division of labor. The **anomic division of labor** gets the most attention. This is associated with conflict between capital and labor, with strikes, and with economic failures. Industrial strife is linked to the problem of meaningless tasks for the worker: "Every day he repeats the same movements with monotonous regularity, but without being interested in them, and without understanding them" (1947: 371). For Durkheim a solution was to make individuals more aware of their part in the wider system and have knowledge of their contribution to the social whole. The employee needed to "keep himself in constant relations with neighboring functions, take conscience of their needs, of the changes which they undergo" (1947: 372).

The **forced division of labor**, the second problematic form he considers, arises when individuals have too little choice and where talents are not matched to tasks. Durkheim writes, "For the division of labor to produce solidarity, it is not sufficient, then, that each have his task; it is still necessary that this task be fitting to him" (1947: 375). What is needed is a system where individuals find a position appropriate to their faculties such that "social inequalities exactly express natural inequalities" (1947: 377) or, put another way, we have a kind of rationally organized occupational meritocracy. This cannot be the case where work is not freely chosen or is contractually unjust due to imbalances in wealth and power. Durkheim sees this as a matter of social justice. The solution to this morass was to do away with constraints such that reasonable ambition and talent could be rewarded and individuals can flourish.

In concluding, Durkheim also mentions **"another abnormal form"** but mysteriously fails to give it a catchy name. This is essentially one of poor coordination within the social system and often involves individuals not having enough work such that the "activity of each worker is lower than it would normally be" (Durkheim 1947: 392). As "solidarity depends very greatly on functional activity of specialized parts" (1947: 390) a lack of activity can generate a shortfall in solidarity. The image suggested but not quite filled out in the text is of inefficient workplaces and complacent bureaucracies where hands are idle, of phony make-work jobs, and of job descriptions that are too narrowly or poorly specified. An efficient division of labor in modernity involves the kind of continual and connected activity that is appropriate for contemporary forms of complex social organization with high levels of dynamic density. To anchor the point, Durkheim makes the kind of organic analogy that is typical of his functionalist logic as it reasons from the nature of the whole to the activity of the parts. Whereas the frog and the snake are simple animals designed to take long periods of rest, sometimes barely breathing and inert, the mammal is designed such that "its relational functions are ceaselessly necessary to each other, and to the whole organism, to such a degree that none of them can long remain suspended without danger to the others and to general life" (1947: 390–1).

In the original publication of the *Division of Labor* Durkheim did not give much attention to solving the problems posed by the abnormal forms. He simply made general comments about the need for meritocracy, appropriate coordination of functions, and improved solidarity. However, in the Preface to the Second Edition of the *Division of Labor* from 1902 (included in Durkheim 1947) he proposed a bold new plan (one that we also see in *Suicide* and in his writings on

Professional Ethics and Civic Morals). Occupational groups were the answer. These were "a moral power capable of containing individual egos, of maintaining a spirited sentiment of common solidarity in the consciousness of all workers, of preventing the law of the strongest from being brutally applied to industrial and commercial relations" (1947: 10). Engaging in some historical sociology he suggests that the guild organizations of the Middle Ages offered an example of what could be achieved. If something like these could be brought back they would provide a secondary group between the individual and the state, and as such be "near enough to the individuals to attract them strongly in their sphere of action and drag them . . . into the general torrent of social life" (1947: 28).

Several themes stand out in the *Division of Labor* that are worthy of our attention insofar as they were to be trigger points for much critique, repair, and elaboration throughout the tradition. We will see these at several points later in this book.

- We find Durkheim laying out his interest in morality and staking his keynote claim that society is integrated through sentiment. This perspective, which he articulated more forcefully than any other scholar before or since, stands in contrast to explanations of social order that foreground power, domination, or rational interests. Punishment, physical force, and compulsion only step up to the plate as a backup once morality has failed – and even this is as an expression of collective morality rather than a tool of brute domination. Put another way, this is an early if somewhat abstract argument for the centrality of "culture" and solidarity in social life. The example was later to be important for cultural sociology, structural functionalism, and systems theory as they attempted to understand how social action and social order could have non-instrumental bases.
- Themes associated with **functionalism** are on display. This perspective tried to move beyond common sense and folk practitioner views. It insists that society is a "whole" or system with interconnected parts. Things happen to assure the survival or equilibrium of that whole with the needs of that whole pivotal to social process. For example, as we saw, punishment is not really about the offender; it is a ritual related to shared social needs to reproduce moral codes and repair the social fabric. People caught up in any particular situation don't see this and would wrongly point to proximate rather than systemic origins, reasons, and causes ("He is a criminal. He has to be punished so he does not do it again!").

19

Such functionalist explanations are now seen as problematic as they not only downplay power, but also marginalize agency and struggle to cope with making sense of change (which is often explained via reference to some exogenous shock to a stable system). Internally to the Durkheimian tradition there has been a feeling among many that the functionalist logic in the *Division of Labor* does not really cut culture loose from social structure, insofar as there are functional homologies between social form, social needs, and collective belief. These problems were not well understood until the later part of the twentieth century. Indeed the functionalist element of Durkheim's theory was to become central for much mid-twentieth-century thought in social and anthropological theory (see chapter 3). This element proved to be a powerful tool for explaining the seemingly inexplicable, such as pervasive witchcraft beliefs in African villages. However, the problems with functionalism were to dog later iterations of "normative functionalism" in the later twentieth century, especially when applied to western industrial societies (see chapter 4).

- Even in this early work elements of a "cultural" Durkheim can be easily found (Erikson 1966; Garland 1990; Smith 2008a). He speaks of collective emotions and interpretations. Punishment is explicitly said to be a ritual that communicates and heals rather than a narrowly instrumental activity. The law is said to have a sacred force. Humans seem to be energized by solidaristic beliefs and collective emotions. For those wishing to argue that Durkheim's last major work *The Elementary Forms of Religions Life* (discussed below) represented an epistemological break from a more deterministic and structural theoretical apparatus, these aspects of the *Division of Labor* remain a problem. Close reading and detailed reconstructions are needed, perhaps arguing that Durkheim failed to fully achieve what he set out to do.

- In the *Division of Labor* there is a use of comparative methods to gain the analytic leverage that comes from looking to radically different social forms. This has been a hallmark of Durkheimian inquiry ever since, whether the context be civilizational contrasts or detailed case-study work on divergently organized institutions. Durkheim has, of course, been critiqued for simplistic or factually wrong accounts of the condition of mechanical solidarity. We now know that small-scale band societies of hunters and gatherers tend to favor reintegration and non-violent punishments. Indeed criminologists have looked to them for templates for benevolent criminal justice reforms involving shaming or community work.

20

Be that as it may, over the years the use of ethnological materials has proven particularly important for theoretical inspiration in the Durkheimian tradition. Although later scholars (including Durkheim himself) made far greater reference to empirical details, accusations of misunderstanding, misreading, and over-simplification seem to go with the territory of interpreting other cultures at a distance.

- The text features some of Durkheim's most beguiling, intuitively appealing, but also fuzzy concepts such as "collective conscience," "dynamic density," "social currents," and even "solidarity." He used and defined these terms in many ways in his works. A sub-stantial field of Durkheim scholarship exists in which individuals attempt to pin the concepts down, locate intellectual origins, trace changes in usage, or discuss problems of translation. Similar dense literatures exist in the study of other theorists. We might think, for example, of Marx on "alienation" and "species being" or Weber on his typology of forms of "power" – or should it be "author-ity"? In this particular book we have a lot of ground to cover and will leave such disambiguation to the expert literature.

- Notwithstanding the possibilities for the *Division of Labor* to be read as a deeply cultural text about morality and the collective conscience, there is some instability. Although Durkheim sought to anchor social structure and solidarity in normative subjectiv-ity, the words on the page often stress the rational, coercive, non-negotiable, or functionally and evolutionarily necessary characteristics of social organization in modernity. Moreover social structure seems to shape culture, morality, and belief in a somewhat unidirectional way as complexity builds into social organization (Alexander 2005). For this reason astute critics of the time such as Sorel (1895) saw the book as broadly consistent with Marxism and only lacking a thought-through model of social class dynamics. This impression of a structural thinker with a material-ist evolutionary blueprint was reinforced rather than supplanted by Durkheim's next book.

The Rules of Sociological Method

In 1894 Durkheim published four articles in the *Revue philo-sophique*. These were shortly afterwards brought together, corrected, and published with a preface in 1895 as *The Rules of Sociological Method* (Durkheim 1964). This has been widely interpreted as a manifesto for sociology as a discipline with its own field of expertise and its own set of conceptual resources. Sociology was to be ring-fenced from rivals philosophy and psychology by Durkheim's insistence that only sociology could understand **social facts**, and social facts could only be explained by other social facts. Durkheim was successful didactically insofar as from the 1950s until the 1990s readings from the *Rules* were a feature of more or less every core course on methods in the undergraduate sociology curriculum. Moreover reference to social facts, such as trends in baby names, suicide rates, ethnic intermarriage shifts, and intergenerational social (im)mobility tables remain to this day a feature of introductory sociology lectures. They give a sense that there are vast collective patterns and forces, and that we individuals are not as sovereign as we may believe or wish ourselves to be. In a way then, the "social fact" was a brilliant meme that has paid off over the generations. But it is more than just a tag. It is also a way of seeing, or methodology. At the heart of the *Rules* is what Robert Alun Jones (1999: 1) sees as Durkheim's commitment to "social realism . . . that social phenomena should be studied *comme des choses*, as real, concrete things, subject to the laws of nature and discoverable by scientific reason."

An executive summary of the *Rules of Sociological Method* would be as follows: Durkheim insists relentlessly and for page after page that sociology is the study of social facts. These are empirical regularities in social life that transcend and weigh down upon individual choice or individual minds. They are "external to individuals" (1964: xlvii) and "external to individual consciousnesses" (1964: xlviii). Because in Durkheim's view "social phenomena are things and ought to be treated as things" (1964: 27) we need to investigate them empirically and not philosophically or speculatively. Our method must give priority to the whole, which is not simply the sum of its parts: "It is to be found in each part because it exists in the whole, rather than in the whole because it exists in the parts" (1964: 9 – note the functionalism in the quote). The overall picture is of social facts dominating and controlling:

> A social fact is to be recognized by the power of external coercion which it exercises or is capable of exercising over individuals, and the presence of this power may be recognized in its turn either by the existence of some social sanction or by the resistance offered against every individual effort that tends to violate it. (1964: 10)

Durkheim identifies two kinds of social fact. **Material social facts** are visible and objective. Examples would be building architecture, and patterns of human association such as crowd behaviors in the movement of bodies in the street. However, sociology was to include the study of the **non-material social facts,** such as ideas, beliefs, and morality, that are shared in a society. These might have a subjective element but they are also in Durkheim's ontology objective, real forces with determinate consequences. From the number of pages he gives over to them these non-material social facts are clearly far more interesting to Durkheim. He repeatedly emphasizes that such non-material social facts are no less external to the individual, constraining on action, and collective in origin. They impose themselves on individuals from the outside and then enter into individual mental life by shaping ways of thinking. He writes, for example:

> A collective emotion which bursts forth suddenly and violently in a crowd does not express merely what all the individual sentiments had in common; it is something entirely different . . . If . . . each individual consciousness echoes the collective sentiment, it is by virtue of the special energy resident in its collective origin. If all hearts beat in unison, this is not the result of a spontaneous and pre-established harmony but rather because an identical force propels them in the same direction. Each is carried along by all. (1964: 9–10)

As Lukes (1973: 12) very usefully points out, the power of the social fact to constrain the individual could take several forms: (i) as laws and rules where there would be a sanction for disobedience; (ii) as a pragmatic necessity such as speaking the language that everyone else speaks; (iii) as objective factors related to demography or the economy that individuals cannot control (a recession, a baby boom); (iv) as shared psychological currents (e.g. crowd behavior as quoted above); and (v) as internalized norms, emotions, values, cultural codes, and expectations. As Durkheim's career progressed he gave more and more attention to the last two. Insofar as these speak to voluntary, motivated action, the vocabularies of domination and constraint that attend to the concept of the social fact as defined in the *Rules* become a little problematic or awkward as descriptors.

Durkheim also distinguishes between **normal** and **pathological social facts.** The distinction has long proven problematic. For example, there are a lot of guns in the United States. Is this normal or pathological? It depends, of course, on whom you ask. Durkheim, however, tries to take a scientific view. He believes that we can objectively identify pathological social facts in terms of their adaptive value for the whole, and also more statistically. Is what we see typical of, inappropriate to, or out of balance with the average for the form of social life where they are found? He writes:

A social fact is normal, in relation to a given social type at a given phase of its development, when it is present in the average society of that species at the corresponding phase of its evolution. (1964: 64)

As Stephen Turner (1986) indicates, this solution is not as neat as it may appear, and in fact "Durkheim has gone from the frying pan into the fire" (1986: 113) insofar as now we have to decide what the comparison set of societies, social groups, or social elements might be and what counts as a useful adaptation. Moreover, there are tensions within Durkheim's theory itself between defining the relevant social type or social unit for the comparison in terms of the collective conscious or with reference to more material social morphology. Nevertheless Durkheim's empirical and somewhat statistical vision is productive in that it allows him to reach some surprising conclusions. For example, he argues that a certain quantity of crime is normal in social life. Drawing on his work in the *Division of Labor* he points out that crime helps moral integration by reviving collective sentiments of outrage. Society needs crime, hence society can or will "invent" crime by moving the bar. He famously writes:

> Imagine a society of saints, a perfect cloister of exemplary individuals. Crimes, properly so-called, will there be unknown; but faults which appear venial to the layman will create there the same scandal that the ordinary offense does in ordinary consciousnesses. If, then, this society has the power to judge and punish, it will define these acts as criminal and will treat them as such. (1964: 69)

Although the general picture Durkheim gives is of social facts as a kind of negative environment preventing free and spontaneous action, we should remember that morality is something to which individuals adhere as an internal environment of action (Alexander 1978; Parsons 1949). Durkheim's tone is consistent with a determinist vision of culture and society dominating the individual, but the theoretical logic at work can also support a more voluntaristic understanding of motivated behavior and choice. This positive, energized vision of social facts is perhaps most manifest when Durkheim speaks of social currents. There seems to be a more active image of attraction and enlistment, especially when he speaks about shifts in opinion and sentiment in a crowd situation (see, for example, the quote beginning "A collective emotion which bursts forth" a page or so above). As I mentioned before, in lectures we often explain social currents in terms of things like fads and fashions in clothing, shifts in popular names for babies, and so forth. The usual image we have of such things is of people like surfers enthusiastically paddling into and then riding the wave, not of swimmers pounded helplessly by the surf. Clearly there are tensions and ambiguities that careful interpreters can find even in this emphatic work. These make for a more nuanced reading experience if we put in the effort (see Gane 1988 for just such a demonstration).

The *Rules* is also significant as evidence for Durkheim's commitment to **positivism**. This is a somewhat scientistic worldview that broadly asserts we can build knowledge by observation of facts, through rigorous method rather than creative intuition, and through general theories involving laws and propositions. But it also has a normative agenda, something that was very present when it emerged in the nineteenth century with thinkers like Saint-Simon and Comte. These scholars, whom Durkheim studied closely, advocated positivism as an optimistic social program for reform. Theirs was an engaged and activist platform that tended to rhetorically oppose itself to introspection, philosophical speculation, and arguments based on syllogism. Originally positivism even had a slightly religious fervor tethered to visions of earthly utopia, but in Durkheim's hands the mood is more relentlessly that of the white-coated lab scientist. The normative agenda to bring about a perfect society takes a back seat here. Still, the idea that sociology could contribute sensible ideas for reform and assist social policy and social integration with expert, knowledge-driven advice remained as another positivist legacy in his thought.

Somewhat lacking in nuance and often monotonous in tone, the *Rules* is a little difficult to love. But nevertheless it is marked by forceful lines and commands our attention. Ugly but effective like bunker architecture, the *Rules* is a solid, reliable intellectual contribution that was seen as a spectacular provocation in its day. Inevitably this brutalist manifesto for positivist sociology has attracted critique. Over recent years it has become the least popular of Durkheim's major works. Mike Gane (1988) has mounted perhaps the most spirited defense, insisting that there is buried subtlety and that we can find this if the argument is understood in the context of Durkheim's detailed intellectual biography. When Gane says that the book is "a treasure house of ideas and methodological suggestions" (1988: 171) few would disagree, even if nearly all would pick another major text as their preferred bedtime reading. Gane also provides the most complete and useful account of the book's critical reception, which he summarizes thus: scholars have seen the work as "naively scientistic, crudely and unreflexively empiricist, a radical or maximalist positivism" and also as oscillating between "empiricism and idealism, nominalism and apriorism, and between subjectivism and objectivism" (1988: 103). So there is plenty for philosophically inclined theorists of whatever stripe to object to. This in itself is enlightening. If Durkheim ever wrote a paint-by-numbers text it is the *Rules*. Yet even here readers are seeing radically different core messages about methodology, epistemology, and ontology.

The political implications of Durkheim's vision in the *Rules* could also be found wanting. Zygmunt Bauman (2005) serves as our representative polemicist for the opposition. For this postmodern skeptic the book was all part of a bid for intellectual authority and power, with Durkheim seeking to establish his authority as a "legislator" who could organize the "society" he had in fact conjured into being as an object of knowledge through his sneaky and ingenious rhetoric and theory. In Bauman's vision the *Rules* shows Durkheim was fully implicated in the misguided projects and hubris of modernity. These could only lead to exclusion and othering thanks to their pride in inexorable classifications, hierarchies, and systems. Certainly the advocacy of positivism was consistent with concepts of social engineering and managed social ordering that were pivotal to Durkheim's vision for the Third Republic. However, most commentators would see the text more modestly as an attempt to create disciplinary autonomy or, perhaps better (and using words of the kind that Bauman typically deploys when he likes something), to create an imaginative and discursive space for the sociological enterprise. That said, Bauman's symptomatic reading does capture something in Durkheim – the spirit of an age where grand narratives and hopes had yet to be shattered by World War I. This was a place and epoch where technocracy and technology, information, education, and planning were associated with freedom and moral progress rather than control and alienation as they so often are today.

Although the concept of the non-material social fact is often used now in cultural theory – notably as a synonym for a culture-structure or a recurring cultural pattern that seems to shape outcomes – the *Rules* remains a modestly problematic text for those who see Durkheim as a cultural theorist. The issue is not only that it seems somewhat determinist in cast. The telling itself is problematic. The book has the Lego-like quality (hence my "bunker architecture" and "paint-by-numbers" jabs a few paragraphs ago) associated with building-block theoretical tracts, and the declarative force of a manifesto. For the most part it lacks the grace and intellectual fluidity we find elsewhere in Durkheim's own work that persuades by virtue of hermeneutic enlistment. It is no accident that in those core courses on theory and method I mentioned on a prior page, the *Rules* was often contrasted to Dilthey-inflected passages from Weber advocating the methodological need for *Verstehen* or interpretative understanding. The week afterward a chapter from *Suicide* citing official statistics could then be contrasted with a reading from *The Protestant Ethic* that attempted to capture the meaning of belief and salvation with reference to Luther. In such contexts straw-man Durkheim represented a robotic interpretation "from without" in his claim that personal beliefs and motivations are trumped by "social forces" that could be understood only with the all-seeing eye of the omniscient sociologist. Or at least that was the Bowdlerized version. Close readings and cherry-picking readings of the *Rules* can be made, of course, that render the text more consistent with his interpretative side. Notably, as we have mentioned, the concept of the non-material social fact would seem to cry out for a cultural turn. Arguably Durkheim did not know quite what to do with this idea or how to square the circle – theoretically or textually – such that positivism and the desire for sociology to be seen as an autonomous science could be reconciled with a vision of internally motivated voluntary action. As we will see, Durkheim redeemed this possibility in his own later work as his thought matured/changed/ adapted/adjusted/shifted . . . (all these words have been used and the choice that is made is usually telling).

Suicide

The year 1897 saw the publication of *Suicide: A Study in Sociology*. Yet it did not appear in English until George Simpson's version came out in the 1950s. *The Elementary Forms of Religious Life* had appeared in translation in 1915, *The Division of Labor in Society* in 1933, and *The Rules of Sociological Method* in 1938. Perhaps this delay reflects Durkheim's early reception as an ethnologist, social theorist, methodologist, and moralist. Today the book is seen as a landmark demonstrating the sociological imagination is at its best when theory and data come together. It is also taken to be an illustration of Durkheim's *Rules of Sociological Method*. As we just noted, *Suicide* has been presented as such an illustration in generations of lecture classes. This interpretation and use are entirely reasonable. Durkheim explicitly noted in the Preface to *Suicide* that the book would feature "the chief methodological problems" raised before in the *Rules* and that these would manifest in this, his new book, in "concrete and specific form" (1952: 37). *Suicide* can also be interpreted as an attempt to beat down Gabriel Tarde, whose writings on social imitation and social influence made him a potential rival in the academy (Collins 2005; Riley 2015: 112); as a territorial challenge by sociology toward psychology; and as a study in the tradition of earlier statistical criminologists or "moral statisticians" such as Adolphe Quetelet and André-Michel Guerry (figures perhaps unfairly not fully acknowledged by Durkheim). These scholars, generally overlooked by social theorists but well known to historians of criminology, had been working with state-collected statistics decades before. They had convincingly shown that there were year-on-year continuities in crime rates and in victim and perpetrator characteristics. Using official statistics they had shown, for example, that the ratio of male to female offenders was around 5:1 or 6:1, that the murder rate increased in summer due to greater numbers of social interactions (Durkheimian translation: dynamic density), and that risk of victimization decreased with age. The moral statisticians even made broadly deterministic interpretations of the regularities they found, suggesting in so many words that the crime exists before it takes place and is waiting for an individual to carry it out. Their findings hold today by and large, but of course the attention in lecture classes rightly goes to Durkheim. This is because, as we see below, he offered the superior theoretical scaffolding for his findings.

Making use of official statistics collected by the French state, Durkheim sought to undermine the common sense notion that suicide can be understood best as an act of the individual will. We tend to think of suicide as an anguished personal decision. After all, there is Hamlet's "To be or not to be" deliberation. Suicide notes are often left and found and read. Encountering stories in the news, we reconstruct personal situations and engage in sympathetic efforts at understanding misery, hopelessness, and depression. Durkheim captures this everyday view when he writes: "Since suicide is an individual action affecting the individual only, it must seemingly depend exclusively on individual factors, thus belonging to psychology alone. Is not the suicide's resolve usually explained by his temperament, character, antecedents and private history?" (1952: 46)

But Durkheim sets out to falsify this kind of explanation and to illustrate the power of social facts. He turns to suicide rates, not individual acts, as the indicator of social forces at work and argues, using statistics from various European nations, that these rates are stable over time. Rates are properties of social groups and categories, hence they are social and collective, ergo ideal for sociological rather than psychological analysis. When we look at these rates we are seeing a positive social fact: "Each society is predisposed to contribute a definite quota of voluntary deaths. This predisposition may therefore be the subject of a special study belonging to sociology" (1952: 51).

Durkheim begins his task of causal identification by elimination. He sets out to demonstrate a lack of correlation of suicide rates with a number of predictors such as climate, quantity of insanity, alcoholism, and race. These alleged causal factors he dubs either "organic-psychic" and "environmental" or "cosmic." Durkheim also pushes back against his rival for intellectual attention, Gabriel Tarde (1843–1904), in a dedicated chapter. Tarde had built his career as a criminologist and social psychologist on the idea that imitation was fundamental to social life. People were driven to copy others and aspired to become like those they emulated. Durkheim asserted that where imitation happens it is subordinate to, a mechanism for, or reflective of the underlying structural environment of social facts.

Durkheim generally does all this work of falsification through simple descriptive statistics. The aim is to show that there is no **concomitant variation** where the contending theory might predict it. The method was most famously advocated by the philosopher John Stuart Mill. He argued that in a situation of concomitant variation, factors relating to cause and effect behave in predictable ways. When one changes the other will increase or decrease, be present or not present. Yet if there is no reliable or stable association then we might suspect there is no causal tie and a hypothesis/theory can be rejected. Perhaps the most common technique of Durkheim's for this task in *Suicide* was to demonstrate that a large amount of variation within an allegedly causal category did not seem to change the suicide rate. There was no concomitant variation of a supposed cause and its effects. His method was broadly consistent with a Popperian agenda of falsification but somewhat naïve by today's standards. Still, it cleared the way for sociology to step into the ring.

When Durkheim turns to his social variables, systematic, predictable concomitant variation starts to appear in the statistics. Properties such as being Catholic or Jewish, being female, or being married seemed to buffer people from the risk of suicide. Other factors amplified risk, such as being Protestant, being widowed, and being exposed to rapid social change. Such findings – or even asking the right question and so knowing where to look – remain a remarkable demonstration of the power of the sociological imagination and the statistical method. Using some of his most beguiling trademark language, Durkheim argued that **suicidogenic currents** were swirling through the collective conscience and that some individuals were swept up in these. Certain individuals and communities were buffered and others more vulnerable by virtue of their moral and social ties, by their aspirations and life experiences, and by the amount of stability and change in their environment.

Durkheim also transcended common sense in developing a typology suggesting that not all suicide was the same. Suicidogenic currents were defined by forces of **integration** and **regulation**. The former refers to shared sentiments and a sense of belonging. The latter considers freedom of action and levels of constraint or social control. The forms of suicide reflected their specific influences. His four-way typology spells all this out.

Egoistic suicide refers to a situation of excessive individuality and low integration. This explains, Durkheim argues, the suicide rate differences between Protestants, Catholics, and Jews. Catholicism and Judaism protect the individual. This has nothing to do with faith or dogma and more to do with community. Catholicism and Judaism are more collectivistic and rely on tradition and ritual. They seem to do a better job at offering a sense of shared belonging. Protestantism is weaker in this regard. Durkheim writes:

> What constitutes this society is the existence of a certain number of beliefs and practices common to all the faithful, traditional and thus obligatory. The more numerous and strong these collective states of mind are, the stronger the integration of the religious community, and also its preservative value ... because the Protestant church has less consistency than the others it has less moderating effect upon suicide. (1952: 170)

He goes on to show that marriage, wars, revolution, and political instability were also able to offer protection to the individual by augmenting participation in collective life. Egoistic suicide would take place when there was low integration in religious, political, or domestic society.

Anomic suicide takes place where individuals lack a moral compass or have limitless desires that are no longer constrained by custom. It is a form of suicide strongly associated with social change and social dislocation and seems more "economic" in origins or more closely tied to modernity. Whereas egoistic suicide is about social integration, a particular focus is given here to social regulation. Durkheim points to the surprising fact that increasing affluence is connected to suicide, as indeed are travel and exposure to the outside world. These weaken customary controls and erode norms before new ones can emerge that provide sensible horizons of aspiration. As Alexander Riley (2015:

118) nicely points out, we encounter anomic suicide regularly in the news. We often read about a younger celebrity going off the rails. After a normal upbringing they have an A-list lifestyle in which every sexual, narcotic, narcissistic, or material whim can be granted thanks to sudden wealth and a coterie of fawning admirers. A sense of proportion is lost. They make poor decisions and do not seem happy or fulfilled despite their wealth. Eventually they feel lost and depressed before they die from a deliberate overdose. The story Durkheim tells is somewhat less sensationalist than such tabloid fodder. He looks to statistics on things like food prices, bankruptcies, steam boiler installations, and world exposition attendance. However, the picture is still the same. A sudden change in circumstances leads to a mismatch of expectations and desires with reality and to a loss of social regulation.

Although these two categories sweep up most cases, Durkheim also suggests that over-investment in the social can generate suicide. **Altruistic suicide** eventuates where the individual values the group more than themselves. This usually involves submission to collective norms, with the person too strongly integrated into the collectivity. Here "the ego is not its own property, where it is blended with something not itself, where the goal of conduct is exterior to itself, that is, in one of the groups in which it participates" (1952: 221). Durkheim gives examples such as the ritual suicide of women on the death of their husbands in traditional India, Christian martyrs who march cheerfully to their execution, ancient Celtic warriors too old to fight who throw themselves off cliffs, and soldiers who are excessively subordinated to the group and lack a robust sense of self such that they take small career setbacks to heart.

Finally there is **fatalistic suicide**. This can be found only in a footnote, as if Durkheim felt the need to balance his typology into a two-by-two table but did not have time to think things through (see Lockwood 1992 for discussion of fatalism as a lost opportunity for Durkheimian theory). Fatalistic suicide occurs when individuals are subject to excessive social regulation and have no more happy future in sight. Durkheim struggled to fill out this category with examples, but it would seem to fit the suicides of prisoners and slaves.

What can be done about suicide? For the most part Durkheim allocates altruistic suicide to tribal life and pre-modernity. The problem we face today, he says, is that rapid social change in an urbanizing and industrializing society has torn away customary sources of social order and moral authority. Foreshadowing some themes later developed in the Preface to the Second Edition of *The Division of Labor* (discussed above, this Preface was written after *Suicide*), Durkheim briefly proposes that professional and occupational associations can offer the modern individual a sense of collective belonging. These would head off anomie, give individuals a notion of their meaningful place in the world, subject them to just the right amount of social regulation and moral integration, prevent excessive individualism, manage the impacts of social and technological change, and generate increased social solidarity in a context of inevitable social differentiation. Multi-tasking indeed.

Durkheim's *Suicide* is rightly acclaimed as a masterpiece. Years ahead of its time, it showcases the use of official statistics as a tool for theory construction and hypothesis testing; demonstrates the conceptual power of typology; diagnoses modernity; and moves beyond common sense with every page turn. It is impossible to measure the impact of this text. It sits as a cornerstone of positivist sociology globally (e.g. for the United States even years ago see Selvin 1958) but, of course, is no longer cited in every item of quantitative research. Many of its lessons have become common sense, and as such no longer require the buttress of citation of a classic. The study has had particularly visible inputs into health sociology and especially the study of suicide. Here alone the citation count is monumental, perhaps greater than in the social theory corpus. More indirectly, *Suicide* foreshadowed all efforts to locate the social and demographic correlates of social attitudes, behaviors, and outcomes. It will still make a worthwhile cited appearance when the specific impact of religion or economic change on a dependent variable is being discussed.

Suicide has been subject to several lines of critique that should be quickly noted here before we move on.

- Durkheim's use of statistics is somewhat primitive or naïve by contemporary standards. As noted, he makes extensive use of John Stuart Mill's method of concomitant variation to identify the hidden laws of social life and to falsify contending explanations of patterns in data. Even elementary statistics classes warn us that persistent correlation does not always equal causation. There are also issues of ecological fallacy and problems where Durkheim wildly assumes what an indirect indicator is tapping. He did not seem to see the need to step toward simultaneous multivariate regression analysis (something that was inordinately difficult in his time due to lack of computing facilities). He did, however, have some awareness of the potentials of the natural experiment, ingeniously comparing suicide statistics around the time of the World Fair that was held in Paris in 1889. This event exposed many

French people to the capital city, to travel, and to other cultures for the first time. It also introduced them to such technological wonders as the Eiffel Tower, which was built as the centerpiece of the event. Durkheim argued the World Fair could promote anomie by changing horizons of experience in people who had otherwise lived sheltered rural or regional lives.

- Durkheim does not reflect on the social origins of the official suicide statistics he used somewhat uncritically. As Jack Douglas (1967) argued, these are unreliable. For example, a suicide is more likely to be covered up or misrecorded in a Catholic setting due to family pressure (suicide is a "mortal sin" and is subject to more stigma) than in a Protestant one. Because statistics are social artifacts they can present a filtered version of real social life. We might be tapping into cross-national variation in norms, recording practices, and statistical conventions more than social reality. At the limit the case can be made that there is no such thing as suicide that can be objectively measured. The ethnomethodologist J. Maxwell Atkinson (1978), for example, suggests that all that really exists is a classification of death by suicide. The label bundles up lots of different deaths, each one unique in some way. As sociologists we need to study the folk reasoning through which coroners arrive at this verdict and construct a sense of definite reality from clues in the event of an unanticipated death. Ironically then, Durkheim was insufficiently sociological when it came to thinking about the nature of the statistics he was using or the existence of the "thing" he was studying.
- Durkheim's typology is not as neat as it might appear. He admits that many suicides might have elements of more than one type and that egoistic and anomic suicide have "kindred ties," but goes on to insist after a minimum of vague discussion: "In spite of their relationship, therefore, the two types are independent of each other" (1952: 258). He briefly mentions, without following through, that one kind is linked to intellectual careers and the other to the industrial and commercial world. But is this really convincing? Much of the problem is that "regulation" is not well managed by Durkheim. Even the noted Durkheim expert Philippe Besnard (1993: 170) admits that "the theory of integration is much more coherent and complete than the theory of regulation" and that "reconstructing Durkheim's theory of regulation is the most difficult aspect of interpreting *Suicide*."

Anyone who has taught *Suicide* will have noticed that anomic and egoistic suicide seem rather similar. They may well have

33

fudged sections of their lecture on these by drawing down an authoritative-sounding quote from Durkheim, hoping thereby to quash any potential student questions that would unpick the key learning objectives of the day's session. For example, we might say that anomic suicide is "more about the economy and social change" or "being balanced and realistic," and egoistic suicide about "social connectedness." Although Durkheim puts one kind of suicide down to social regulation and the other to the normative, one to the relationship of horizons of desire to reality and the other to a sense of moral integration, the distinction seems scholastic. There seems to be a lot of covariance. Individuals who are poorly integrated, depressed, and isolated seem by definition to be somewhat anomic. Much the same point can be made for altruistic and fatalistic suicide. Why should the death of an Indian widow on the funeral pyre of her husband be seen as altruistic and not fatalistic, if the alternative is social exclusion in a context of misogyny and poverty? Durkheim even speaks of the "obligatory" nature of altruistic suicides. It seems easier just to collapse the fine points of the argument that produces his two-by-two table and say that suicide is due to over- or under-integration in society, that this has moral, solidaristic, and aspirational elements, and that we need to help individuals find a Goldilocks Zone somewhere in the middle. Needless to say, a cottage industry of Durkheim scholarship has emerged that goes over and over the typology attempting to clarify what he really was trying to do and often blaming poor readers for their own error (for a more balanced look see Besnard 1993; 2005). The truth, I believe, is that the typology is not as cleanly worked through as we would like.

- The typology is not evenly weighted and this diminishes its elegance. Empirically, egoistic and anomic suicide seem to do nearly all the lifting when it comes to what we see in the world around us. They are also discussed at length. In contrast, fatalistic suicide and altruistic suicide are not properly developed by Durkheim (Besnard 1993). Both seem somewhat unusual. As hinted in the bullet point above, empirical examples of either can be challenged. In lecture contexts examples of altruistic suicide include the custom of *suttee* or *sati* in India (where the widow throws herself on her husband's funeral pyre), Japanese kamikaze pilots in World War II, and suicides in cults like Jonestown. However, elements of selective reporting and myth shape the stories we have received about these. Digging deeper often shows compulsion was present.

- Durkheim's statistical analysis demonstrated that women have lower suicide rates than men. Moreover marriage, divorce, and widowhood have differing impacts on women and men. Essentially men benefit from marriage more than women. We can see this from the fact that being divorced or widowed seemed to buffer women from suicide. The finding is consistent over time and also matches with much feminist work on marriage as an oppressive institution. Unfortunately, in attempting to explain and discuss his findings Durkheim drifts into lines of gender essentialism and social conservatism that have irked generations of feminists. Unlike the widower, the widow's "sensibility is rudimentary rather than highly developed ... very simple social forms satisfy her needs ... man is a more complex social being, [who] can maintain his equilibrium only by finding more points of support outside himself" (1952: 215–16). What could have been an opportunity to praise women for their fortitude and autonomy has somehow become yet another case arguing man = culture, women = nature (we touch on this theme again in the next chapter).
- Experts in other professions have argued for clinical factors as significant, notably that depression can have an organic basis in things like brain chemistry. And of course, as Lukes (1973: 221) points out, it is individuals who undertake the final act of suicide. Likewise Jack Douglas (1967) finds Durkheim inadequate and suggests that patterns of motivation and meaning need to be studied. Douglas identifies themes of revenge, escape, and sympathy in suicides. The big problem is that in attempting to generate distance from psychology Durkheim never fully explained how suicidogenic currents could lodge in the individual and generate more efficient, localized causes, such as depression, or changes in cognitive function, personality, or even logical reasoning and self-narration, suggesting that death (not something else – say migration, prayer, or study) was the best way forward. Many people reading *Suicide* leave the text feeling both inspired about the power of sociology and that somehow there is a missing step or connection to the personality, self, or existential depth of a life narrative.

Toward the *Elementary Forms*

Durkheim's final major work, the last of our "big four," is *The Elementary Forms of Religious Life*, which was published in 1912.

Before we can get to that book we need to return to his career. Keenly aware of the need to found a school of thought and to institutionalize sociology Durkheim started on *L'Année sociologique* (approximate translation: "Sociological Yearbook") in 1898. This was to be a journal consisting of original articles and theoretically informed book reviews from contributors including not only Durkheim but also his advanced students and like-minded scholars. The material was nearly all from within the paradigm and dedicated to advancing the study of sociology in the Durkheimian mode. A close reading of Fournier's biography as well as a glance at the tables of contents in the *Année* show Durkheim doing much of the heavy lifting over the years, assisted somewhat by his talented nephew Marcel Mauss (whose work is discussed in chapters 2 and 3). It is clear that the *Année sociologique* became a burden that sucked up Durkheim's time and energy as he cajoled contributors to meet deadlines, and edited their texts (Smith 2014b). The price was very high, which is to say a reduced output from Durkheim himself. Nevertheless the *Année* was a worthwhile intellectual exercise that produced a handful of short classics (we review these in the next chapter). It is notable that many scholars produced their best work for the journal and were never able to hit the same intellectual heights again even if they lived for another two or three decades (another theme we return to later). This suggests that Durkheim's mentoring, the deadlines, and the sense of belonging to a team were in fact significant factors in generating high-quality, theoretically generalizable output. Durkheim had indeed hit on a formula for paradigm building. Also significant is that involvement in *L'Année sociologique* played a major role in Durkheim's own intellectual shift toward a religious sociology. Via reviews and editorial work he was able to spend time thinking through and toward a new set of ideas. So the team-building activity was costly, but was also productive. It was anything but a dead loss or a failed strategy.

The productive time in Bordeaux eventually paid off. The year 1902 saw Durkheim return to the Sorbonne in Paris, and in 1906 he took up the Chair in the Science of Education (note: yet again not "sociology" – he was able to include the word "sociology" in his job title only in 1913). The importance of this move to Paris cannot be overstated. Durkheim arguably reduced his productivity and increased his administrative load. However, he was able to gain influence. As Charles Lemert (1981: 7) notes, "to be French is to think of Paris as the center of France." It was, and is, at the core of struggles for authority in intellectual and academic fields. To remain in the provinces is to be something of a loser. With his arrival at the

Sorbonne Durkheim became a player and more than just a person in Bordeaux producing scholarship of above average interest. He was now in the very center of French academic life. He was also better able to manage his team and recruit and develop the best students through face-to-face contact and personal influence. Speaking of which, what was he like as a person and teacher?

Reading his deeply serious and earnest books today it might be surprising to learn that Durkheim was something of a charismatic figure. In his day he was a titan at the center of an intellectual network. His lectures were eagerly awaited and, as figure 3 shows, were attended by a spectrum of society of diverse ages and genders, not just male undergraduate students. There are also several women present in the image, suggesting he had an open and inclusive orientation for his day. We find several themes in accounts of Durkheim as a person (the following information and quotes are derived from Fournier 2013: 420ff.). The motifs and vocabulary elements line up such that they seem non-random and not simply the consequence of individual experiences or impressions. Some found Durkheim cold, austere, and mechanical. Gilbert Maire, who supported Durkheim's rival Henri Bergson, found him to be "sort of an automaton" and Hubert Bourgin also highlighted the "severity" of his lecturing style. This set of representations matches those from the ENS days of Durkheim as stern but also as having a passion for serious thought. A second language cluster describes him through religious imagery. Durkheim himself likened a good teacher to a priest with strong faith and joked with Célestin Bouglé about lecturing from a pulpit, as his lectern had an ecclesiastical look. Amazingly enough we have an image of this (see figure 4). Although low-quality, the photograph captures his demeanor. Xavier Léon spoke of him as an ascetic and mentioned a metallic tone of voice "expressing a burning faith which inspired this heir to the prophets to shape and carry the convictions of his listeners." Bourgin also saw him as a "secular priest" and wrote of "falling under his spell" during tightly argued lectures. He mentions meeting the scrawny Durkheim in his study and, like Léon, describes him as "ascetic." Bourgin continues that before him was: "a cold hard face, lit up by his deep eyes, and intense, gentle power that demanded respect, attention and even submission, and that required the same very bare simplicity that you could see before you, sovereign, imperious and inspiring trust." As if taken by Bourgin during his encounter, figure 5 gives a clear sense of this aspect of Durkheim's persona. Although an intense personality, an organized thinker, and – as we can see in the images – possessed of a dapper sensibility, Durkheim was not a neat freak. As figure 6 shows,

Figure 3 Durkheim lecturing at the Sorbonne *c*.1911. The presence of notebooks suggests this is a regular class, not a public lecture or ceremonial event. Yet we see a surprisingly high proportion of women and mature-age students in attendance. This diversity is indirect evidence of Durkheim's progressive views.

Figure 4 Durkheim at the lectern *c.*1908. Note the characteristically intense expression.

he kept a messy desk that was overflowing with books and papers. This is not the bureau of a slacker or organization man but that of a workaholic. The overall picture we have from our accounts and images is somewhat contradictory but can be reconciled. Rather like an inquisitor, Durkheim was charismatic and magnetic on account of his severity and seriousness. He was inclusive but did not play to the crowd. He used the force of ideas and the example of his austere personality to persuade through dignity. He lectured systematically and logically. He worked unbelievably hard.

Perhaps we can make our own judgments from sound as well as the images presented in this book. A brief section of Durkheim's talk "Des jugements de valeur," given in Bologna, Italy, to the International Philosophical Congress, was recorded (see Durkheim 1911 in French to read along with the recording, 1974b for an English version) and can be found on the Internet with a little searching. We hear that slightly high-pitched and metallic voice intoning quite fast and

Figure 5 Durkheim standing in his office *c*.1911. Clearly he was a precise dresser. The photograph also captures his penetrating eyes.

Figure 6 Durkheim working at his desk, Paris *c*.1911. This is a remarkable, informal image of immense significance. With its piles of literature stuffed with placeholding sheets of paper the image fully captures Durkheim's intellectual energy and his workaholic tendencies. It is a little startling to realize these were almost certainly the ethnographic source books for the *Elementary Forms*, which he was finishing up at the time.

rhythmically. The timbre is not unlike that of the French President Charles de Gaulle. Durkheim tends to pair up phrases and sentences, following each pair with a short silence. This gives an urgent but also slightly liturgical feel to his lecture delivery. The talk itself, we read, was a great success and the audience response supports the vision of a charismatic Durkheim. According to one report the crowd "fell under his sway and then spontaneously rose to its feet. They crowded around the platform, reaching out towards the orator as though they had been drawn to him" (Xavier Léon cited in Fournier 2013: 583).

The Elementary Forms

It was in Paris that Durkheim worked with tremendous resolution to produce his late masterwork, ***The Elementary Forms of Religious Life***, which appeared in 1912. As Frank Parkin notes, this is no ordinary academic tome and it is "rightly considered to be his most ambitious and startling work." Parkin continues, "Anyone who, on a first reading of the *Elementary Forms* fails to register any intellectual *frisson* must be made of very stern stuff" (Parkin 1992: 41). The intrigue starts before we have even turned a page. The word "elementary" in the title might refer to (i) primitive or *early* forms of religion in an evolutionary sense (see Fields 2005: 162); or (ii) *simple* forms of religion that lack theological or organizational complexity; or (iii) *foundational* aspects of all religions, anywhere, anytime, no matter how complex. We have to read the book to find out which of these is the case. Over time the third understanding has come to predominate in scholarship. The book is said to expose the basic building blocks of all religions or quasi-religious beliefs rather as we might identify the universal elements in a periodic table or break down a complex molecule into its constituent atoms. For such reasons, the noted Durkheim scholar William Watts Miller (2012) refers in a very deliberate way to *The Elemental Forms* and not to *The Elementary Forms* throughout his study of Durkheim's evolving thinking.

When contrasted to the other three major monographs it can sometimes look as if *The Elementary Forms* came out of nowhere and represented a chaotic, random, or at least sudden change of direction for Durkheim. This impression comes from a shift in intellectual style, vocabulary, research topic, and, some would say theoretical logic (see Alexander 1978; 2005; Parsons 1949). The experience is particularly jarring for readers who are only familiar with the "big four" and not with Durkheim's wider range of outputs. As we have seen, the three earlier major works tend to stress the coercive, constraining quality of external social facts – or at least they facilitate this reading of Durkheim's social theory through imagery, word choice, and intellectual articulations. Although he stresses the significance of morality and solidarity in them, Durkheim does not engage in the kind of deep interpretation that would show rather than tell. Relative to the other works the *Elementary Forms* represents a transformation in the presentation of evidence. Durkheim does more to take us along with him textually in the manner of a Clifford Geertz. Also there is a stronger sense of active engaged individuals, of meaning rather than social structure shaping social life, and a stronger push toward capturing the subjective quality of collective and intimate experiences. When detailed textual analysis is combined with citation to the famous letter of 1907 speaking of a "revelation" and a "dividing line" in his thought (see below) the case can be made in a powerful way that Durkheim developed an almost completely new social ontology (e.g. Alexander 2005).

Still, arguing for a full-fledged intellectual and epistemological break might be taking things too far. Durkheim never disavowed his earlier works and tended to insist on the unity of his oeuvre. Indeed his very final essays indicate a return to the themes and style of the *Division of Labor* (Watts Miller 2012; see next chapter). There are also deep intellectual correspondences we can find. Durkheim's earlier works can be re-read in light of the *Elementary Forms* and we find in them plenty of reference to the centrality of religion and the sacred as a kind of origin point for all kinds of social things (most notably the law but also education, punishment, property, contract), to the role of morality/culture in forming solidarity, to the need for motivated individuals to sustain society, and to the signifying and ritual aspects of culture.

An intriguing footnote in the *Elementary Forms* adds even more complexity to the mix. Contradicting his letter of 1907, this sees Durkheim pushing back against critics and using the opportunity to insist that there was deep continuity in his work.

> I hope this analysis and those that follow will put an end to an erroneous interpretation of my ideas, which has more than once led to misunderstanding. Because I have made constraint the *external feature* by which social facts can be most easily recognized and distinguished from individual psychological ones, some have believed that I consider physical constraint to be the entire essence of social life. In reality, I have never regarded constraint as anything more than the visible expression of an underlying, inner fact that is wholly ideal: *moral authority* . . . the main object of the question treated in the present work is to discover in what form the particular kind of moral authority that is inherent in all that is religious is born, and what it is made of. (1995: 210, italics in original)

However, should we take him at his word? Perhaps the footnote is evidence of "protesting too much." How are we to reconcile what others saw ("an erroneous interpretation of my ideas") with what Durkheim himself declared? What may well have been happening was a complex articulation of theory construction, academic reception, and self-understanding. Perhaps the best answer to this riddle comes from Jeffrey Alexander (2005). He claims Durkheim really and truly thought he was doing one thing in his earlier work – that is, generating a voluntaristic sociology of moral integration – but could not quite deliver this due to lingering morphological determinism. Durkheim could never really see this failure himself. So he tended to blame his audience for being bad readers when they took him for a positivist and determinist in their book reviews. Durkheim became frustrated. It would take his move toward/discovery of a symbolic, ritual, and religious sociology to get the theoretical intent, the textual construction, and the received message to line up. However (and here we must really speculate), he could not bring himself to disown his earlier body of work (either to himself or to the public) by admitting that he had changed tack in a radical way or that his labor had been in vain. Rather he preferred to see his later work as a new set of understandings that augmented and developed his earlier ideas with fresh theoretical and empirical resources.

Regardless of whether scholars stress continuity or change in Durkheim's thought, it is agreed by everyone that William Robertson Smith's (2002) study of the *Religion of the Semites* had a major impact upon him. This had been published in 1889, just five or six years before Durkheim read it. Although trained in theology, the Scotsman Robertson Smith took a broadly sociological and comparative approach to the religions of the Middle East as he attempted to reconstruct their history and to understand how belief shaped social life among the Semitic tribes. The aim was to shed light on the Old Testament through a kind of comparative anthropology. Robertson Smith considered core ethnological themes of the time like taboos, totemism, sacrifice, and classification, showing how they were all interconnected in tribal social life. The text was to exert a profound influence not only on Durkheim but also on the British structural functionalist tradition in anthropology we turn to in chapter 3.

The ability of *Religion of the Semites* to impress Durkheim was no doubt shaped by a similarity to Fustel de Coulanges's *The Ancient City* insofar as both explored in a "joined up" and empirical way the evolution of culture, belief, and custom. They showed how religious activity had profound connections to social structure, be it among the Hebrews or in the Rome of Antiquity. However, as Robert Alun Jones observes, Robertson Smith allowed Durkheim to develop a "far more capacious" (1993: 38) concept of religion than that of Fustel de Coulanges. His mentor from the ENS had an understanding that was too tied to ideas about duty and ancestor worship. In a sense it was too buttoned down. Durkheim's exposure to ideas about taboo, sacrifice, feasting, and wider community life helped him to move toward a more comprehensive, envigorated religious sociology.

We know that Robertson Smith was important because Durkheim provides an emphatic endorsement. In the famous letter from 1907 (already alluded to, here it is at last), much cited by Durkheim scholars, he speaks of Robertson Smith's impact while preparing a new course of religion several years before.

[I]t was not until 1895 that I achieved a clear view of the essential role played by religion in social life. It was in that year that, for the first time, I found the means of tackling the study of religion sociologically. This was a revelation to me. That course of 1895 marked a dividing line in the development of my thought, to such an extent that all my previous researches had to be taken up afresh in order to be made to harmonize with these new insights . . . [This re-orientation] was entirely due to the studies of religious history which I had just undertaken, and notably to the reading of the works of Robertson Smith and his school. (Durkheim quoted in Lukes 1973: 237)

The details of the 1894–5 course remain sketchy. What is clear is that although Robertson Smith was pivotal in a Damascene way, he was not the only incident on the road to the *Elementary Forms*. This was not just the case of a single profound reading experience leading to the scales falling from Durkheim's eyes. Durkheim's interest in religion was encouraged also through Marcel Mauss and their collaboration on the essay *Primitive Classification* (discussed in the next chapter). This appeared in *L'Année sociologique* in 1903 and dealt closely with ethnographic information as well as with theoretical ideas about evaluative cultural codes. Further, we should mention that Mauss and another student, Henri Hubert, had published significant extended essays on magic and sacrifice in the *Année* (also see next chapter). Their mentor's micro-managing editorial style and desire to develop the talent in his team ensured not only that he was deeply familiar with these studies, but also that he had made intellectual inputs into the published product.

Durkheim had outputs too under his own pen that indicated a ten-year obsession with the Australian ethnography that would form the backbone of the evidentiary base of the *Elementary Forms*. These substantial notes and placeholders took advantage of *L'Année sociologique*'s regular publication of theoretically motivated book reviews. An essay on totemism (the worship of animals, plants, or other things emblematic of the social group; see below) appeared in 1902 (Durkheim 1902). This signaled Durkheim's entry into one of the biggest debates of his era. Scholars of religion and ethnology were struggling to understand just what was going on, and how totemism could be made amenable to generalizable social or religious theory. Controversies swirled as to whether or not totemism was a proper religion or was a form of magic; whether it was the origin of all religion (or any); and whether and how totemic species were related to practical or survival needs, to ritual, and to sacrifice. Durkheim also published on Aboriginal ethnographic material in the *Année sociologique* of 1905 and again in 1906 (Durkheim 1905; 1906). The first of these two items was a twenty-nine-page review of complex materials suggesting that Durkheim was already highly motivated and in the thick of it. Clearly he needed to invest a lot of time in technical details to write this essay. He went deep into kinship data and theory concerning rules of exogamy (incest taboos, prescriptive rules about marrying out of the group, and details on just who could be married to whom in societies with multiple "marriage classes") and in this way Durkheim arrived at an understanding that logical operations of a mathematical kind must be behind what was going on. This intuition was noted by others in subsequent decades and, like his essay on totemism, fed into the thought of anthropologists like Radcliffe-Brown and Lévi-Strauss on kinship systems and the workings of the primitive mind (Watts Miller 2012: 95; see later chapters). These later scholars redeemed the promise of using totemism and kinship to uncover formal and highly abstract operations in cultural systems as Durkheim had hinted. Even more groundwork for the *Elementary Forms* can be found in Durkheim's lecture series of 1906/7. A detailed table of correspondences (Watts Miller 2012: 101) with the *Elementary Forms* suggests that most of his intellectual problems had already been solved by that date and that he was ready to begin writing up from 1908 onward. Beyond this work on the Australian context, Durkheim's lectures on property from as early as 1898–1900 also provide an indication of the religiously directed shift in his thinking following the reading of William Robertson Smith (Jones 1993; see also chapter 2).

Of course these earlier works and passing remarks add up to cumulative intellectual steps, each addressing just one or two pieces of a puzzle that required an extremely complex solution. As Kenneth Thompson (2002: 137) points out, the *Elementary Forms* was Durkheim's "most mature and sophisticated deployment of theoretical strategies" for the study of religion. Within a larger structuralist framework "he employed three types of explanation: causal, interpretative and functionalist." It is a magnificent, complex intellectual synthesis of theory building, information organization, and sociological accounting. And Robert Alun Jones (2005: 80) indicates that this is a book that "advances two outrageously ambitious theories and at least a dozen subsidiary hypotheses, and whose interpretive possibilities sometimes seem endlessly bewildering." In the *Elementary Forms* Durkheim argues (predictably enough given that he is, well, Durkheim) that religion is not about individual beliefs. It is a fundamentally social thing. Moreover, we are wasting our time if we seek to evaluate religions as true or false. The important thing is to study them as something real and enduring, as a social fact. Perhaps it was the most important social fact of all, for Durkheim argued somewhat audaciously that religion was at the basis of all knowledge.

In the *Elementary Forms* Durkheim insists that every religion is made up of "intellectual conceptions and ritual practices" (1995: 99) or "beliefs and rites" (1995: 34). At the core of these is a binary classification: "The division of the world into two domains, one containing all that is sacred and the other all that is profane – such is the distinctive trait of religious thought" (1995: 34). The translation of the two words **sacred** and **profane** has caused all kinds of problems due to slight misalignments between English and French. They are not synonymous with "good and bad" or "good and evil" or "pure and polluted" (Kurakin 2015), although we will see that this kind of interpretation has proven fruitful in cultural sociology (see chapter 5). Rather, the sacred is contrasted by Durkheim with the mundane, the ordinary, the everyday, the utilitarian, the unremarkable, the practical, and the functional. What makes things even more complicated is that Durkheim emphatically notes that the sacred also includes the idea of danger, or, better, that there are two sides to the sacred that cannot be easily separated. It can be a positive force that can protect the individual, community, environment, and cosmos but it is also unpredictable, capricious, volatile, malevolent, and potentially vindictive. It needs to be handled with care, managed, and controlled. So Durkheim argues not only that the sacred must be separated from the profane, but also that it is surrounded with taboos, prohibitions, and secrecy. Our emotional attitude toward it is also special. There are attitudes of fear, reverence, and awe and a sense of contact with the transcendent.

In order to illustrate and understand the operations of religion Durkheim turned to a new empirical resource. He believed that methodologically it made sense to look toward the earliest and most stripped-back forms of religious life so that complexity was reduced and the essential elements of religion would be at their most visible. In an era when evolutionary thinking on stages of social development was baked into anthropological thought, Australian totemism was believed to offer "the most primitive and simplest religion that can be found" (1995: 93). Layers of doctrine and distracting theological disputes could only get in the way if Durkheim was to explore Christianity, Judaism, or any other major world religion. In addition, he believed the selection was justified by the fact that "the most thorough documentation we have concerns Australian totemism"

(1995: 93). He was lucky that reports from W. Baldwin Spencer and F. J. Gillen had been arriving in Europe from the central deserts of Australia. Deep in the middle of the continent, isolated cattle stations, missions, and a new long-distance telegraph line had initiated colonial contact with previously isolated groups engaged in a hunter-gatherer small-band lifestyle. Gillen was a telegraph operator and Spencer a scientist at the University of Melbourne. Together they formed an effective research team, making arduous field trips and documenting the languages and customs of scattered Aboriginal peoples in the bush or at points of administrative and religious control. This work was to culminate in a book that struck Durkheim as a resource without peer when it came to detailed, credible, firsthand information – *The Native Tribes of Central Australia* (Spencer and Gillen 1899), which focused largely on the Arunta (variously in the ethnographic record "Aranta," "Aranda," "Arrente") people and their neighbors.

Durkheim's exploration of Aboriginal beliefs follows Spencer and Gillen (as well as other writers on Australia, much ethnology from North America, and a highly technical, specialist debate in anthropology and comparative religion that extended from the Victorian age through to the 1960s) in giving centrality to the **totem**, the "very archetype of sacred things" (1995: 118). This is generally a plant or animal, or a related image or object that is considered sacred by a social group and that is the emblem of the group. One such object is the ***churinga***, which is usually an oval or oblong stone or piece of wood that is marked or engraved with a totemic symbol. This could actually be more sacred than the species it represents. The totem is believed to have great powers – for example to heal the sick or to cause sickness, to allow game to proliferate, to bring rain – and is surrounded by prohibitions. Contact with the *churinga* may only be possible for initiates and the object must be kept hidden. The totemic species depicted on the *churinga* must not be eaten. In Durkheim's view **totemism**, which we might define as the set of beliefs and practices associated with totemic worship, reveals the qualities of the sacred in a direct way. The totem is the carrier of a more abstract sacred force that flows through it and that gives energy to that which it touches. Moreover, the totem sits at the heart of culture insofar as it is part of a classificatory system. Totems are associated with clans and phantries (kin groups, each with its own totem), and relations between clans and totemic symbols in turn provide a bedrock for wider cosmologies, hence knowledge. Most important of all for Durkheim, the totem is an expression of the collective conscience of the society. The totem somehow captures and holds it.

48

But just how does the totem come to be endowed with this incredible power? The answer lay not just in thought but also in social activity. For Durkheim, as we quoted above, religion consisted of both rites (actual human activity) and beliefs (ideas, mental representations, classifications). Hence the concept of **ritual** ("rites") is as central to the *Elementary Forms* as that of the sacred ("beliefs"). The Aboriginal tribes would be scattered for much of the year and engage in the activities of profane time: "food, hunting, and fishing are not occupations that can stir truly strong passions. The dispersed state in which society finds itself makes life monotonous, slack and humdrum," Durkheim writes (1995: 217). However, at special times of year the tribes would come together. There would be a change in the dynamic density and the group would enter into socially classified sacred time. In larger groups and with more intensive social contact the tribes would engage in intensive rites known as a **corroboree**. This would pivot on the celebration of the totem. Involving dancing, chanting, percussive music, mythical storytelling, using bullroarers (noisy ceremonial items spun around the head on a long string), contact with the elaborately carved and decorated *churinga* (sometimes also the bullroarer), and even collective sexual activity, these rites would generate tremendous excitement among the Aborigines.

> [A] sort of electricity is generated from their closeness and quickly launches them to an extraordinary height of exaltation ... from every side there are nothing but wild movements, shouts, howls, and deafening noises ... these gestures and cries tend to fall into rhythm and regularity ... Boomerangs are knocked against one another; bull roarers are whirled ... The sexes come together in violation of the rules governing sexual relations ... the ceremonies are generally held at night, in the midst of shadows pierced here and there by firelight, we can easily imagine the effect that scenes like these are bound to have on the minds of all those who take part. (1995: 218)

Durkheim famously dubbed the social energy illuminated by this frequently used quotation **collective effervescence**. There would be a sense of mystical and empowering contact with sacred forces. These would be transferred onto the totemic symbol (plant or animal) that was at the center of the ritual activity, or into sacred objects of material culture that were connected to the totemic symbol (often the *churinga*). The totem would then "store" this sacrality and operate as a reminder for the group. This focus on action and energy suggests that sitting somewhere behind Durkheim's thoughts about collective effervescence were ideas from his time on the topic of **dynamogenesis** (Jones 2005; Watts Miller 2012). This referred to the ways that energies in people could be uplifted in various social contexts when offered a stimulus. Experimental psychologists of the time had noted that individuals performed strength tests better when given a sound or image as they were exerting themselves. In everyday life we see this enacted when we play pumping music at the gym – say the theme from *Rocky* – or put motivational images of great leaders over our desks, or believe in the power of positive thinking. The concept of dynamogenesis had already been adopted by the pragmatist philosopher William James, where it played a central role in his theory of religious experience (Watts Miller 2012: 156). Durkheim was intimately familiar with James's work (Jones 2005: 93; see also next chapter, on pragmatism). Although the term does not appear in the *Elementary Forms*, Durkheim mentioned dynamogensis explicitly in 1913 at a meeting of the French Philosophical Society (Durkheim 1913) where he seemed to be trying to set the record straight on what his book from the year before was really about. Here he suggests that simply having a mental representation of God would give an individual "an ardor for life, an enthusiasm that he does not experience in ordinary times. He has more power to resist the hardships of existence; he is capable of greater things and proves it by his conduct" (quoted in Jones 2005: 80). Once we are aware of dynamogenesis, it is easy to find in the *Elementary Forms* passages where Durkheim attempts to communicate the energizing and motivational power of the collectivity. He writes:

> This stimulating and invigorating effect of society is particularly apparent in certain circumstances. In the midst of an assembly that becomes worked up, we become capable of feelings and conduct of which we are incapable when left to our own individual resources. When it is dissolved and we are again on our own, we fall back to our ordinary level and can then take the full measure of how far above ourselves we were. (1995: 212)

Durkheim goes on to allude to heady events such as those of the French Revolution, the Crusades, and Joan of Arc's uprising as exemplifying this process. In some ways Durkheim's collective effervescence was a specification of dynamogenesis, but one that gave particular attention to morals and ideals as well as collective action and sociality.

If dynamogensis lurks in the background, a pivotal concept that we see in print many times in the *Elementary Forms* is that of **collective representations**. The term had first appeared as early as 1897 (Lukes 1973: 6) but became more important in Durkheim's later work. Collective representations are shared ideas, classifications, myths, and symbols. The verb "to represent" in French is reflexive ("represent to oneself") and so it also captures the way that society thinks about or imagines itself into existence (the subtleties are not unlike those attending to "collective conscience"; see above). It ties nicely to the idea of the non-material social fact and is an important resource for those wishing to see Durkheim as a cultural theorist. For Durkheim there was a dynamogenic force in collective representations. They could motivate individuals, powering them up through a sense of sacred energy and collective belonging.

Durkheim's analysis of religion exposes a classic case of misrecognition. The real source of religious power lies not in the totem but in the social group and in collective life: "Religious forces are in fact only transfigured collective forces, that is, moral forces; they are made of ideas and feelings that the spectacle of society awakens in us" (1995: 327). This idea is often summarized in lazy textbooks with radically simplifying sentences to the effect that religion is society worshipping itself or that God is society. Yet the fact remains that participants in the delirium and ecstasy of ritual do not see the true, "social" cause of the sacred. The operant outcome of this ignorance and belief is solidarity, civilization, and morality. Durkheim sees such religious thought as a positive social achievement, not as evidence of faulty rationality. So there is an uplifting subtext to the book that can seduce the reader with a sense of society flourishing and bootstrapping its way toward transcendence as it escapes the profane, mortal world. The poet T. S. Eliot (1916: 2), a meticulous reader if ever there was one, noted this, observing that although Durkheim had publicly disagreed with the idealist philosopher Henri Bergson, there was "a suggestion of Bergsonism" in his words. Henri Bergson (1859–1941) was a leading French thinker of the time whose writings gave emphasis to creativity, intuition, experience, and freedom as fundamental to human existence. He was resolutely opposed to mechanistic and deterministic visions of action and social life. If Eliot's reading is correct, it suggests a very different Durkheim had emerged from the one who had written the *Rules of Sociological Method*.

We have covered the main ideas about religion, ritual, collective effervescence, and the sacred. Yet it should be noted that the *Elementary Forms* is chock full of lesser but highly tractable, productive concepts. The **soul**, to which a large number of pages are given over, is said by Durkheim to have a social origin. It is connected to his thinking about *homo duplex* (see next chapter) wherein the person has both sacred and profane attributes. The soul, which is a sacred aspect of the individual, is associated with collective life, totemic forces, and *mana*. This is a multi-tasking Polynesian word that variously refers to magical powers, supernatural forces, taboos, ritual protections, and charismatic prestige. Durkheim also engages in a classification of rituals. **Negative cults** are associated with restrictions on activity and with efforts to keep the sacred and profane separate. For example, there might be taboos or injunctions against certain activities such as eating or sex, or seeing, hearing, or speaking certain things before encountering the sacred totem. Often we find forms of suffering here, such as self-inflicted pain or even torture. These prepare the individual for the often-dangerous contact with higher powers. **Positive cults** involve actions rather than restrictions on actions. The example Durkheim considers most extensively is sacrifice. Here there is an act of communion or communication with the sacred. Mimetic (copying) actions also reproduce, encourage, and honor sacred forces. In exploring positive cults Durkheim gives particular attention to the *intichiuma* ceremony described in detail by Spencer and Gillen. This involved efforts to ensure the proliferation of the group's totemic species through mimetic actions of dancing, singing, and communal eating. Durkheim speaks of these using terminology such as "drama" and "performance" and so captures the creative, aesthetic, and emotionally engaging nature of ritual (we return to this theme in chapter 5). **Commemorative rites** stress the continuity of the present with the past. They remind tribal members of their history and connect a community to its mythological origins (the term is popular today in collective memory studies). **Piacular rites** (a concept probably invented by Durkheim) refer to mourning. They reflect collective suffering and control the sacred dangers embodied in the recently dead ancestor (a theme also addressed by Durkheim's student Robert Hertz; see next chapter). These frequently involve pain in Aboriginal society. The mourners might flagellate, burn, or cut themselves. This activity serves as a sacrifice to the dead and, far from being debilitating, reminds the survivors of their own sacred energies – presumably in a dynamogenic way. The purpose of such piacular effort, of course, is to rebuild group solidarity after a loss, and it is no surprise that this section of the *Elementary Forms* was to later inform Radcliffe-Brown's thoughts (see next chapter) about the connection between emotions and a determinate social structure.

Although the *Elementary Forms* is based on a study of "primitive" religion, Durkheim stressed time and time again that the principles he identified applied also in the great world religions and in modernity. For Durkheim, the Christians and Jews of his own time were engaged in similar tasks of managing the sacred and generating collective effervescence. It is of the greatest importance that he stresses his findings were not just about primitive society or even just about religion. Indeed *The Elementary Forms* stands out as a contribution to a "religious sociology" (the sacred is everywhere in social life) rather than the "sociology of religion" (the study of religious aspects of social life narrowly conceived as "the study of religions"). Durkheim argued that conceptions of the sacred were social in origin. Hence anything that comes to represent the group or that is a manifestation of the collective conscience in a sense has a religious quality. The sacred and society are inextricably linked and social life is propelled by collective representations that are internalized by actors. In one of his most often-quoted passages he writes:

> There is perhaps no collective representation that is not in a sense delusive; religious beliefs are only a special case of a very general law. The whole social world seems populated with forces that in reality exist only in our minds. We know what the flag is for the soldier, but in itself it is only a bit of cloth. Human blood is only an organic liquid, yet even today we cannot see it flow without experiencing an acute emotion that its physicochemical properties cannot explain. From a physical point of view, man is nothing but a system of cells . . . yet society conceived him and requires that we conceive him as being endowed with a *sui generis* character that insulates and shields him from all reckless infringement – in other words, that imposes respect. (1995: 229)

The image here is a radical one and it is no accident that this seems to be the favorite Durkheim quotation for cultural sociologists today. Shared mental representations and classifications form the basis for action, motivation, and morality. Social life is steered by the idea, by culture, by the surplus of meaning that is put onto materiality. Such valuation was the property of arbitrary social constructions. Durkheim underlined the point with reference to the price of a rare postage stamp in a collection. These insights were to inspire later thinking by Lévi-Strauss and others as they argued that society could build a cultural system from whatever came to hand (see chapter 4), and they would go on to shape cultural sociology after the cultural turn via the radical claim that that not only meaning but also society itself is constructed via symbolic or imaginative activity.

For a long time the *Elementary Forms* was given a lukewarm reception. Reviewers complained that Durkheim had over-reached in seeing the origins of all thought, knowledge, and science in religion (see Fournier 2013: 62). Durkheim's published response in 1913 is illuminating, as perhaps it highlights aspects of the book that he feels reviewers had not noticed. He wrote of the role of religion in "raising up" the individual, of the "duality of man" (*homo duplex*), and – as already noted – of the dynamogenic or motivational and empowering force of religion. Other reviewers, arguably caught up in abstruse debates about ethnology rather than seeing the bigger contribution to social theory, were concerned about points of detail concerning totemism. For example, it could be claimed that Durkheim underestimated the role of material conditions in primitive belief. These sorts of complaints – of very little interest to us today – were to continue for years and were even made by scholars who were deeply influenced by Durkheim. For instance, Radcliffe-Brown argued that totemic species were not entirely randomly selected but tended to be more visible or important in the proximate environment.

Although not acclaimed as a revolutionary work in its time, the contributions and reputation of the *Elementary Forms* have grown such that now it is considered a foundational classic and almost oracular source of authoritative insight, not only in social anthropology but also in sociology and religious studies. For those interested in social and cultural theory it is widely seen as Durkheim's most significant book. Why so?

- The study is chock-full of concepts that have proven highly adaptable and fruitful for empirical research. These include the sacred and profane, ritual, and collective effervescence.
- The *Elementary Forms* encourages different ways of thinking than Durkheim's other works. Although Durkheim occasionally intones about social facts and objectivity, this work is infinitely more subtle or musical than the *Rules of Sociological Method*. As Eliot noted in spotting the Bergsonian resonances, it seems more humanist. Yet if there are transcendental notes, there is also a pragmatic and empirical focus on real bodies in real social interaction. People as social actors who can bring about results are strangely absent from Durkheim's other, earlier works. These tended to focus on system-level and higher-order explanations. The shift toward ritual opens up not only to functionalism and semiotics but also very nicely to symbolic interactionist and processual sociologies, to cultural sociologies of "performance," and even, some would say, pragmatics (e.g. at the limits of the case that is generally made, Rawls 2001).
- There is a detailed interrogation of cultural systems as an interlocking complex of beliefs, signs, and myths. Durkheim seems to

be shifting here to a structuralist, communicative mode of analysis that seems strikingly contemporary when contrasted to the almost Victorian language games of, say, *The Division of Labor*. With this move Durkheim seems, in certain passages at least, to be uncanny in his anticipation of the cultural turn that swept the social sciences in the late twentieth century (see chapters 4 and 5). Society exists and functions due to the institutionalization of a set of somewhat arbitrary and non-utilitarian ideas and beliefs that carry information and value. There is a surplus of meaning that drives action and that has little to do with survival or profane economic life. As we will see in chapter 5, these factors have decisively shaped much of the more recent reception of this masterful text.

- However, we must also be aware that the *Elementary Forms* was read for the next six decades through a functionalist lens. In this understanding, rituals happen so as to integrate society; people do not realize the reasons they are acting; the sacred is a force for moral unity; cultural life is all about maintaining social stability. In this reading, continuities with Durkheim's arguments about the social functions of punishment for the wider community were often in the foreground. We trace this reception dynamic in chapter 4.

With the publication of the *Elementary Forms* Durkheim hit his last intellectual high point. Although he was to write some more essays, he became less productive by his own high standards. His life was increasingly governed by melancholia and by the effects of a stroke. The deaths of his student Robert Hertz and his son André in World War I seemed to sap his energy. He was diagnosed with neurasthenia, which Fournier (2005: 57) describes as "a clinical state of mental hypersensitivity and physical debility, resulting from continual mental exertion." To these symptoms we might add nervous exhaustion, fatigue, irritability, and general emotional disturbance. Neurasthenia is not recognized today as a medical condition, although much of what it describes is also captured by our equally diffuse concepts of depression and anxiety. Perhaps the illness is fitting, at least for those influenced by the epistemological relativism of the cultural turn. What better illustration could there be of the arbitrary ways a culture will classify the world around it than to die of a disease that does not exist? Durkheim passed away in November 1917 at the age of fifty-nine. By today's standards Durkheim had not even made it to retirement age. Yet he made the most of his short years thanks to deep thought, originality, leadership, strategy, and hard work. The incredible burst of high-level academic productivity in the twenty or so years from 1893 to 1912 seems in hindsight somewhat miraculous. As this book will show, Durkheim may have been dead but he was never forgotten.

Chapter 2
Durkheim's Other Works and the Contributions of His Students

The variety of outputs – individualism – socialism – ethics – the state – sex/gender/family/marriage – pragmatism – education – the body – punishment – classification – Mauss – Hertz – Hubert – other students in the Année team.

In our prior chapter we sketched Durkheim's most substantial contributions. These are found in the four major books that are the core of his legacy. Yet these tomes do not exhaust his output. Indeed there seems to be a bottomless pit of smaller works. Some continue and expand the lines of thinking in the major studies. Others bring in new topics or provide the best evidence we have for his views on certain issues. In this chapter we will introduce the multiple reviews, lecture series, and commentaries that need to be acknowledged as important in their own right. We will at times connect these to themes that are perhaps subordinated or scattered in his four major books.

The chapter will also begin our move away from Durkheim and toward the Durkheimian tradition. It highlights how Durkheim was the leader of a research team. The contributions of his colleagues and students in the last two decades of his life are the first signs of an evolving Durkheimian paradigm that was beginning to take on a life of its own. This moved into ever-new territories, generally more anthropological and more concerned with symbolic and religious life. We consider these elaborations also in this chapter. The main argument: even without the four great monographs Durkheim would have been considered today a noted minor theorist, a significant intellectual networker, and the originator of one of the most productive and original scholarly groups in the history of the social thought.

If they are not full-length scholarly monographs written as such, then what exactly are the products we are going to be talking about in this chapter from Durkheim and his students? When it comes to format they are: book reviews with developed arguments; responses and rejoinders; notes; extended essays from the *Année sociologique* that could later be published as short, stand-alone books; and lecture series and lecture notes that could be collated and published as a book posthumously (the empirical topics for these being education, pragmatism, morality, socialism, and politics and the state). Such product in all its material forms tends to fall out into the following themes:

- reflections on the problem of social integration and the nature of morality in modernity;
- efforts to clarify epistemological foundations for a discipline or science of sociology;
- critical analyses of rival thinkers and paradigms;
- ethnologically inspired comparative studies, usually regarding the nature of religious phenomena.

Generally speaking, Durkheim's leading students made their most significant contributions to the last of the above bullet points, the most empirical one. Durkheim's efforts, as might be expected, involved all four. He was far stronger than all his students at abstract social thought.

This chapter is organized as follows. First we run through the remainder of Durkheim's thought by name-checking key concepts. This is a fairly speedy "need to know" exercise. Often there are overlaps with and elaborations upon themes we introduced in the prior chapter. Still, the case could be made that the most important statements he had on many topics were outside the major monographs; hence the title for this section that is given below features the word "remaining." We are looking here at themes that took a back seat before in chapter 1 and at minor works that express these particularly well. As we finish with Durkheim we turn to his students and look at their most significant works.

Durkheim's Remaining Ideas and Works

Individualism struck Durkheim as a distinctive feature of modernity. In *Suicide* he had highlighted the dangers of excessive egoism and flagged that people needed to be connected to collectivities in meaningful ways. However, his understanding was that egoism and individualism were not one and the same. Nor did individualism necessarily challenge a valued collective life. Rather individualism was a positive thing where it was a shared, core, and appropriate social value. This was the case in the mature condition of true modernity. In the crucially important essay "Individualism and the Intellectuals," first published in 1898, Durkheim (1970) responded to the Dreyfus case in a somewhat oblique way. He defended Dreyfus indirectly and cryptically by elaborating ideas about individualism rather then engaging in a direct discussion of the matters filling the newspapers. His argument was that a utilitarian and economistic version of individualism needed to be contrasted to a moral individualism that was a sign of social progress. These ideas about individualism are also clearly expressed in book 1, chapter 5, of the *Division of Labor*.

Durkheim's most enduring meme in "Individualism and the Intellectuals" was that the human person is a sacred entity existing in a **cult of the individual** and that our morality demanded this sacrality be protected. He writes:

> The human person . . . is considered sacred, in what can be called the ritual sense of the word. It has something of that transcendental majesty which the churches of all times have accorded their gods. It is conceived as being invested with that mysterious property which creates a vacuum about holy objects and keeps them away from profane contacts and which separates them from ordinary life . . . It is a religion of which man is, at the same time, both a believer and a god. (1986c: 81)

The idea of the "vacuum" was taken up by Erving Goffman (see chapter 4). He was to discuss much later how certain prohibitions and small marks of respect surround the individual in everyday life like a protective bubble. Durkheim also indicates in the essay that individualism, within the context of a more abstract concept of common humanity, is a shared civic value. To respect the individual is to respect society more widely. True individualism is best described not as a source of anarchic self-interest but rather as a moral force that if honored can generate social integration. He writes:

> A verbal similarity has made possible the belief that *individualism* necessarily resulted from *individual*, and thus egoistic sentiments. The religion of the individual is a social institution like all known religions. It is society which provides us with this ideal as the only common end which is today able to offer a focus for men's wills. (1986c: 81)

As Durkheim expands upon such ideas in "Individualism and the Intellectuals," he connects them with his thinking in the *Division of Labor*. In traditional contexts life was more collective. As society became more complex people started to develop divergent interests and ways of seeing. Society had evolved to the point where respect for these differences and for common humanity was an appropriate cultural form for our age. He further expounds that Christianity played a role in this process, with its emphasis on the individual's choice of faith and inner sentiment over the merely formulaic observance of rites. The resulting cult of the individual was a pivotal dimension of the collective conscience or collective morality today. It saw the individual accorded respect and autonomy. When it was correctly specified, these individuals would be guided by a shared social morality and be able to combat egoism and the narrow pursuit of self-interest that were so destructive to social life.

Durkheim's thoughts are barely sketched out but they have monumental implications. In a twist reminiscent of the gymnastics of an ENS entrance examination (discussed in chapter 1) they square the circle. Whereas common sense places individual and society in tension, Durkheim suggests that becoming a true individual can mean fulfilling a social value. Growing individualism in the right circumstances equates to growing sociality. It is a win–win situation. He was right on the money. In the world today discourses of human rights are fundamentally shaped by the assumption that freedom of expression and identity are inalienable, and that an entitlement to creativity and personal growth are universal, shared, collective values of humanity. We measure the worth of entire nations and of smaller collectivities such as universities, churches, or families by looking to whether they allow individuals to achieve, flourish, and prosper (become "truly themselves") or whether they subject individuals to repressive group norms. The idea has proven especially fruitful as a way to understand the evolution of rights in fields such as gender equality, mental health, criminology and punishment, education, and childhood (Joas 2013; see chapter 5). Likewise Roger Cotterrell (1999) looks to the law in light of Durkheim's remarks. He reconstructs individualism as increasingly important to Durkheim's vision of regulation. According to Cotterrell, over time Durkheim came to replace the more mechanistic and repressive view of law in the *Division of Labor* with a more culture-driven vision of ideas organized around individual freedoms shaping legal change.

Durkheim's orientation to **socialism** also inspired much of his writing and was at the core of a lecture course largely dedicated to the proto-sociological thinker Henri de Saint-Simon (1760–1825). This lecture course later came out as a book (Durkheim 1958). Some have seized on the thoughts and texts as evidence of a "radical Durkheim" (Gane 1992), a somewhat progressive figure calling for change and looking industrial society squarely in the eye. In truth, Durkheim's relationship to socialism was complex and challenges any easy reading of him as a reactionary or a conservative. Those arguing he is conservative draw upon his views on gender and marriage (see below), the priority he placed on social order and gradual transformations, and his disapproval of strikes, social conflict, and Marxism. It still remains a source of slight discomfort for his advocates that Durkheim tended to see in a negative light things that others might have interpreted as a struggle for justice or as evidence of a critical social awareness of power and inequality (e.g. strikes). Yet Durkheim was perceived in his day as liberal and progressive. He not only stood up for Dreyfus but was a friend of the prominent trade unionist Jean Jaurès (1859–1914). Durkheim saw in socialism the possibility of a form of solidarity and collective morality that would confront the problem of anarchy and egoism in the world. But then again, he was clear that he did not condone or hope for revolution, which he saw as yet another indicator of anomie.

Durkheim took socialism to be a social fact like any other – and so it was worthy of study. It had correctly intuited that there were necessary interconnections between the various parts of society, and so was in a sense a doctrine appropriate to or reflecting its time. It was also symptomatic of the incomplete and difficult transition toward organic solidarity. He gave socialism praise as superior to communism, which he conceived as having pre-modern origins. Communism was in his view utopian, divisive, and not correctly adapted for the France of modernity. According to Durkheim, Saint-Simon was a more useful guide than Marx. Saint-Simon had understood the need for a form of centralized and coordinated social organization that recognized the significance of science, knowledge, and industry in the regulation of social life and the production of social goods. However, Saint-Simon, in Durkheim's reading, had placed too much faith in individual economic interests as a source of social harmony.

If for Durkheim revolution was not an answer, then what was? Only more active involvement by professional and occupational associations could generate the solidarity, morality, and constraint on desires that would bring peace and happiness. In dealing with the fallout from the anomic division of labor, he broadly advocates a kind of social engineering that would restore balance to society through building a shared morality, not through redistributing wealth. Insofar as Durkheim was a socialist he would likely have approved of Swedish-style social democracy or corporatism in which labor, capital, the state, and experts on morality such as himself sat down together in an effort to identify problems and reach sensible, consensual conclusions. We see these ideas about the positive possibilities of occupational groups and guilds scattered throughout his work and career (Watts Miller 2012), most notably in an early review of a book by Albert Schäffle from 1885 (Durkheim 1978); in the 1896 series of lectures on Saint-Simon we have just reviewed; and in the concluding pages of *Suicide* from 1897 (Durkheim 1952). They are most visible in the Preface to the Second Edition of the *Division of Labor* published in 1902. They are even present in his last completed article, "The Politics of the Future" from 1917 (Durkheim 2009).

A much-studied 1897 review of a book by the Italian thinker Antonio Labriola provides further insights into Durkheim's thoughts specifically on Marxism. Here Durkheim approves of Marxism's understanding that there were hidden collective and structural causes and laws behind social life of which individuals might not be aware: "We believe it to be a fertile idea to explain social life not by the conception that those participating in it have of it but by those deeper causes that elude consciousness" (Durkheim 1986a: 132). However, he argued that religion and not economics provided the key to the interpretation of solidarity and the collective conscience: "In the beginning everything was religious. But we are aware of no way in which religion can be reduced to economics" (1986a: 135). The timing of this critique of Marxism that puts religion first, 1897, is consistent with the account of reading William Robertson Smith as a revelation around about 1895 – although we note that religion was also held to be the origin of many things in the *Division of Labor* (from 1893).

Much the same grudging praise and censure is to be found in Durkheim's summary and critique of a book by an occasional *Année sociologique* team member, the talented Gaston Richard. Durkheim reiterates his talking point that socialism is not a "science" (unlike sociology, of course) but this did not mean it should be ignored: "If it is not a scientific theory of social facts, it is a social fact of the utmost importance that sociologists must seek to understand. Whatever one may do, it exists, and not without reason; it expresses a state of society" (Durkheim 1986b: 127). He claimed that only sociology (another characteristic move in the mode the *Rules*) could provide a truly scientific set of insights into the causes of the malaise of which socialism was an expression. Durkheim's own analysis of these origins, which was set out in his lecture series on socialism from 1895 and 1896, was that although rampant self-interest was present in the world, and socialism had to its credit seen this, the roots were moral and not economic.

We can find related themes concerning social disorganization and modernity in Durkheim's wider writing on **professional ethics and civic morality**. His thoughts are mostly found toward the end of *The Division of Labor* from 1893 and in *Professional Ethics and Civic Morals* (1957), which came out much later. The latter book, first published in Turkey, was based on lecture courses given in various years. These were initially collected in 1934 from Marcel Mauss, who had them in storage, by the young Turkish sociologist Hüseyin Kubalı. He was interested in writing a thesis on the concept of the state. The papers from Mauss were augmented after World War II by further manuscripts. Kubalı located these at the *Musée de l'Homme* with the help of Durkheim's daughter. The lectures are an expression of Durkheim's concern to strengthen the vulnerable and divided Third Republic. For Durkheim, a core problem in modernity is that economic desires can run rampant among "the manufacturer, the merchant, the workman, the employee, in carrying on his occupation" (1957: 12). There needed to be a "check on egotism . . . it is therefore extremely important that economic life should be regulated" (1957: 12). Where was this regulation to come from? Durkheim looked to medieval guilds for inspiration and suggested a solution: "Whilst the craft union or corporate body is nowadays only a collection of individuals who have no lasting ties to one another, it must become or return to being a well-defined and organized association" (1957: 13). If developed, these could meet fundamental social needs to regulate production, enforce standards, provide solidarity, community, and welfare, set ethical standards, and engage in orderly collective bargaining. There would emerge a positive and collective morality based on an awareness of a shared mission, a defined contribution to society, and a set of common interests.

This brings us to **the state**, which was to operate at a yet higher level of socially integrative generality than the occupational association. Durkheim's views here are scattered, yet again, in *The Division of Labor*, his writings on socialism, and his views on professional ethics and civic morals (for a useful collection on these kinds of issues that means bringing just one book back from the library, see Giddens 1986). For Durkheim the state was an expression of the collectivity and the collective conscience as well as a force through which these were renewed. In contrast to popular passions, it was marked by a relatively cool and deliberate mode of thought and offered a buffer against impulsive shifts of opinion and hot sentiments. Durkheim claimed that centralized elites with competence and expertise were often best suited to select and implement policy. Clearly he is influenced here by the traditions of French technocracy and the elitist social-engineering beliefs of the ENS and the other Parisian *grandes écoles* that have persisted to this day. He also suggested that the state could be supported by those guild-like groups he advocated as pivotal for a new mode of industrial-political-moral organization. These would also play a significant "cooling" role in the democratic process, appearing there as representatives of professional and occupational constituencies.

Durkheim's perspective on the state is somewhat unusual in sociology even if it is broadly in line with social contract theory in political philosophy. In much sociology today the state is seen as operating on behalf of capital, as a self-interested organization that aims to expand its own power and dominate society, or as an ecosystem of poorly coordinated contending organizations and policies engaged in some kind of internal Darwinian struggle for supremacy. Durkheim was indeed wary of the despotic potential of the state, referring to this as a monstrosity in his famous 1902 Preface to the Second Edition of the *Division of Labor* (Durkheim 1947). However, he argued that the state has historically operated as a liberating force with strong connections to collective morality. It has freed individuals from the bounds of tradition and established itself as a guardian of the cult of the person. As such, the state stands with and not against individualism. He writes: "If the cult of the human person is to be the only one destined to survive, as it seems, it must be observed by the state as by the individual equally" (1957: 69). Moreover, the state was a stepping-stone toward a universalism of a cosmopolitan kind in which national pride could be based on the ability of the nation to respect or institutionalize universal values related to justice and morality, rather than on success in war and domination over other nations. Getting the balance right was difficult. What was needed – here we go again – were those occupational groups and associations that would mediate between individuals and the state, heading off tyranny, administering welfare, and permitting the growth of healthy moral sentiments. These "secondary organs ... seem necessary to prevent the State from tyrannizing over individuals" and would permit a system where "the State, whilst remaining distinct from the mass of the nation, is closely in communication with it" (1957: 106).

For similar reasons Durkheim was skeptical of the socialist vision of the state, which tended to collapse the distinction of state and civil society. Turning its back on societal differentiation, this move was against the flow of history.

Somewhat neglected are Durkheim's writings on **property** (a point well made by Riley 2015), perhaps because they are buried in his writings on law and on ethics. A nice selection is included in *Professional Ethics and Civic Morals* that has a very different feel from the material on the themes that are in the title of that book (Durkheim 1957). When dealing with property, Durkheim both demonstrates and moves beyond the influence of Fustel de Coulanges, prefigures the *Elementary Forms*, reprises some themes in the *Division of Labor* about the evolution of practices from religious origins, and shows that he has been listening to Marcel Mauss on taboo (Jones 1993). Pivotal in Durkheim's concept of property is the idea of the sacred: "So there is a sacred basis for property being property" (1957: 152). Historically everything belonged to the group. This is the source of sacred power. As property devolved to clans and then individuals this sense of the sacred never went away. Modern property seems to be enclosed in a magic circle demanding avoidance. For example, if we see something belonging to someone else we cannot just take it, we feel as if we should ask permission to touch or even photograph it, and we feel guilty if we mistakenly walk off with it; we are uncomfortable if we have to retrieve a football from somebody's lawn; and so on. The threshold rites, which take place when one enters a house, are according to Durkheim a visible sign of this sacred envelope. These are a way of managing the transition from the profane to the sacred realm. Even today we will wipe our feet or tidy up our appearance before entering a building.

It is at times striking how Durkheim's thoughts on property, seemingly written up in the years 1898 to 1900 (see Durkheim 1957: x), feature vocabularies and treatments similar to those on *mana* in the *Elementary Forms* or, much later, *The Gift* by Marcel Mauss (see chapter 3). There seems to be a special force in the object itself. For example, when writing on the early evolution of the notion of property in soil and farming Durkheim says: "The things were sacred in themselves; they were inhabited by potencies, rather obscurely represented, and these were supposed to be their true owners, making the things untouchable to the profane" (1957: 159). Property makes abstract beliefs tangible and helps individuals feel this sacred power, which is, of course, society itself. Hence we find a little later on in the lecture: "The gods are no other than collective forces personified

65

and hypostasized in material form. Ultimately, it is society that is worshipped by the believers; the superiority of the gods over men is that of the group over its members" (1957: 161). Although well known to Durkheim specialists, this theme in his work remains under-appreciated and under-utilized by contemporary cultural theory as it looks at issues such as the household, iconicity, or material culture.

Property is generally obtained by **contract** or by inheritance. Durkheim took a dim view of inheritance, especially of large quantities of wealth, seeing it as incompatible with modern ideas of justice. However, he is very interested in the theoretical and moral possibilities of contract. Here again Durkheim stresses the role of the sacred. Early exchanges involved oaths to the gods, sacred promises, or sacrifices to seal the deal and to impose moral bonds on the parties. Prefiguring work on the performative aspects of language use, such as Austin's (1962) identification of illocutionary and perlocutionary speech acts whereby people "do things with words" such as promise, pledge, curse, command, or banish, Durkheim shows such activities amounted to a "ritual contract" that was every bit as real as an exchange of goods themselves. Over time these ritual trappings fell away. Yet even today parties to an exchange, as well as the exchange itself, will still have something of the sacred attached that gives the contract extra force. In addition, "the contract by solemn ritual has moreover not wholly passed away" (1957: 195). Such rituals are still found in contexts of "supreme importance" (1957: 195) and make contracts even harder to break. Durkheim gives the example of marriage: "Now marriage is a contract by solemn ritual not just because the religious ceremonies provide the evidence and record the dates, etc. It is above all because the bonds that have called forth moral values of a high order cannot then be broken at the arbitrary will of the parties" (1957: 195).

Durkheim insists that all contracts stand on an unexamined collective foundation. Common sense ideas about mutual competence, trustworthiness, and the authority of the law sit behind every contract. In contrast to the *tabula rasa* views of classical economics, he insists that there is a kind of **precontractual solidarity** that makes contract possible in the first place. True enough, Durkheim points out that in modernity contracts have become more individualized and are less collectivistic. Still, they are tethered to the idea of the individual as sacred. The valid contract in law must respect the individual and so be the result of free will and not coercion or duplicity. These ideas about property and contract have perhaps never been developed to their full potential even though they have gained close attention in the sociology of law (Cotterrell 1999). There seem to be many possibilities for fusion with the Durkheimian tradition on consumption and material culture, as embodied for example in the work of Douglas and Isherwood (1979; see chapter 4), or on economic cultural sociology more generally (chapter 5).

Durkheim's is hardly the first name that comes to mind when we think of pioneering sociological theorists of **sex, gender, marriage and the family**. Perhaps this is because many of his ideas read as uncomfortably essentialist and patriarchal in today's intellectual environment. I suspect that Durkheim's perspectives on sex/gender in particular have a "third rail" quality that sees them left well alone even by ardent devotees. They could easily become a distraction that would shift attention away from efforts to highlight bigger contributions. Mike Gane (1983: 232) documents this wariness and speaks of a kind of "half-avoidance." It does not help that Durkheim's thoughts are widely dispersed and so have little immediate visibility. His reflections about sex and gender in particular are buried in subsections and paragraphs under headline treatments of themes such as law, morality, suicide, and social evolution. They might have attracted more attention had they been concentrated in a single key monograph or extended essay, or if more writings had survived into the present.

The low profile belies the fact that the thematic cluster of sex/gender/marriage/family was surprisingly central to Durkheim's intellectual concerns. This remains the case even when we set aside his many thoughts about kinship systems and deem these as belonging to a separate endeavor connected to ethnography. Fournier (2013: 457) states that "Durkheim took an interest in anything to do with kinship, the family marriage and the relations between men and women." Consistent with this opinion, Lukes (1973: 179) reports that Durkheim's second and most frequently repeated lecture course was on the family. Lukes notes that according to Mauss this was Durkheim's "most cherished work" alongside the lectures on morality. Durkheim apparently kept the pages of his family lecture course with him when traveling and intended to return to the topic in a concentrated way in his later years. Illness and death prevented this ambition being fulfilled.

We can gain an inkling of Durkheim's ideas on sex, gender, and the family in the early pages of the *Division of Labor*, in discussions of sexual differences in suicide rates in *Suicide*, and in the many book reviews he wrote for the section on "Domestic Organization" of the *Année sociologique*. The most important of these reviews are on works by Jacques Lourbet, Charles Letourneau, Marianne Weber, and Edward Westermarck. Drawing upon the framework to appear later in the *Division of Labor*, Durkheim's lectures on the family from 1888/9 understood the modern conjugal family to be the product of societal evolution and institutional differentiation. The lectures are now lost but we have a solid account of them from Durkheim's student Georges Davy (see Lukes 1973: 179–86). The modern family, Durkheim says, had emerged from prior stages involving clans, extended families, and patriarchal groups wherein various functions, solidarities, duties, and religious beliefs had been fused. Aspects of these earlier incarnations remain, as we can see in the sanctity afforded to marriage contracts and to sexual fidelity today, as well as in the way the family still imposes a sense of duty on its members. Likewise in its early pages the *Division of Labor* identified a sexual division of labor that had emerged over time, as the two sexes took on different social functions within a wider context of intensifying social complexity. Women's role saw them retreat to the domestic sphere and as a result develop lower levels of sociality. Durkheim had a positive view of marriage. It prevented the anomie and instability that would accompany a sexually profligate lifestyle, regulated relations between the sexes, and calmed potentially turbulent moral and emotional dynamics. As for the family, this today provided a basis for moral education and renewal and was a control on unrestrained egoism. By playing a pivotal role in a wider societal division of labor it freed up men for economic and administrative activity outside the home.

Durkheim was in many ways a progressive who wanted to see more equality for women – eventually. He worried how increased involvement in public life could be attained without disrupting the valuable role played by women in family life via this sexual division of labor. This potentially troubling concern for integration over freedom is overshadowed as a negative check mark by his essentialist thinking about gender and mind. For example, in a review Durkheim pushed back against Letourneau's argument that over the course of history patriarchal culture had disempowered and mentally enfeebled women and that legal changes could fix things. Yet his argument was not that Letourneau had disrespected women's achievements or failed to understand the fundamental intellectual equivalence of the sexes. Rather Durkheim asks and answers the question thus: "Will equal rights be enough to do away *ipso facto* with hereditary inequality? The problem seems to me to be more complex. Legal equality must result from mental evolution rather than coming before it" (quoted in Fournier 2013: 457). The mental inferiority and lower levels of sociality Durkheim attributed to women meant that in his opinion their sexual and social needs were more basic. In the prior chapter we noted that this simplicity, in his analysis, buffered women from suicidogenic currents. Such a constitution also meant that women could be more easily satisfied with domestic family duties, solidarities, and monogamy. Men, by contrast, are more "social" or more oriented to the entirety of society. They must feel they are part of wider political life and so must participate in occupational groups and professional associations.

A product of his epoch, Durkheim has an uncanny ability to say the wrong thing and prick the "just doesn't get it" nerve when it comes to sex and gender today. His equation of women with nature and man with culture, the assumption of essentialist, organically rooted differences in cognition and emotion, and the functionalist justification of the public/private split hits the trifecta of errors that have been exposed so relentlessly by late twentieth-century feminist theory. As Jennifer Lehmann (1993: 10) puts it:

> Durkheim believes that women, unlike men, are essentially asocial in nature. Therefore, he takes the conservative patriarchal position that they should remain in the home, ostensibly outside of society, where they belong. Durkheim invokes group attributes and biological determinism when he discusses women, as opposed to the individual attributes and social determinism he imputes to men ... [this] leads him to a dual theory of human labor, in which the functions of men and women *should be* specialized, into natural reproduction and social production.

Even Mike Gane (1983), who was an advocate of a "radical" Durkheim with a message for the Left, agrees his views are essentially patriarchal.

Be that as it may, at least it cannot be said that Durkheim ignored the topics of marriage, family, sex, and gender. Nor can his thinking be written off as being "only" or "merely" a thoughtless echo of the patriarchal views of his time. Unlike many (male) scholars he took the private sphere seriously enough to engage in concerted theoretical efforts (see Gane 1983 for a detailed account). He showed the intimate sphere of family, sex, and gender had to be understood historically and relationally with regard to the social organization of the public sphere – an unquestioned starting point for feminist inquiry today. Durkheim pioneered in thinking about sexuality as a potential source of vital energy that could generate social solidarity and morality as well as tension and violence. Further, in *Primitive*

Classification and the *Elementary Forms* he showed how sexual activity, sex, and gender were significant features of symbolic systems and a resource for ritual life. In a sense they were a foundational building block for culture in both material and semiotic ways. Probably courageous scholars could revisit Durkheim's uncomfortable legacy and find neglected ideas worthy of careful revision and reworking.

If Durkheim's thoughts about the themes we have just considered are widely scattered, those on **pragmatism** form a very coherent set. Yet it is a body of thought that we can only see indistinctly, as if through a glass darkly. Durkheim developed his analysis of pragmatism quite systematically just after the publication of the *Elementary Forms* in a lecture series of 1913–14. Mauss wrote about the lecture course in the *Année sociologique* of 1925. He noted that Durkheim had admired pragmatist scholars like Dewey and James as intellectuals and believed that the young men of the time should be introduced to this exciting new line of thought. Yet Durkheim had disagreed with their message. Mauss lamented that the lecture series was lost and appealed for any information, papers, or manuscripts that his readers might have. His appeal was successful. Unfortunately the items he collected were lost yet again during the German occupation of Paris in World War II. However, two sets of student notes fell into the hands of Armand Cuvillier via a publisher. He reconstructed the lectures and published them in French in 1955 (Durkheim 1983; see Cuvillier 1983). It should be noted that we do not have Durkheim's own words. Nor do we have the lecture notes that Cuvillier used. It is difficult to pull apart the mutual influence of Cuvillier, Durkheim, and the anonymous student note takers, although what we read has the clear voice of Durkheim. Still, the lecture notes seem suspiciously detailed unless the students were prodigious at shorthand.

For Durkheim, pragmatism tends to equate truth and value with narrow utility and is too individualistic. He asserts there needs to be more space for theoretical inquiry, for pure knowledge, and for the power of the mythological and ideal to be understood (as had just been demonstrated in the *Elementary Forms*). In Durkheim's reading, truth carried a sense of moral obligation, was often a painful challenge rather than something that could be bent to meet human needs, and was determined impersonally and collectively rather than individually and subjectively. The crux of the argument comes in the eighteenth lecture when he writes:

> Mythological truths have been, for those societies that believed in them, the conditions necessary for their existence . . . By the very fact that the

70

collectivity accepts them, mythological ideas are no longer subject to individual contingencies. Hence their objective and necessary character ... It is the same with trust as with moral rules. Moral rules are not made with the purpose of being useful to the individual ... Truth is similar to moral rules, in having an impersonal and necessitating character. (Durkheim 1983: 86–7)

Experts nearly universally agree that Durkheim took a respectful but negative view of pragmatism as both an analytic and a normative intellectual project. Yet it is worth a digression to note that this has not prevented a few scholars (e.g. Rawls 2001) from swimming against the tide and arguing, using dense theoretical work, that his ideas about culture, action, and social order (especially in the *Elementary Forms*) have a pragmatist core that is amenable to a situational micro-sociology. The possibilities for this kind of use of Durkheim have been demonstrated in a less radical mode by those looking at ritual, symbolic life, drama, and emotion as contextually emergent or contingent or as involving creative action choices (see chapter 5, e.g. the discussion of Collins on interaction ritual, Alexander on perfor-mance). That said, many of the standard talking points of pragmatism are used today to take deliberate aim at Durkheimian visions of an organized semiotic culture: symbol systems are incomplete or contra-dictory or not even worthy of the term "system"; people use culture without knowing what it means; meanings emerge from repeated use and from context; the "symbolic" is a residual category for habitual behaviors that neither informants nor anthropologists can explain; we should look at what people "do" with culture to coordinate action or reach goals in practical situations rather than try to "decode" it. Among those who are steered by these claims (e.g. Bell 1992; Sperber 1975; Swidler 1986), the general consensus (contra Rawls) is that the Durkheimian tradition sits on the anti-pragmatist side of the fence, over-estimates cultural system coherence and integration, and wrongly insists that meanings precede actions.

For much of his life Durkheim followed a track in "pedagogy." He struggled for a long time to convert his official job titles so as to include the word "sociology." One senses that for most of his career Durkheim was multi-tasking. He had adapted to the labor market by cultivating an interest in **education**. He did enough in the field (the "day job") to be credible as a major scholar and to justify his rank and pay check, while at the same time continuing the advocacy of sociology that was his major passion. These words do not mean that Durkheim did not care about education or do brilliant work, but rather that his agenda in education studies was always subordinated to a bigger, more ambitious sociological agenda. We can trace the beginnings of his concern with education to an early research trip to Germany. This had been to investigate best practice in university settings so as to modernize research in France and make it competitive. Durkheim was especially impressed by the scientific and laboratory approach of Wilhelm Wundt, arguably the founder of modern psychology with his rigorous empirical work on perception and cognition (which, as it happens, has latent ties to dynamogensis). Sitting behind all this activity was the more specific fear: France had been outpaced by its neighbor, Germany, in science, industry, and military capacity. It had been humiliated, somewhat to its own surprise, in the Franco-Prussian War of 1870–1. The belief was widespread that France needed to fix its education system in order to compete economically and to ensure national security (see Riley 2015: 132–3).

For Durkheim, education was a key plank in his normative agenda of defending France, shoring up the Third Republic, and preventing instability and disunity. It was no use just inculcating students with knowledge. Educational institutions also had to be implements of moral integration. Like many others of his time, Durkheim believed that education under the control of the state could be the foundation of a secular morality that would replace the influence of Catholicism. This morality was keyed in turn to ideas about *laïcité*. This concept is still very visible in France today and is often associated with news stories about controversies at the boundary of state, civil society, and religion. It goes a little further than thoughts about the need for church and state to be kept separate (e.g. a teacher cannot wear a religious symbol like a crucifix in school) and calls for abstract, universalist civic values (rationality, liberty, equality, etc.) to play an active role in shaping social and political decisions, laws, and policies. In developing such views on education we see elements of those social-engineering tendencies that can also be found in Durkheim's writings on Saint-Simon, on professions, and on collectivistic democracy. With the correct policies and forms of organization Durkheim believed that France could become a stable, unified, and great power that was also moral, just, and fully modern, rather than an anomic, disorganized, backward, and internally fractured nation (a set of anxieties structured in a binary way that has continued to this day in France).

Durkheim's thoughts on education can be found in several places. *Education and Sociology* (Durkheim 1956) consists of four chapters, two of them from contributions to a dictionary of pedagogy and the other two from lectures. *The Evolution of Educational Thought*

(Durkheim 1977) is taken from a core lecture series from 1905 for aspiring teachers at the top high schools in France. *Moral Education* comes from a different lecture series, that of 1898–9 (Durkheim 1973), which was more or less repeated at the Sorbonne in 1902–3 and 1906–7. Considered as a whole, in these works Durkheim understands education as having a core mission organized around the comprehensive socialization of children. The task was to instill the "social" into the not yet fully formed individual so as to make good citizens and to head off possibilities for anomie and egoism. The idea was to develop an attachment "to one's country, providing that the country is conceived not as a narrowly selfish and aggressive personality but as one of the agencies through which the idea of humanity is realized" (Durkheim 1973: 207).

Durkheim's work on the evolution of education (captured in Durkheim 1977) is generally neglected but offers a nice empirical example of his approach to historical matters. As such it is an early instance of investigations in the functionalist tradition that focus on **differentiation** and social change. These would become widespread in the Parsonian era (see chapter 4). Differentiation is the process in which the components of society, or society and culture, split apart from each other and become more complex. Durkheim's work here is far less factually detailed than what we would likely find in an equivalent text by scholars such as Foucault or Weber. However, it does make a stab at empirically grounded historical analysis. Durkheim traces the evolution of education since the Middle Ages in a very sociological way with an eye to shifting religious doctrines, emergent humanist values, and the rise of science. He shows that in the Middle Ages, Ancient Greece, and Ancient Rome, education was bundled up with other aspects of social life. However, Christian education in the Middle Ages differed from the other two forms in that it had a stronger focus on moral discipline and on the cultivation of the personality (this claim is very empirically debatable – the Greeks and Romans were obsessed with building character and virtue). In modern France the explicitly religious element has been removed, thanks to science and abstract humanism, but traces remain in a program intended to generate a secular sense of morality. Durkheim offers a normative endorsement for this continuing agenda. The education system is rightly charged with the function of managing diversity and self-development. As such, it is central to both social integration and self-actualization in a context of moral individualism.

In speaking about education, social adjustment, and the cultivation of a better individual, Durkheim is flirting with his ideas about *homo duplex* that we mentioned in passing in the last chapter. These refer to the duality of human nature. The individual is both a unique being with a particular history and set of sense impressions that are connected to a single, unique material body, and also a carrier of collective representations, shared morality, and identity – what we might think of as culture. Without this social element the person is not whole. Durkheim's general view was that the under-socialized individual could not quite be trusted. Passions, desires, and egoism could easily take over. The social element of the self was needed to hold these in check and to ensure a balanced and well-rounded person who could contribute in a positive way to society. Durkheim tended to associate the body with the passions and the pursuit of pleasure, and the soul with regulating social influences. This makes it sound as if society is repressive of the individual. But in yet another move reminiscent of an entrance exam to the ENS, Durkheim argues that true freedom comes from surrender to the social, which releases individuals from slavery to passions and permits self-control. It is interesting to note that somewhat similar arguments were to be made a few years later by Norbert Elias, who in effect places Durkheim's argument about the life course in a societal evolutionary perspective by showing how hot emotions had been tamed over the centuries in a civilizing process. Impulse control is liberating.

Homo duplex as a concept received a major boost in visibility and relevance from the more general revival of **body** theory and research starting in the 1980s (Shilling and Mellor 1998; Shilling 2005). It is worth a quick digression here. Chris Shilling argues that for Durkheim the body was a medium through which society was constituted and reproduced, but in a different way from that to be found in Foucaultian visions of discipline and control. For example, in Durkheim's studies of totemism he placed an emphasis not only on meaningful totemic prohibitions on the body but also on positive, expressive acts such as cutting and painting. These were a way in which the distinction of the sacred and profane, so fundamental to the idea of society, could be anchored and reproduced in deeds and flesh, then become part of the collective conscience. And Durkheim's theory of ritual looked at how coordinated bodily activities could generate strong pro-social emotions (see discussion of Collins, chapter 5). These embodied emotions, emerging from or identified as collective effervescence, are then fixed onto totemic symbols.

In Shilling's reading, Durkheim also offers a resource if we take him less literally and think about the wider implications of his work in light of more recent body scholarship. For example, there are strong connections through to studies of *habitus* (via Mauss and Bourdieu, of course); to investigations of moral individualism and the ways this is regulated through embodied emotions like shame; to studies of bodies and ritual in political life; and to moral classifications that mark out preferred and deviant bodies (Shilling 2005). All things considered, Durkheim's theory offers a powerful way to connect individual experiences and embodied materiality to collective thought, social emotions, and group identification.

Returning from the body to the topic of education, Durkheim's somewhat earnest tomes on the subject demonstrate he was anything but an advocate for permissive, expressive, fun-based learning. To the contrary, he insists that the teacher must exert strict authority so as to subordinate the will of the student. Discipline was essential as a tool for instilling a sense of duty, a sense of limits, and a restriction on desires. When fully completed, disciplined education would have a more positive aspect. There would be a sense of respect and an active attachment to society, the nation, and in the case of France the Third Republic. Personal autonomy could come from being realistic in aspirations (there is an echo of the analysis of anomic suicide here) rather than having limitless or foolish expectations, in being able to reason and understand the world, and in accepting and recognizing the power of the group and the need for morality. In effect we needed the social side of *homo duplex* to come into play to get things right. Teachers were there to literally "perform" or enact this task in front of the class.

In *Moral Education* Durkheim reprises some of his thinking about **punishment** from the *Division of Labor*. The full implications of these two works for a more general theory of punishment were only realized much later by David Garland (1990). He also paid attention to Durkheim's essay "Two Laws of Penal Evolution" (reproduced in Gane 1992). Garland reconstructed Durkheim not as an "end in itself but as a first step towards the construction of a more adequate framework for the analysis of penality" (1990: 23). The distinction is important. Whereas Durkheim scholars see an improved understanding of Durkheim as the task, for sociologists with expertise in substantive fields (here it is criminology), detailed readings have always been made with an eye to what can be taken from Durkheim or how his ideas might play into contemporary debates or theoretical armatures. Time and time again we have seen Durkheim with fresh eyes as a new topic is brought into the frame. In this case just thinking about Durkheim as a theorist of punishment allows us to see that he "took punishment to be a central object of sociological analysis and he accorded it a privileged place in his theoretical framework, returning to it again and again as his life's work progressed" (Garland 1990: 23). By the end of his task of sifting and rebuilding, Garland has shown Durkheim to be offering the major foundational statement for a normative and moral vision of punishment in social theory. This can potentially be opened out into a fully developed vision of the act as ritualized, expressive, religious, and emotive. According to Garland, Durkheim's approach, although not without its own problems relating to power and consensus, can be shown as standing in opposition to the rational, control-oriented understandings of Foucault and Marxist political economy. Building on this work, Smith (2008a) pushed Durkheim even further round the cultural turn than Garland, arguing that particularly in *Moral Education* there are intimations of a later, more semiotic and religious vision of punishment. Going through *Moral Education* carefully, Smith finds vocabularies and statements that align with ideas about signification, pollution, and the sacred.

We saw in the *Division of Labor* that punishment was an angry and expressive outburst of the collective conscience directed toward social repair. Likewise in the school setting as described in *Moral Education*, punishment is not primarily about changing the offender – although this too is part of its remit. It is a sign or gesture to the group that the sacred order of the schoolroom is to be upheld. There is a communicative purpose regarding the teaching of morality. Further, punishing the student is an expiation of the symbolic harm of the initial infraction. As Durkheim puts it:

> the teacher must prevent the weakening of the class's moral convictions by demonstrating in an unequivocal way that his feelings have not changed, that the rule is always sacred in his view . . . such is the principal function of punishment. To punish is to reproach, to disapprove. (Durkheim 1973: 175)

Durkheim's thoughts on punishment are further elaborated in the short book on *The Two Laws of Penal Evolution*, which first appeared in *L'Année sociologique* in 1901 (in Gane 1992). This slightly amended the logic of the *Division of Labor* by suggesting that power played a role as well as social complexity. Durkheim now associated the most cruel punishments with absolutism and the centralized state rather than primitive society. Given this finding, *The Two Laws* stands as a relatively unexplored pathway along which to pace out connections from recent cultural Durkheimian punishment theory through to more Foucaultian understandings of bodies and sovereignty, especially in early modernity.

Durkheim's wider views about **morality**, so central to his work on punishment, education, and other areas, were rerun in a paper from 1906 on "The Determination of Moral Facts" (Durkheim 1974a). Here, however, he underscores the role of the sacred and makes arguments that are a little closer in feel to those of the *Elementary Forms* than to the *Division of Labor*. He hits some of his best talking points one after another in this relatively short essay. Morality comes from society, not God. It is both constraining and yet also inside us. We submit to it but in so doing come to be free of illusion and unrestricted wants. This morality has a sacred force. In modernity the individual is sacred and there is a "cult of the individual." A science of moral facts can emerge in sociology that can explore collective morality. This can be an empirical activity as well as a theoretical one. We can look to data sources like the law, popular maxims, and philosophical and literary works to see how morality is configured. As this list-like paragraph makes clear, "The Determination of Moral Facts" is an amazingly impressive condensation of so many key ideas. But more than this: it also joins them up into a unified vision of morality, self, and modern society.

The discussion of value in Durkheim's 1911 paper "Des jugements de valeur" (Durkheim 1911), translated into English as "Value Judgments and Judgments of Reality" (Durkheim 1974b), has an even stronger *Elementary Forms* quality. This was the lecture he gave in Bologna, Italy, that engendered an enthusiastic audience reaction and was partially audio-recorded (see chapter 1). Rejecting a crude mechanistic or neo-Darwinian alternative that sees value emerging from social needs and functions, Durkheim suggests that there is independence to the sphere of values. As in the *Elementary Forms*, he points to items that have high social value but little material value, such as flags, idols, and fetishes. Their value comes from their connection to ideals. Such ideals are culturally constructed by groups in periods of excitement and intellectual creativity such as the Renaissance or the French Revolution. Here the collectivity is swept along by the force of the ideal and a sense of the social is internalized by the individual. Periodic reminders in the form of festivals and celebrations allow these sentiments to be revived. Society is more than just the material. It is a set of ideas and collective representations that is both real and ideal. Likewise value has its origins in the reality of collective life. In this paper we see the model of collective effervescence and sporadic cultural vitality playing out that was to be a hallmark of the *Elementary Forms*, which a year or so later was to reprise the theme about the social energies behind innovative periods in history. It offers a model that is more dynamic that that of *Primitive Classification* (below) insofar as the engine of ritual activity is introduced as a motor of cultural change. We also find traces of this idea as far back as Durkheim's lecture series of 1905, where he connected the turmoil of the French Revolution to new ideas and to collective effervescence (Watts Miller 2012: 99). Such a focus on periods of creativity reminds us of Ann Swidler's (1986) claim in her famous "tool kit" paper that taken-for-granted cultural schemas are actively reworked into new constellations during what she calls "unsettled times."

After the publication of the *Elementary Forms* Durkheim's productivity dropped off. He was sick and preoccupied by World War I. As a patriot he penned some essays on behalf of the French cause. Often considered mere "propaganda," these in fact illustrate, albeit to a limited extent, Durkheim's capacity to engage in a cultural sociology of the events of his own times. Of course there is much that is objectionable, such as crude denunciations of the German mentality and a refusal to understand the diplomatic complexities, cascade effects, and failures of leadership that rendered all nations partly responsible. *Who Wanted the War?* (Durkheim and Denis 1915) offers an explanation that pins the blame squarely on German militarism. It involves a reading of diplomatic documents that largely absolves Britain, France, and Russia and accuses German and Austria of duplicity, mendacity, and lack of restraint. A follow-up pamphlet, *Germany Above All Others* (Durkheim 1915), is a little more subtle. It sees the war not only as a grab for power but, rather, as the product of a cultural pattern. He speaks of ideas, feelings, the moral system, and mentalities. Durkheim argued that civil society was insufficiently developed and respected in Germany and that obedience to the state and to pan-German ideology was paramount. Although generally considered second-tier work that debases Durkheim's legacy – and to reiterate, it certainly does not consider the complex diplomatic and geopolitical origins of World War I – the thrust of Durkheim's interpretation is arguably not so very different from that of more acclaimed work diagnosing Germany's national pathologies, such as Adorno's study of the authoritarian personality in the wake of World War II. Still, it is perhaps disappointing or surprising that the essays on World War I show little sign of the vocabulary of the *Elementary Forms* (Eulriet 2010) that was deployed by his student Robert Hertz in his letters home from the trenches (Hertz 2002; see below).

Durkheim's last publication in his lifetime was "The Politics of the Future" from 1917 (Durkheim 2009). This reiterated his calls for economic life to be subject to moral regulation after the war and advocated one last time for socialism and increased state activity. Plans for a final major work have been reconstructed from notes made in 1917. These were discovered by Marcel Mauss after Durkheim's death and published in 1920. As Watts Miller (2012) explains it, Durkheim's intention seems to have been to consolidate his thinking on ethics, drawing on his many prior writings and organizing them into a two-volume book. The overall feel is of a return to the intellectual preoccupations and style of the *Division of Labor*. There is an inquiry into moral life and into the preconditions for a society that is shaped by ideals and a sense of duty. This finding somewhat cuts against argument that there was a decisive break in Durkheim's thinking that led to the *Elementary Forms*.

Contributions from the *Année sociologique* Group

With Durkheim's death, and having run through his treatment of various issues in less visible but still very notable works, we are in a position to turn toward the students and collaborators in the *Année sociologique* group (see chapter 1). Collectively they helped propel Durkheim toward his religious sociology thanks to an interest in ethnology and in themes relating to belief, sacrifice, ritual, classification, and the sacred. Perhaps more importantly, they demonstrated that Durkheimian thought was a paradigm with a tool kit of concepts and a replicable intellectual orientation, rather than simply the product of an individual mind *sans pareil*. Put another way, the intimidating aura that often surrounds the thought of a great intellectual was dispelled by visible signs that others could pick up his ideas and run with them.

In this process something was gained and something was lost. A perceptive comment made by the British Durkheimian anthropologist E. E. Evans-Pritchard (we look at him in chapter 3) gets at this. Durkheim's students were in many ways more scientific and empirical than their teacher: "In Durkheim's writings facts are still sometimes subordinated to an *a priori* philosophical doctrine. This is much less so in the essays of Hubert and Mauss and in Hertz's writings" (Evans-Pritchard 1960: 12). Durkheim often tended to play on two registers: one analytic and the other normative. This makes his works a little dense and convoluted at times as he flips between them or harmonizes. Sometimes adversarial and programmatic foot pedals were in the mix as well. The team had far less ambition when it came to the moral reform of France or battles against Marxism, pragmatism, psychology, and philosophy. Those themes tended to drop out. Fugal distractions removed, the students could get down to the task of neutral analytic inquiry into social process in a more focused way, and without being diverted into polemics, prescriptions, or turf wars.

In agreement with Evans-Pritchard, another noted anthropologist, Louis Dumont, remarks that Marcel Mauss (1872–1950), celebrated author of *The Gift*, which we discuss later in this book, "was a philosopher and theoretician who always turned towards the concrete and who understood that it is only in close contact with given facts that sociology can move forward" (in Mauss and Beuchat 1979: 1). We see evidence of the empirically grounded intellectual style Dumont wittily highlights (speakers of French would see that he puns on *données*, the French word for "facts," and *don*, the French for "gift," with this statement) in perhaps the most influential of Durkheim's minor works, **Primitive Classification**, which Durkheim and his nephew co-authored. The essay draws deeply upon Mauss's expertise in ethnology and was first published in the *Année sociologique* in 1903 (Durkheim and Mauss 1963). There are jabs at philosophy and psychology, probably from Durkheim's pen, but these are the least developed and somewhat marginal aspects of a text that builds new theory with reference to empirical detail. The study was a major stepping-stone. As Rodney Needham (1963: xxix) put it, there is an "early formulation of ideas later more famously expressed in Durkheim's *Les Formes élémentaires de la vie Religieuse*." It showed that theoretical advances could come from studying non-western cultures, gestured toward a more semiotic model of culture, opened up the idea of a sociology of knowledge, and, most obviously, placed the study of **classification** center stage. With the decision to "isolate classification as an aspect of culture to which sociological enquiry should be directed" (Needham 1963: xl) it set the stage for Claude Lévi-Strauss, Mary Douglas, and others in the second half of the twentieth century who would be so influential in the "cultural turn."

We cannot help but speculate whether Durkheim's early career trip to Wundt's laboratory sparked his concern with the topic, insofar as classification is a fundamental dimension of thought. Be that as it may, with his explorations of classification Durkheim would continue his lifelong crusade against psychological explanations that failed to consider the determining qualities of social facts. Durkheim and Mauss assert that classification is one of the most fundamental aspects of culture and of human mental life. Moreover, they claim that psychological and pragmatic explanations fail to hold water.

And although Kant had insisted that humans had some kind of innate mental resources into which sense impressions were organized – such as an ordering system of time and space – Kant did not explain where these came from.

As we might expect, on turning to data from the totemic systems of Australia's Aboriginal people Durkheim and Mauss argue that classifications are fully "social" in their origin. The social structure, when expressed in relationships between totemic groups, was refracted into models of the natural world.

> The first logical categories were social categories; the first classes of things were classes of men, into which these things were integrated. It was because men were grouped, and thought of themselves in the form of groups, that in their ideas they grouped other things. (Durkheim and Mauss 1963: 82)

From these origins, more complex cultural systems are built up that align and oppose elements in cosmologies. Even the most abstract concepts like time and space have their roots in social structure. A crude example might be that a society organized into two clans would recognize two seasons. Unfortunately, in *Primitive Classification* it is nearly impossible to find an example as definitive as the prior sentence. In his introduction to the English version, Rodney Needham famously demonstrates that almost none of the examples in the book actually work and that it is beset by messy *ad hoc* argumentation to deal with exceptions. Durkheim and Mauss come up with elaborate excuses and explanations for one classification system after another that doesn't quite match social structure in a homologous way. Another serious issue for the philosophically inclined is that Durkheim and Mauss only trump Kant by sleight of hand (Giddens 1978). Even if they had shown that collective systems of classification match social form, this would have told us little about the ways that the brains of individuals process information to make sense of the world. Really there are distinct levels of analysis – individual information processing and sensory awareness, and the collective organization of knowledge about the natural world. Nevertheless the book is of the utmost importance for the evolution of cultural theory. It points to the religious and binary qualities of classification. As Durkheim and Mauss (1963: 86) put it:

> Things are above all sacred or profane, pure or impure, friends or enemies, favorable or unfavorable, i.e. their most fundamental characteristics are only expressions of the way in which they affect social sensibility ... it is this emotional value of notions which plays the

preponderant part in the manner in which ideas are connected or separated. It is the dominant characteristic in classification.

From this perspective any cognitive sociology must take account of the wider cultural meanings and emotions that are ordered in a system. The book also highlights the systematic qualities of primitive thought, considered as "logical operations" (Durkheim and Mauss 1963: 88), and the ways that complex cultural forms can be built out of really simple elements. In sum, *Primitive Classification* is in many ways a precursor to more than just the *Elementary Forms*. It also directly inspired the structural anthropology of Lévi-Strauss, the classification analyses of Mary Douglas, and the middle-range empirical study of codes, distinctions, and value that is common in anthropology and sociology today (we come to these in chapters 4 and 5).

Mauss was to make other contributions during Durkheim's lifetime. Notable among these was the essay co-authored with or assisted by the ethnologist and explorer Henri Beuchat (a talented and productive scholar who sadly died of starvation and cold in a field expedition in 1914), entitled *Seasonal Variations of the Eskimo: A Study in Social Morphology*, which appeared in the ninth volume of the *Année* (Mauss and Beuchat 1979). The book is not as well known is it should be, perhaps because it was translated into English as late as 1979. Although appearing a couple of years after the essay *Primitive Classification*, this text for the most part still reflects the middle-period Durkheim's concern with social morphology and how social density and organization influence morality and solidarity. Yet at the same time it prefigures a concern in the *Elementary Forms* with the movement between particular kinds of time. Mauss suggested that "social life does not continue at the same level throughout the year; it goes through regular, successive phases of increased and decreased intensity" (1979: 79). In the summer the Eskimo (Inuit) were dispersed in small family groups and engaged in hunting. This was a more utilitarian time of "profane existence" (1979: 79) marked by individualism and task orientation. In winter the groups came together to live in villages. Here they engaged in intensive religious activity (shamanism), ritual, communal feasting, and storytelling. In this season there was a "state of continual excitement and hyperactivity ... the group becomes more aware of itself and assumes a more prominent place in the consciousness of individuals" (1979: 76). For Mauss this was evidence that dynamic density influenced morality and behavior and that there were rhythms to social life. He writes:

social life in all its forms – moral, religious, and legal – is dependent on its material substratum, namely with the mass, density, form and composition of human groups . . . Eskimo societies . . . offer a rare example of a test case which Bacon would have regarded as crucial. Among the Eskimo, at the very moment when the form of the group changes, one can observe the simultaneous transformation of religion, law and moral life. (Mauss and Beuchat 1979: 80)

Aside from influencing Durkheim's thinking about profane and sacred time and their relationship to collective effervescence and ritual activity, the book stands as an important forerunner of the Mary Douglas grid/group perspective (see chapter 4). Individuals seemed to change their behaviors and outlook according to the form of social structure in which they were embedded. The entire group culture, its morality and norms and relationship to the sacred, underwent a radical shift during the movement from atomized structural isolation to intense cohabitation and solidarity. Mauss, of course, continued to make important contributions after Durkheim's death and we recount these in the next chapter.

The work of **Robert Hertz** (1881–1915) stands as perhaps the best example of what individual team members could achieve without Durkheim as a co-author. Durkheim thought highly of him as an intellectual and mentioned his "brilliant mind" in a letter to Octave Hamelin (Fournier 2013: 463). Indeed Hertz did better than Durkheim and ranked first in his class on graduation from the ENS. He was attracted to socialism and fascinated by the dark side of human life. Durkheim worked hard to bring him into the *Année* group and to convince him to knuckle down to serious scholarship instead of devoting his career to teaching in semi-peripheral institutions. Hertz was killed in 1915 in World War I and his writings were later brought together into one volume, edited by Marcel Mauss, that appeared in 1928. He was an ardent patriot. His letters home to his wife Alice showed that he understood the war in terms of themes relating to sacrifice and sacred duty – elements of vocabulary and framing that we noted above were strangely lacking in Durkheim's own war propaganda writings (Eulriet 2010; Hertz 2002).

Hertz is considered to have written two works of the first rank. One appeared in volume 10 of *L'Année sociologique* in 1907 and is entitled "Contribution to a Study of the Collective Representation of Death"; the other, from 1909, is "The Pre-Eminence of the Right Hand: A Study in Religious Polarity," which came out in the *Revue philosophique*. For reasons of convenience these seem to be generally referred to together by English-speaking audiences through the title of the 1960 translation, *Death and the Right Hand* (Hertz 1960). The study of **death** is an early inquiry into symbolic pollution – a category that would later become especially central to cultural anthropology. Looking closely at funerary practices (as Durkheim would a handful of years later in his treatment of piacular rites in the *Elementary Forms*), Hertz argued that death was a social event and not simply a biological one.

> Where a human being is concerned the physiological phenomena are not the whole of death. To the organic event is added a complex mass of beliefs, emotions and activities which give it its distinctive character ... The body of the deceased is not regarded like the carcass of some animal: specific care must be given to it and a correct burial; not merely for reasons of hygiene but out of moral obligation ... Thus death has a specific meaning for the social consciousness; it is the object of a collective representation. (Hertz 1960: 27–8)

Turning especially to ethnological information from Indonesia, Hertz notes the impurity of the corpse. He observes that in many tribes the dead body and its associated soul are seen as initially dangerous and are subject to ritual exclusions. The soul has not fully migrated to the land of the dead and so it remains in part an "importunate guest whose proximity is dreaded" (1960: 36). There will be a provisional burial and putrefaction. The corpse will be left alone as "It is only when the decomposition of the corpse is completed that the newcomer among the dead is thought to be rid of his impurity and deemed worthy of admittance to the company of his ancestors" (1960: 35). A second and final ceremony of the burial, usually of dry bones, can now take place.

The essay on the right hand has become significant for structuralism with its arguments about the classification of **left and right**, and for the sociology of the body – notably the claim that the body is a universal source of symbolism (see Needham 1973). Hertz notes that in nearly all societies the right is valued over the left, and that the left is symbolically polluted or considered tricky. The right is associated with justice, the male, the beneficent, life, the strong, the noble, and the active. The left is connected to the female, weak, capricious, dangerous, and diabolical. This dualism he says is not due to biology but rather a social classification of the sacred and profane that sweeps up right and left in its path. The profane body is given deep social meanings: "It is because man is a double being – *homo duplex* – that he possesses a right and a left that are profoundly differentiated" (1960: 112). The connection to discussions of the body in the *Elementary*

Forms, published just a few years later, are evident. So is a humanistic impetus toward structuralism. Hertz concludes: "The obligatory differentiation between the sides of the body is a particular case and a consequence of the dualism which is inherent in primitive thought" (1960: 110). From here to Lévi-Strauss it is a very short step.

All things considered, Hertz epitomizes the qualities we find in the best short items by Durkheim and his group: the use of the comparative method; a capacity to generate and display multiple, first-rate ideas on one page after another; the anchoring of theory in empirical examples; and a capacity to inspire whole lines of research decades later. Fittingly for a work on the pathways to immortality, *Death and the Right Hand* (Hertz 1960) almost magically outpunches its slender page-weight and has become a much-cited classic that lives on.

After Mauss and Hertz it is probably **Henri Hubert** (1872–1927) who most demands our attention on account of his contribution to the wider group project of developing a religious sociology. Hubert was a close friend of Mauss and one of the most dependable members of Durkheim's team when it came to performing editorial duties, volunteering for extra work at short notice, and taking deadlines seriously (Smith 2014b). Mauss and Hubert shared an interest in comparative religion and so had control over the content of the *Année sociologique* in that field. Their most notable collaboration was a study on **sacrifice** published in 1899 (Hubert and Mauss 1964). Looking mostly to Hinduism and Judaism and reading ancient religious texts, they attempted to figure out the elementary logic of an activity that had been central to the work of William Robertson Smith, and hence was now pivotal in debates about religious evolution. Their important conclusion was that "sacrifice is a religious act which, through the consecration of a victim, modifies the condition of the moral person who accomplishes it or that of certain objects with which he is concerned" (1964: 13). The sacrifice in their vision was also a means of communicating between sacred and profane worlds. The analysis is quite structural. Mauss and Hubert identify phases of the sacrificial ritual (entry, destruction, etc.) and the actors (the sacrificer, the sacrifice itself, etc.). There is a strong focus on belief in the sacred as a non-material social fact or consequential social construction. The essay sets much of the agenda for the *Elementary Forms* in connecting ritual and a sacred cosmology within a broader understanding of communicative, symbolic action.

Hubert and Mauss (2001) went on to collaborate on a long item on a "general theory of magic" that appeared in the seventh *Année sociologique* in 1904. They had both worked on the topic independently before deciding to pool resources. The item, the only one in volume 7, is resolutely Durkheimian. This is not surprising insofar as Durkheim micro-managed this collective product of two of his best students (Fournier 2013: 454). The basic point is that **magic** is a social fact sustained by collective representations. Hubert and Mauss distinguish magic from religion (thus engaging with one of the longstanding debates of the time in anthropology and comparative religion) by a number of criteria. For example, magic is oriented toward practical and immediate ends. It is all about doing things. The most significant contribution to the wider paradigm is the discussion of *mana* as a sacred force maintained by collective belief. These ideas in turn were to feed through to the *Elementary Forms* when it discussed totemic power and the human soul, and also to Mauss's later masterwork *The Gift* (discussed in the next chapter). Surviving the war, Hubert became increasingly interested in the ethnographic prehistory of Europe, notably of the Celts and Germans. He became closely involved in museum work and lost his theoretical creativity.

Célestin Bouglé (1870–1940) was most noted for his contributions on **caste**. Perhaps the most pivotal of his analyses appeared in 1907 in *L'Année sociologique* (Bouglé 1907). Together with other essays it has been collated into a book wider in scope that is generally known as *Essays on the Caste System* (Bouglé 1971). The evolution of his work involved some tensions. Bouglé had initially emphasized the legal and economic aspects of India's caste system and downplayed the religious elements relating to the sacred. Written critique from Durkheim and Mauss led to a revision, although even this does not go as far as Durkheim might have liked. A review by Durkheim and Renier in volume 11 of the *Année* indicated regret that Bouglé had not gone "more deeply himself into the problems" and that he had presented a "framework awaiting content" or "provisional inductions" (quoted in Bouglé 1971: xiv). The fact is that Bouglé was not a strong theorist and could not match Mauss, Hubert, or Hertz for imaginative insight even when gifted the low-hanging fruit of the caste system. It is hard to think of easier material for a rich cultural analysis of codes, symbols, myths, and rituals, not to mention the binary of pure/impure. Bouglé may have failed at writing hermeneutically satisfying cultural theory but he did provide an adequate and somewhat detailed sociological account of doctrine and its corresponding social system. This stands as an important early Durkheimian treatment of the religious and cultural origins of stratification, although Bouglé does not emphasize the significance of pollution as much as did later commentators (e.g. Srinivas 1962). Had Bouglé done so Durkheim might have been more impressed. Still, the overall picture he provides matches the Durkheimian vision of a total social fact that under-pinned all aspects of social life, such as law, economic production and consumption, and belief. Aside from this work Célestin Bouglé was generally unproductive of top-level scholarship. However, he was a pivotal survivor of World War I who as an academic administrator kept the Durkheimian school a visible presence in the interwar years (see next chapter). Bouglé was appointed director of the ENS in 1935 and also occupied Durkheim's Chair at the Sorbonne. Yet for all this power he never enjoyed the same scholarly reputation as Mauss. Among his students was Louis Dumont, the noted author of *Homo Hierarchicus* (Dumont 1970) and an expert on Indian anthropology. Dumont pushed beyond Bouglé in the direction of cultural relativ-ism, arguing vigorously that non-western cultural systems needed to be understood on their own terms. For example, he asserted that ideas about basic human equality were not found in many cultures. A member of the Oxford group of British anthropologists, M. N. Srinivas, was also to keep India on the agenda for neo-Durkheimian inquiry into caste, culture, and religion (see chapter 3).

After Mauss, Hertz, Hubert, and Bouglé, there are also numerous more minor figures who contributed less frequently to the *Année*. We note them so as to be comprehensive and to indicate the depth of the team that Durkheim assembled around himself during his lifetime. With one or two exceptions these figures are of more interest to spe-cialists in Durkheim studies or experts in particular substantive fields (law, history of French education, etc.) than to the wider audience in social and cultural theory.

Georges Davy (1883–1976) lived an amazingly long time. He had institutional positions of increasing power at the Sorbonne and in various august bodies of higher learning. It is somewhat mind-boggling to think that Davy met Durkheim in 1903 or 1904 when he was a student at the Sorbonne (Fournier 2013: 581) aged around twenty, yet he retired at the height of the atomic age and lived to see the birth of punk rock. Indeed the landmark first concert in France by the Sex Pistols took place in Paris only six weeks after he died. I make this seemingly flip and intellectually irrelevant remark so as to underscore a point made near the start of the first chapter: Durkheim is not a distant figure. In fact we are all only three or four handshakes away from the start of it all. One connection I recently confirmed with Steven Lukes and the ritually enacted was me–Lukes–Davy–Durkheim. Many others are possible even today. Durkheim is not a distant figure belonging to another age.

Although he wrote on law, Davy's major contribution was in fact to be in maintaining the memory of the intellectual giant. His edited textbooks and chapters on Durkheim have something of the feel of hagiography as he summarizes and expounds on the vision of the great master (e.g. Davy n.d.). Davy focused on a teaching and administration career and was never a star intellectual. However, he had real power by virtue of his academic posts, and through these he could continue to keep Durkheim's legacy alive. For example, from 1940 to 1956 Davy was Director of the *jury de aggregation de philosophie* (a competitive civil service entrance exam), and he was also for some time Dean of the Faculty of Letters at the Sorbonne.

Paul Fauconnet (1874–1938) was also a devoted student and a fairly regular contributor of reviews to the *Année* and elsewhere. He co-authored minor items with both Durkheim and Mauss. A contribution with Mauss (Fauconnet and Mauss 1901) famously defined sociology as the study of institutions. Fauconnet's thesis and major work, "Responsibility: A Study in Sociology," was finished in 1914 but only published by Felix Alcan after the war (Fauconnet 1920). Durkheim had touched upon the issue of **responsibility** (legal, criminal, moral, individual, collective, etc.) in his lectures at Bordeaux in 1894. He gave Fauconnet his lecture notes and asked him to explore the theme. The result is an undervalued but fascinating, detailed, historical and comparative study of interconnections between law, punishment, and morality that, broadly speaking, amplifies the messages of the *Division of Labor*.

Considering his huge reputation today Maurice Halbwachs (1877–1945) was a comparatively minor and low-profile figure in the group during Durkheim's life. Halbwachs published quite widely and, compared to many others, had a lower level of brand loyalty to the *Année sociologique* itself. Perhaps this is because he had studied with Bergson at the ENS. That said, along with Simiand (below) he edited the economics sections of the *Année*. He also contributed several reviews, including of truly significant books by Sombart and Schumpeter. Like Simiand he conducted empirical research on economic life that was "Durkheimian," but only to the extent that it was based on an effort to assemble social facts and make general arguments. His second doctorate, defended in 1913, was on class and standards of living. It was ahead of its era in claiming sociologists should look at consumption as a way to think about class, but at this point in time Halbwachs did not push the envelope theoretically. As a survivor of World War I and as Chair at Strasbourg and later the Sorbonne he had growing institutional power. His most significant achievement was to come in the 1920s. He revisited the Durkheimian topic of suicide in a substantial monograph. He also published truly original and imaginative work on collective memory that had little connection to his former output as an economic sociologist. We turn to this breakthrough in the next chapter.

Paul Huvelin (1873–1924) was formally qualified in law. His most significant contribution to the group was a single article published in the *Année sociologique* volume 10 (Huvelin 1907). Here Huvelin argued for connections between law and the sacred and asserted that many early punishments took a magical form, such as curses. This imaginative work can be seen as extending Durkheim's own interest in both the religious origins of law and the specifics of Roman law. It also bore the stamp of Mauss and Hubert's work on magic. Huvelin, who wrote several other works on the history of law that were less indebted to Durkheim, died in Syria while on a diplomatic and political mission.

Gaston Richard (1860–1945) took over Durkheim's chair in Bordeaux. He wrote multiple reviews for the *Année sociologique* relating to law and punishment but like Halbwachs published only a small proportion of his output there. Richard remained a productive scholar throughout his long life, writing on feminism, the family, law, education, empire, and other topics long after Durkheim's death. Perhaps his most courageous product was a review published in the *Année* itself in 1898 of Durkheim's very own *Suicide* (Richard 1898). He critiqued the master's work as showing too little interest in imitation and as making a false distinction between the individual and the social (because the individual is social, something that Durkheim argued himself many times, as we have discussed earlier in this chapter – *touché*). This review tells us much about the academically honest editorial policy of the journal and also Richard's intellectual independence – he seemed to be both in the group and outside it. As Fournier notes, "Richard had the least compunction about making public some of his differences with Durkheim" (2013: 443). Perhaps this is because he was a contemporary and colleague and did not see himself as a student. Richard was always something of an outsider to the team (Besnard 1983) and seemed to break with it around 1907. His early career magnum opus was the book *Socialism and Social Science* (Richard 1897), which offered a critique of Marxism as reductionist and unscientific. This book in turn offered Durkheim (1986b) material for a review with which he could clarify his own stance (this review is discussed above in this chapter). It remains one of our more important sources of information when it comes to Durkheim's views on socialism.

François Simiand (1873–1935) was an ardent Dreyfusard. More than other prominent members of the group, he took an interest in industrial modernity and economic life. Although producing somewhat uncharismatic works he was highly productive and did much to carry the legacy of Durkheim's interest in social statistics. Much of his reputation was to be with historians, from whom he received "more appreciation . . . than from sociologists and economists" (Karady 1981: 39). To this day Simiand is a figure not much noticed in the world of social and cultural theory, so it may be surprising to discover that there are several monographs dedicated to his work. Philippe Steiner (2011) in particular has argued for Simiand's significance, alongside that of Durkheim, Halbwachs, and Mauss, in helping the Durkheimian school to develop an elaborated and pioneering theory of economy and society. This can be reconstructed from their surprisingly varied and extensive writings dealing with industrial organization, political economy, economy and culture, economic knowledge and statistics, and consumption and lifestyle.

Simiand's most notable early output, symptomatically, was an eighty-or-so-pages-long discussion of the price of coal that appeared in the *Année sociologique* (Simiand 1902). He was also interested in wages, money, and economic cycles. Although his writings on economic life are, to be honest, far less interesting than those of the more brilliant Simmel or the more historical Weber, he remains significant as the early Durkheimian most interested in inequality and the least interested in the ethnology of pre-modern societies. It is less well known that, in contrast to orthodoxy in the humanities, Simiand also advocated a data-driven science of history in place of a more "arts" conception. In a lecture in 1903 entitled "Historical Method and Social Science" he argued that scholars should collect social facts and strive for generality. He asserted that historians were too obsessed with chronology, individuals, and events. This is the standard mantra among comparative and historical sociologists today when they distinguish themselves from (most) historians, and it is notable that a member of Durkheim's school (not yet another Marxist or Weberian) was among the first to articulate the point with precision in a public debate and publication (Simiand 1903). Surviving into the 1930s, Simiand was institutionally significant in the *Collège de France* (elected 1931) and the *École practique des hautes études* and so, like Bouglé and Davy, helped keep the Durkheimian perspective visible.

Like the atmosphere around a planet, the membership of

Durkheim's circle thins out such that locating a decisive in/out boundary is impossible. Many people contributed just a review or two. We bring this section to an end with three representative individuals who contributed a little more than that bare minimum to *L'Année*, either with editorial work or through writing: **Dominique Parodi**, **Paul Lapie**, and **Hubert Bourgin**. These figures are indicative of the multi-tasking universe of followers surrounding Durkheim and whose work, like that of Gaston Richard, was not always strongly marbled with Durkheimian thinking. Lapie (1869–1927) wrote on a variety of topics. Most notably he was an early contributor on gender issues. His book on the topic of the family (Lapie 1908) argued in a broadly progressive way for the greater inclusion of women in the workforce and for gender equality. As such, it stands as an under-utilized resource for arguments that the Durkheimians were in fact radicals and represents something of a Durkheimian counterpoint to Durkheim's own conservative views on these topics (see above). Lapie became involved in the administration of the primary education system after the war and continued to write and research on psychology, morality, and education until his death in 1927. Dominique Parodi (1870–1955) had a long life. He had power as General Inspector of Public Instruction from 1919 to 1934 and wrote second-tier work on positivism, morality, and democracy. Hubert Bourgin (1874–1955) was a very productive individual with an amazing capacity for hard work. He had a vibrant and creative early and mid-career as a historian, activist, socialist, and education theorist. Unfortunately in his later years the one-time Dreyfusard and socialist became an unpleasant public intellectual, moving to the nationalist far right and pronouncing anti-Semitic, pro-fascist opinions. For our purposes it is important that he wrote a precise account of Durkheim's lecturing style and personal charisma (see Fournier 2013: 420–1 and our account in chapter 1), and contributed an essay on the butchery industry in nineteenth-century Paris to volume 8 of the *Année* indicating how it fused elements of tradition and modernity. In a sense this essay indicates how an empirically grounded Durkheimian inquiry into occupations or a case study of occupational change and detailed social history might have proceeded.

What are we to make of the work of Durkheim's students in the period through to 1917? The group was clearly significant in the evolution of a religious sociology and in bringing ethnological materials to the table as a resource. There are moments of real theoretical brilliance as well as several mid-range empirical extensions of the paradigm that have had lasting impact. The group also pioneered the production of intellectual works that were more purely analytic and with less attached baggage related to turf wars (with pragmatism, psychology, etc.) or normative agendas (fixing the Third Republic, heading off anomie). In this sense their work was more "modern" than much of Durkheim's.

Yet given that so many of these scholars were part of the group for a full ten or fifteen years before the outbreak of World War I, they actually look quite unproductive. Although there was an elite level of recruitment there were too many one- and two-hit wonders, too many individuals who – as I suppose the paragraphs above testify – can be reduced without too much guilt to a book or an idea in a ten-minute segment of a lecture today. Thus the collectivity unwittingly highlights Durkheim's remarkable productivity. If we looked only at Durkheim's minor works and at the lecture series that we covered in the first part of this chapter, these would dwarf the collective output of his students and colleagues in terms of volume, creativity, and depth of thought. The group project was successful, but it could have done better. At least it kept Durkheim motivated. Broadly speaking, the students and fellow travelers in the *Année* group we have been discussing fall into three patterns:

(i)   promising and brilliant but killed in World War I (Hertz);
(ii) produced their best work for *L'Année sociologique* or with Durkheim's guidance and never did much of lasting importance afterward; if they remained productive this work was second-rank (Bouglé, Davy, Fauconnet, Hubert, Huvelin, Lapie, Parodi);
(iii) continued to be creative and productive and to do top-quality work (Halbwachs, Mauss, arguably Simiand) that has left a legacy; we return to these three scholars in the next chapter to look at that contribution.

Given the institutional centrality of many of the group and the fact that those in category (ii) remained active if not creative scholars during the 1920s and 1930s, we are looking at the story of a lost opportunity. Their trajectory indicates just how significant Durkheim was as an intellectual totem, as a taskmaster, and as a source of ideas. Without Durkheim the group lacked direction and drive. It was lost. The history has a "be careful what you wish for" feel to it. As a cult of outsiders with a mission, struggling to initiate careers, build a reputation, and get a foothold in academia, to find a job and a salary, these scholars had been creative and hardworking. Once insiders in the French academic system they became complacent gatekeepers, overburdened administrators, rote teachers, and esoteric fact collectors, most of whom could no longer fire up intellectually to generate theoretically innovative work. We elaborate this story at the start of the next chapter.

Chapter 3
Durkheimian Thought, 1917–1950

*France – the fate of Durkheim's team – Mauss:
the gift and the body – Halbwachs and collective
memory – Bataille and the Collège de sociologie
– Britain and structural functionalist anthropology –
Radcliffe-Brown – Evans-Pritchard – the United States
– Parsons – Merton.*

The story of the Durkheimian legacy from the end of World War I through to the start of the Cold War is one involving three nations: France, the United Kingdom, and the Unites States of America. Each was to have a different intellectual context, a different uptake, and a different set of contributions. The paradigm was to slowly decline in authority and creativity in France but attain scholarly recognition in the Anglophone world. We return first to where we left off in the last chapter: France.

France

It is often said that Durkheim's group was wiped out by World War I and with it went his paradigm. As Johan Heilbron (2015) makes clear in his detailed study of the period between the wars, the narrative we tell ourselves should be far more complex. In fact there were good chances for Durkheimian sociology to become both dominant and innovative in France through the 1920s and 1930s. If we count the blessings, they were many. True enough, Durkheim's son

André, the talented Robert Hertz, and some less significant figures died in the trench warfare. Yet nearly all the core members of the *Année sociologique* team were still around in 1919. These survivors include Mauss and Hubert, who, along with Hertz, had been the best practitioners of the breakthrough to the cultural and religious sociology Durkheim had worked toward. Nor were the remainder of the team scattered and structurally isolated. Many Durkheimians and fellow travelers of the *Année* group were resident in the same city, Paris, and held situations of institutional power during the interwar years. For example, Mauss occupied a Chair at the *Collège de France*, and Durkheim's Chair at the Sorbonne was held at various points by Fauconnet, Bouglé, Halbwachs, Davy, and Simiand. Taken as a whole the group was not unproductive as they moved one by one into middle age. Articles were written and books published. There were also what we might think of as legislative protections for the paradigm. Sociology itself was a minor but also recognized specialism that lingered on the fringes of more prestigious disciplines like philosophy and jurisprudence. Thanks to the efforts of Durkheim's team after his death, it was incorporated into the official curriculum here and there, thus guaranteeing jobs and an audience for lectures.

Success seemed over-determined. And yet they blew it. As Victor Karady (1981: 34) notes, although the "survivors of the cluster continued to dominate French sociology until the Second World War" they did so "without passing on the Durkheimian intellectual heritage to their direct successors in the second half of the twentieth century." The forms of Durkheimian sociology that were to persist tended to be empirical, esoteric, fact-driven, or moralistic. There was a loss of intellectual vitality and theoretical innovation. Although a critical mass of scholars remained and scattered important publications continued to emerge (we discuss these outliers later), something was missing. There had been a diminution of shared energy and creativity. Part of the problem was that Durkheim had provided a charismatic focus. Yet as Max Weber famously discussed, problems of succession dog this form of social power. Perhaps Durkheim had been implicitly aware of this when he tried to routinize intellectual production with the *Année sociologique*, shifting as it were to a more enduring bureaucratic form of organization. However, he had done too much lifting himself at the *Année*. The hands-on management style that had taken up so much of his time (Smith 2014b) did not help when it came to achieving a separation of his own personality from the power of office or the work of intellectual labor. Marcel Mauss, the anointed successor, was certainly talented but perhaps in a different way and was unable to replace Durkheim. Factors external to the group dynamic and group history played a role too.

Younger scholars turned away from sociology, which was seen as unfashionable and conservative. One reason for this was precisely because sociology was now taught as a small part of a standard, nationally approved philosophy curriculum. This led to an intensified focus on themes of morality, social integration, and service. The bargain was costly. Institutional power offered Durkheim's survivors guaranteed employment and visibility but at the price of restricted intellectual scope. Students could not expect to be inspired by the required courses. Droning homilies about duty and the higher cause of the nation contributed to a widespread view of sociology as ideal-ism. Durkheim's more compelling and politically neutral emphasis on a scientific program of empirical research, on building social theory, on the sacred, and on the dynamics of group interaction was pushed to the side. As Collins (2005: 117) puts it, "sociology was presented as moral teaching, of the preeminence of the group over individual selfishness, of respect for collective institutions, and above all as French national patriotism."

Paul Nizan's (1981) polemical essay *Les Chiens de garde* from the early 1930s was not entirely unfair when it portrayed a discipline dominated by out-of-date and unambitious thinkers working in the service of the state, of a closed-minded patriotism, and of needless hostility to more dynamic German ideas. As if this was not bad enough, Nizan went further and argued that Durkheimian thinking was part of a problematic set of flawed ideologies that had plunged France and Europe into the disaster of World War I. Given such a negative image of Durkheim and sociology it is perhaps unsurprising that there was a recruitment crisis for talent. This impacted not only Durkheim's group but also the legacy of his one-time competitor René Worms. By the time Nizan was writing, sociology as a whole was looking a bit like a deeply mistaken, somewhat tarnished *fin de siècle* fad.

What of talented, charming, and interpersonally charismatic indi-viduals such as Bouglé and Fauconnet? They became sucked into administration and rote teaching. As they became more institutionally central they became more intellectually irrelevant. Consistent with their role in training future schoolmasters and leaders of the nation, the Durkheimians in key academic positions produced unambitious textbooks and other works popularizing the sociological outlook, summarizing and praising Durkheim's major lines of thought, or melding sociology with a conservative social philosophy of social morality. These were not true research publications. Nor were their jobs the ones that gave the most creative intellectual opportunity. As Karady (1981: 35) put it, "a good number of the teaching posts granted by state-sponsored faculty and graduate school networks in the social sciences were held by members of the *Année* group. But these posts themselves remained, throughout the period, utterly marginal within the university system." Income and organizational importance were secured but creative energy was wasted.

Those in research positions had a more empirical outlook that did manage to push knowledge forward. However, they had a somewhat esoteric set of interests. Given France's empire and colonial ambitions, the study of other cultures remained a pertinent, comparatively well-funded concern even in Paris. Rather than studying the social organization of modernity, Mauss and Hubert became increasingly involved with comparative ethnology of an armchair variety. Their published outputs often involved accumulating and reporting detailed knowledge on particular culture areas or aspects of civilizational history rather than theorizing it up in creative ways. The exceptions to this ethnological activity were Halbwachs, who held the Chair at Strasbourg as early as 1919 and who worked in valuable ways on social memory studies and on suicide, and Simiand, who plugged away on the empirical study of economic life. Both were engaged in the study of modern society. What united all the research scholars was a concern for social facts that took priority over the discussion of morality. This was a positive thing intellectually. Yet they had less public and student visibility than the academic administrators, as these researchers knuckled down to the highly scholarly but less than revolutionary task of compiling and sifting through information and writing for niche audiences.

In a sense, by 1930 two tendencies in Durkheim's own thought were drawn out, but in a modestly dumbed-down way. One was the line of thinking that had been concerned with sustaining the Third Republic. Here sociology was a moral-philosophical enterprise that was, at least in Durkheim's hands, both explanatory and programmatic. Durkheim's other interest was in a comparative, analytic sociology of culture and civilizational development that went back to his mentor Fustel de Coulanges. Here the search was on for social facts and for generalizable theory on societal process and evolution. The teachers took up the first strand and preached morality, the researchers the second and collected facts. But what was missing in both was a third strand we see in Durkheim. This was the one that displayed colossal theoretical ambition and that sought to create a generalizing science of society and social process, to discover laws and identify principles of structural and cultural organization. The other two lines had been made relevant and vibrant by this third one. Individual studies had been tied to, indeed made subordinate to, a cumulative agenda that was all about explaining how society works. This was the program that had been set out in Durkheim's major and minor works and in the collective output of the *Année sociologique* on his watch.

And what of that journal? Two more volumes of the *Année sociologique* were published in 1925 and 1927 with Mauss at the helm. Viewed *in toto* these fell short of the high bar set by the volumes from before the Great War. The average age of contributors increased (see Heilbron 2015: 95) and there was not enough energy from new blood or fresh thinking. The want of renewal compounded the stasis arising from the advantage of secure, salaried employment and the initial lack of serious opposition in the intellectual ecology. What we might think of as a decadent period set in. Sometimes these phases can be productive and experimental, or produce analytically flawed but luxuriant, imaginative texts or artworks. But the French Durkheimians didn't manage this metamorphosis between the wars. They squandered their historical opportunity to focus resources and energy and to push forward cultural theory at an unprecedented rate. After World War II it was game over. Halbwachs, who was perhaps the most creative figure, was killed by the Nazis. Davy remained as Dean of the Sorbonne but was not intellectually productive. The *Année sociologique* was revived under a new title, but no longer had a core Durkheimian mission or identity. New thinkers and paradigms took over French sociology and social thought. Some of the most promising talent like Raymond Aron – and later Alain Touraine – turned to Weber and Marx for insight. Others, like the eclectic and brilliant Edgar Morin, looked to anti-foundational continental philosophy. And of course existentialism and structuralism lured in most of the talent as the 1950s progressed. We come to structuralism in the next chapter.

Cutting against this theme of a dismal decline, however, are a scattering of texts and lines of influence. It was not all bad news. Simiand continued to write substantial analyses of economic life that were a little wooden but at least pioneering (for a more generous appreciation see Steiner 2011). He gained a Chair at the *Collège de France* and so had a good measure of power and respect. Marcel Granet (1884–1940) had been a sometime member of Durkheim's team. He eventually became recognized as a great Sinologist and had lasting influence in that field. If this book were about the study of China over the last century he would have a central place in it. Hubert likewise took the ethnological/area studies route and became an expert on prehistoric Celtic civilizations before his death in the late 1920s. It was Mauss and Halbwachs, however, who continued to author texts that have had a generalizable legacy for cultural theory itself and that have inspired entire fields of sociology and anthropology. We turn to them next.

If the younger **Marcel Mauss** had been chided by Durkheim for his lack of application to the serious business of scholarship (he took full advantage of what Paris had to offer – a not altogether poor choice at an existential level given that the *fin de siècle* was a Golden Age in the city), the somewhat older Mauss of the 1920s onward was an unselfish figure. He spent of a lot of his time and energy editing, compiling, revising, and publishing works left unfinished by Durkheim, Hubert, and Hertz and in taking on the lead role as editor of *L'Année sociologique* when the team members made efforts to revive it. Later he moved heavily into administration like so many of Durkheim's successors. Perhaps because of these responsibilities he finished several important extended essays but never a truly substantial landmark book. But it is also clear that he loved reading and learning. In the manner of a comparative anthropologist he accumulated a vast stock of ethnological knowledge and linguistic skills, with which he could make dazzling comparisons and leaps during his lectures. With the leverage of this erudition he could enlighten Sanskrit scholars on the meanings of their texts or demonstrate that Malinowski had made errors of interpretation (Evans-Pritchard 1954). It is entirely symptomatic of his magpie qualities that the eighty pages of actual text in the English translation of his essay *The Gift* (1954) are supplemented by some fifty pages of small-type endnotes, most of them detailing arcane matters from, or one senses *for*, the ethnographic record. Yet at the same time this essay, *The Gift*, shows Mauss was blessed with Durkheim's capacity to move beyond details, to work with concepts, and to build arguments analytically through a comparative method.

Mauss is, of course, best known for the text we have just drifted into discussing. Published in the relaunched *Année sociologique* of 1925, *The Gift* remains a landmark for cultural theory. Looking to ethnological materials, Mauss uncovered the hidden logic of **gift** exchange and went beyond particularities to discern a general or even universal pattern. For Mauss, modern society was characterized by market and contract and was individualistic. By contrast in his view gift exchange and collective action were fundamental to economic life in traditional societies. He writes:

In the systems of the past we do not find simple exchange of goods, wealth and produce through markets established among individuals . . . for it is groups, and not individuals, which carry on exchange, make contracts, and are bound by obligations . . . what they exchange is not exclusively goods and wealth, real and personal property and things of economic value. They exchange rather courtesies, entertainments, ritual, military assistance, women, children, dances, and feasts . . . we propose to call this the system of total prestations. (1954: 3)

Exploring this universe in the spirit of Durkheim as a "total social fact," and drawing on his own vast ethnological knowledge, Mauss explains that gifts (by which he means not only items of material culture but also, as we just saw, services and honorific gestures) are not really "free." We might feel they are freely given but in fact there are strong social obligations to give them. They also come with moral obligations for reciprocity. This is because gifts carry within them a particular kind of spiritual force. Borrowing a term from the Maori language, Mauss insisted that the gift contains *hau* (essentially for our purposes a variant of *mana* – although I note that there is a long, scholarly, and esoteric debate about the meaning of both terms). There is strong pressure to accept a gift. A gift must be returned in some way. The return has to be delayed and cannot be of the same object. Turning in particular to data from Polynesian and Melanesian societies (but supplementing this with materials on India, Native Americans, and Germany) Mauss insisted that behind this circuit of exchange was a powerful spiritual and moral force, not a series of rational calculations.

For Mauss this system was central to the emergence of solidarity and peaceful coexistence amongst peoples. He read the study of the gift as something from which lessons could be learned for the construction of a peaceful world where "people can create, can satisfy their interests mutually and define them without recourse to arms . . . oppose one another without slaughter and to give without sacrificing themselves to others" (1954: 80). At the same time as having this positive message, Mauss is aware of the strategic uses of gift obligations, most notably in his discussions of competitive **potlatch** activity in the tribes of the Pacific Northwest. This is a ritual in which material goods, such as blankets, weapons, and cooking vessels, are "needlessly" destroyed in displays of wealth and power. Such a secondary theme gives the book a peculiar instability as it wavers between solidaristic and instrumental visions of action and ritual exchange. The tension is never fully resolved and, as Mauss points out, is well expressed in the German word *gift*, which means both "gift" and "poison."

The Gift has been recognized as a classic in anthropology since well before its English translation in 1954 – a translation made at the behest of E. E. Evans-Pritchard. It has been the foundational text for social scientific studies of altruism, reciprocity, and morality (e.g., famously, blood donation), and been pivotal for the evolution of social exchange theory, for thinking about ritual process, for the study of goods and material culture in everyday life, and for the cultural sociological approach to the economy more generally (for a representative selection see Osteen 2002). Much critique comes from within the empirical subfield relating to altruism. For example, it has been argued that gifts to strangers such as street beggars, or those made anonymously such as blood donations, do not come with expectations or obligations for any return. *The Gift* has also generated dense, extended, scholarly critique from theorists of the level of Derrida and Bourdieu, and inspired Mary Douglas in her thinking about the world of goods and their connection to family ritual (see chapter 4). There were further impacts via Bataille (also discussed below). This is a remarkable achievement for what is really just an extended essay. It indicates Mauss himself had a special gift. Like Durkheim and Hertz, he had a capacity to be right on target and to spot and theorize things of universal significance that nobody had really noticed before.

Given that anthropology is often implicated in the colonial project, it is worth a digression here to consider the origins of the essay – to look at the deep backstory, as it were. As Grégoire Mallard (2018) points out, *The Gift* has a context relating to France's own colonial situation. Mauss saw gift giving as a model through which relationships between the colonial powers and their colonies could be imagined. Mauss was aware of abuses such as those perpetrated by the Belgian empire in the Congo. He was especially critical of the activities of chartered companies that had monopoly-like advantages, engaged in horrific violations of human rights, and took without giving back. Often such exploitation was couched ideologically in the language of a "gift" or involved coercive contractual exchanges, for example through predatory lending and company-store monopolies. In writing *The Gift* Mauss was reflecting on this situation, hence, Mallard claims, the attention he gave to the double-edged aspect of the gift as both solidaristic and also competitive or poisoned.

Mallard reveals Mauss had been tracking inquiries into abuses in the Congo as far back as 1900, long before the publication of *The Gift*. Atrocities there were well known to leftist, Dreyfusard intellectuals around the turn of the century. The dots are joined in a later book entitled *La Nation* that was published posthumously (Mauss 2013) and that reflects Mauss's career role in training future colonial administrators at the *Institut d'ethnologie*. As Lévy-Bruhl (1925) had put it, this organization saw its mission as being to develop a more rational, modern, and compassionate form of colonialism. In *The Nation* Mauss considers what it would take for colonies to become independent, complex nations. He pushed for a kind of altruistic colonialism that would allow positive development to take place. Falling short of recommending political independence, he called for genuine, constructive, nation-building contributions to replace fake "gifts" from corporate agencies or colonial powers. He also asserted that there could be a kind of beneficent nationalization of extractive and manufacturing industries. This story is indicative of the mindset of many Durkheimians working in a colonial context, including the British anthropologists we consider later in this chapter. Far from being active racists and imperialists, they attempted to understand, validate, and respect traditional cultures – much as Durkheim had done in his own work. While the primary impetus for writing was intellectual, there was also a belief that their knowledge-work would facilitate benign forms of colonialism. If such views might now strike us as politically naïve or paternalistic, this does not discharge us of the responsibility of trying to understand their motivation "from within" and to see that far more damaging alternatives (racial hierarchy theory, eugenics etc.) were decisively rejected by these cultural theorists.

Mauss's other sole-authored work with longevity and impact is less than twenty pages long: "Techniques of the Body" (Mauss 1973). This is another astonishing bull's-eye for Durkheim's nephew. The paper was first given as a lecture in 1934 to the *Société de psychologie*. Like *The Gift* this is a splendid read. The charm in this case is enhanced by the fact that Mauss frequently draws on personal experience, offers meandering exposure to ethnological curiosities, and writes in the first person. There is something of the feel of Herodotus or Dampier here. Although Mauss does not labor the language of the social fact (perhaps with a diplomatic eye to his psychologist audience), the overall thrust of the paper is to suggest that the way we use our bodies as a tool, technology, and expressive medium is decisively shaped by society in ways of which we are unaware.

Mauss observes that while we may believe bodily movements are determined by the confluence of biological constraints with a quest for mechanical efficiency, the way we use the body is in fact very malleable cross-culturally. Much of the text is given over to telling examples from practical activities (i.e. crucially not aesthetic activities like dance). For example, he recalls that during World War I, French and British soldiers marched and dug holes differently. Women in France and America walked in contrasting ways, although he suggested that cinema had lately exported the American style to France. The way that people swam had changed radically in his lifetime from breaststroke to crawl. Even an immobile state such as a sitting posture or a biological fact like sexual reproduction (he boldly discusses sex positions) could carry the imprint of society. Mauss highlights the importance of education and imitation in the process of learning particular uses of the body, and notably makes use of the term *habitus* (famously picked up much later by Bourdieu) to capture the way these are routinized into second nature.

The essay is somewhat disorganized but perhaps because of this it is chock-full of ideas, some of them still hardly exploited. For example, in a clear nod to dynamogenesis (see chapter 1) Mauss notes that an Aboriginal hunter in Australia would run with the assistance of magical incantations. These would help him chase down animals. This observation suggests to Mauss that we might look to investigate "the psychological momentum that can be linked to an action which is primarily a fact of biological resistance, obtained thanks to some words and a magical object" (1973: 75). In other words, meanings can motivate performance as well as shape physical actions. Cultural theory, as well as sports coaches, could do far more to investigate how superstition and belief connect to effective task activity.

The essay "Techniques of the Body" is rightly seen as a classic in the substantial sociological subfield devoted to the body that has emerged since the 1980s. It is one of the first texts explicitly arguing that the body is "social" with reference to scholarly data. It undercuts the idea of the mind as "culture" and the body as "nature," but in a way that complicates rather than falsifies the core binary of *homo duplex*. Mauss also demonstrates a thesis with cross-cultural data (still a standard method of exposition in body sociology), and posits mechanisms through which bodily habits are transmitted and reproduced. For all these reasons his thinking fits nicely with the core mission of social science's never-ending challenge to biological determinism. The short length and accessibility have also made the essay ideal for teaching purposes, ensuring that it remains widely read even today by undergraduates.

Aside from any specific writings, Mauss was also supremely important personally as a conduit between the Durkheimian epoch and French thought in the second part of the twentieth century. He was a visible figurehead and revered teacher of many. The most important student of all was the brilliant Claude Lévi-Strauss. The first collection of Mauss's essays in France appeared in 1950, entitled *Sociologie et anthropologie*, and it is no accident that Lévi-Strauss, at this point in his career still something of a young lion, offered a long, complex introduction (Lévi-Strauss 1987). He praises Mauss for his "deep influence" and speaks of his productive thinking that was "so dense as to become opaque at times, of his tortuous procedures, which would seem bewildering at the very moment when the most unexpected itinerary was getting to the heart of problems" (1987: 1). This seems a bit rich coming from the master of complex structuralism and inscrutable writing – clearly something rubbed off. In this introduction Lévi-Strauss moves through the other essays in the book quickly and, indicatively, devotes most of his time to *The Gift*, calling this the masterwork of Marcel Mauss and suggesting that, like Moses seeing the Promised Land, it had stopped just short of a more formal and mathematical analysis of exchange dynamics (of the kind that he himself had pioneered when looking at marriage classes and exogamy). The line from Durkheim to structuralism is clearly indicated in this statement of regret at missed opportunities. So is the fact that the author of *The Elementary Structures of Kinship* (Lévi-Strauss 1969b), a milestone that had been published just a year before, was publicly associating himself with the tradition and heritage of Durkheim by writing the preface. We return to the connections between the master of structural anthropology and the Durkheimian tradition in the next chapter.

Only one other member of Durkheim's group was to be as influential in the long run as Mauss. This was **Maurice Halbwachs**. We last saw him in chapter 2 sharing editorial responsibility for the economic life materials in the *Année sociologique*. Yet his most lasting contribution was to be in a very different field. As Mary Douglas put it, "Halbwachs's gift to Durkheim was to unpack and separate clearly the elements of social life that contribute to **collective memory**. His concept was of a flexible, articulated set of social segments consisting of live individuals who sustain their common interests by their own selective and highly partial view of history" (in Halbwachs 1980: 1). The key ideas are contained in the essay "Les Cadres sociaux de la mémoire," which was originally published in 1925, and in another paper with which it is generally bundled from 1942 that was entitled "La Topographie légendaire des Évangiles en Terre sainte: étude de mémoire collective" (Halbwachs 1980). This considered the encounter that Crusaders and pilgrims had with the Holy Land in the Middle Ages. Halbwachs distinguished collective memories from personal, autobiographical memories. He also separated out the collective memories of real groups from the abstracted, context-free chronology that makes up more objective, written, official, and academic historical memory (the distinction is now challenged, of course, by studies exploring how history books and textbooks also select from the past and are shaped by familiar sociological variables). For Halbwachs, collective memories tended to be emotionally invested, selective, meaningful, and associative. They had a focus on continuity, whereas historical memory was cold, was more objective, and stressed change.

> Every collective memory requires the support of a group delimited in space and time. The totality of past events [i.e. historical memory] can be put together in a single record only by separating them and by severing the bonds that held them close to the psychological life of the social milieus where they occurred. (1980: 84)

It is all too easy these days to think of collective memory in terms of statues and monuments, or shared "official memory" related to national experiences and legitimizing state narratives – and indeed this is the path that much work took during a revival of interest in the course of the 1980s and 1990s. A close read of Halbwachs shows a flexible thinker generating one idea after another and with great sensitivity to the micro-level. He points to face-to-face storytelling, individual biography, friendship groups, the family, associations, works of fiction, and institutional processes as playing a role. Many of these are not official or "public" memories in any simple sense but rather are living group memories that overlap in complex ways working at different levels. They are shared, socially shaped, and collectively maintained in associative life. Sociology, in his view, can study the processes and techniques through which all such group memories are formed.

Drawing a little on functionalism, Halbwachs insisted that collective memories reflect current group needs for solidarity and belonging. Materiality, he said, could play a role in the process of connecting collectivities to helpful cultural forms. For this reason some of Halbwachs's more interesting ideas concern the relationship of memory to the built forms and spaces that can anchor it. For instance, he asserted that cities are repositories of memory (e.g. street names) and also that collective ideals can be built into the materiality of the city itself. An example presented itself to him in the case of Jerusalem as captured by the Crusaders. Finding that the real city did not conform to the imaginary city of God they had carried around in their heads, they set about reconstructing it in the image of their myth.

Halbwachs's ideas have underpinned the emergence of memory studies as a field, particularly since the 1990s. There has been much infilling of lacunae and conceptual clarification, with attention being given to themes such as memory contestation, multiple memories, memorialization, genres of commemoration, and the role of politics and power. There remains for much of the literature a core concern with Durkheimian themes such as the role of the sacred and ritual, myth and collective representation, and of course the power of the group. At the same time as being a productive field, many of the themes considered in highly imaginative ways by Halbwachs have been somewhat neglected, notably those concerning community memories, personal memories, small group memories, and local memories. We return to collective memory in chapter 5.

After Mauss and Halbwachs, the third major contribution from France to the forward movement of Durkheimian thought was perhaps the most creative of all globally in the interwar period. It is entirely indicative that it came from outside the institutional core of French academia. This was the work not of salaried moralists but of marginal libertines and free thinkers. Georges Bataille and Roger Caillois spearheaded a short-lived group known as the *Collège de sociologie*. This was a bundle of interdisciplinary energy and excitement that captured the spirit of the late Durkheim. It was densely networked into the very core of the ultra-hip, avant-garde intellectual and artistic world of 1930s Paris, and produced works in a dizzying variety of genres, not all of them formally academic. As Stephan Moebius (2006; 2020) points out, the *Collège* was far from being deferential to Durkheim. This was no effort to summarize and deify in the manner of the textbooks and introductory chapters of Davy or Bouglé. The *Collège* (which – just to be clear – was not a proper, degree-granting college or institution but a club or informal intellectual group) believed the Durkheimian tradition had become too positivistic or science-oriented and was a little too concerned with ethnology. The *Collège* wished to establish a sociology of the sacred that was more visibly applicable to modernity and that took into account human subjective experience. Further, there was a political impetus insofar as there was a belief that the sacred could be mobilized against fascism and that it could form the basis for a revolutionary reworking of society. There was more than a whiff of anarchism about the *Collège*.

The brilliant instinct of **Georges Bataille** (1897–1962) was to pick up on Durkheim's vision of an unruly, dangerous, even erotic "**left sacred**" as expressed in the *Elementary Forms* and in Hertz's essays on death and bilateral symbolism. Bataille was also inspired by Mauss's analysis of the gift and of the potlatch tradition involving an "irrational" mass destruction of material goods. A final element was the papers by Mauss and Hubert on sacrifice and Mauss's work on the Eskimo, the latter offering a snapshot of a sacred time of ritual excess (all these works have been discussed earlier in this book). Bataille took this Durkheimian cultural-sociological orientation, melded it with elements of surrealism, and stirred in some non-technical Freudian psychology. The result was a series of extraordinary creative essays that attempted to capture the ways the sacred manifested in social life, much of the time in experience-near, embodied, personal contexts related to sex, violence, or death that seemed to go beyond words (Bataille 1985). For Bataille, taboos invite transgression, are somehow strangely compelling, and are a vital force in the maintenance of the social, even (or especially) when boundary lines are crossed. In his worldview emotions of disgust and desire, often associated with taboo, offer valuable insights. They run through social life and their spontaneous eruption indicates the continuing proximity of the sacred to human experience. Bataille's account of the social world also includes a cosmic vision of circulating forces that curiously prefigures the recent ideas about Gaia held by some ecologists. Solar energy, he says, is filtered up through natural and then social systems to generate a material surplus that must be consumed in culturally shaped activities of war, luxury, eating, and sex. He writes:

> The living organism, in a situation determined by the play of energy on the surface of the globe, ordinarily receives more energy than is necessary for maintaining life . . . if the system can no longer grow, or if the excess cannot be completely absorbed in its growth, it must necessarily be lost without profit; it must be spent, willingly or not, gloriously or catastrophically. (1988: 21)

This process was explored in his most important work, *La Part maudite* (English: *The Accursed Share*), a collection of experimental essays written in the 1940s and later assembled as a book. Here Bataille (1988) claimed to be studying political economy – although for sure this was not political economy of the kind we find in Macro-Economics 101 lectures. Bataille later noted that his friends, knowing his personality, were baffled when he told them this was his topic. He then had to explain carefully that he "did not consider the facts the way qualified economists do" and that he had "a point of view from which human sacrifice, the construction of a church or the gift of a jewel were not less interesting than the sale of wheat." He then had "to try in vain to make clear the notion of a general economy in which expenditure (the consumption) of wealth rather than production was the primary object" (1988: 9). The activity of theorizing luxury and consumption had a normative twist. Bataille was contemptuous of modernity's focus on zero-sum competition and accumulative, mean-spirited bourgeois capitalism. By contrast he could praise the Aztecs for their rich sacrificial ceremonies and the elaborate ritual courtesies they extended to human victims. In a model demonstration of anthropological relativism, he saw their use of human sacrifice as a profound and knowing form of cultural expression.

> Sacrifice restores to the sacred world that which servile use has degraded, rendered profane . . . Destruction is the best means of negating a utilitarian relationship . . . The victim of the sacrifice cannot be consumed in the same way as a motor uses fuel. What the ritual has the virtue of rediscovering is the intimate participation of the sacrificer and the victim . . . The victim is a surplus taken from the mass of useful wealth . . . he is the accursed share, destined for violent consumption. (1988: 55, 56, 59)

The case of Aztec human sacrifice was one in which we could learn a more general lesson. The "free expenditure" of surplus energy and goods through ritual generated meaning, solidarity, and authentic human relationships. The **"accursed share"** has the capacity to unleash vital, life-enhancing social forces. Other than in sacrifice and potlatch this energy could also be expended in erotic activity that was not aimed at procreation, in feasting, and in festivals and creative acts that had only aesthetic, existential, or communal value.

The shadow of Bataille was to influence later thinkers such as Baudrillard and others on the non-utilitarian economy, and an entire cadre of poststructuralist feminists in the celebration of the female orgasm and the "excess" of style and imagery in female literary creativity (Cowell 2002). He has always appealed to humanistic philosophers, although his ideas have proven hard to translate into projects for a more routinized academic production, even in qualitative cultural sociology. One reason, as the quotations above show, is that his writings are inflected with an arts sensibility. Like artistic/political manifestos by underground radicals, the texts are hybrids that defy easy classification. They are at the same time a set of propositions, an attempt to outrage, and a creative exposition that attempts to give force to the ideas via a vortex-like cascade of imagery, syntax, rhythm, and imagination (see, for example, Bataille 1985). It is no surprise that Bataille has long held an appeal for revolutionary anarchists, artists, intellectuals, and students for whom doctrinaire and scientific Marxism is problematic, too rational, too dried out, or too constraining of individual free expression. This is well demonstrated by Bataille's influence on Situationist protest in the 1960s. Indeed the Situationist journal that had twenty-nine issues from 1954 to 1958 was called *Potlatch* in a clear reference to the anti-materialism, anti-capitalism, anti-modernism, anti-rationality, and creative destruction that Bataille had valued (Debord 1959).

Roger Caillois (1913–78) was one of the most talented students of Mauss. Like Bataille he had a strong literary bent (indeed he was a novelist, wrote an autobiography, and was a champion of Latin American literature to the extent that a major literary prize is named after him), and like Mauss he had an interest in human cultural diversity as expressed in the historical and ethological record. Caillois had an early brush with surrealism and was friends with such luminaries as André Breton, Max Ernst, and Salvador Dali. However, he moved away from the group, teamed up with Bataille and Leiris (below), and was a key player in the *Collège de sociologie* and its journal *Acéphale*. The word means "headless," and in fact is often used in anthropology to denote tribes without clear hierarchies and political authority structures, such as the Nuer (see a few pages below – we actually have a quote featuring the word "acephalous"), and in anarchist thought to denote a form of rule without a centralized state. Somewhat later in life, during the 1950s, Caillois wrote *Man, Play and Games* (1961). This was much influenced by and, to be realistic, overshadowed by Johan Huizinga's (1949) more famous *Homo Ludens*. Like Huizinga, Caillois sets out to provide a comprehensive typology of play as a kind of social universal. The analysis fits well with Durkheimian notions of ritual as distinct from profane everyday life. Caillois argues that play is separated from routine, involves ordinary rules of social behavior being set aside, is voluntary, and has no practical utility. According to Caillois games tend to fall out into common patterns. They can involve: (i) *agôn* (competition); (ii) *alea* (chance); (iii) *mimicry* (copying, imitation); and (iv) *ilinx* (thrill-seeking or disorientation). The book is an under-utilized resource. Play is something that has not been fully explored in the Durkheimian tradition but Caillois offers a way to start to think about this socially widespread, deeply meaningful activity that is hiding in plain sight. From play it is but a short step to theory on drama, performance, irony, role distance, and self-actualization. Unfortunately Caillois does not always make the connections. For example, he does not join play closely enough to its ritual possibilities or fully understand the "serious" quality of play, as Geertz (1973) was to do only a few years later.

Roger Caillois (1959) should be thanked by students for writing *Man and the Sacred* as it is in this book that we find perhaps the single most coherent or reader-friendly statement of the beliefs of the *Collège*. First published in 1939, the work lays out a vision of the sacred as a universal building block of social life, using scattered ethnological examples as well as theory. He talks through how the sacred is opposed to the profane, has a certain duality or ambiguity, is often experienced in the violation of an interdiction, and generates intense emotions including fear. According to Caillois the festival is a location where such transgression is institutionalized. In this sense the book is a pivot point that links the *Elementary Forms* with scholars like Bakhtin and Turner as they discuss carnival and liminality.

Lastly we should mention **Michel Leiris** (1901–90). Like Caillois and Bataille, Leiris was something of a total intellectual. He achieved the almost impossible feat of having a more impressive address book and non-academic CV than either of his two colleagues. Leiris was a creative writer of fiction and poetry who split with the surrealists under the positive influence of Bataille and in an effort to escape André Breton's overbearing personality. He wrote also on art, opera, and jazz and completed a multi-volume autobiography. Due to his sophistication and aesthetic sensibility Leiris was a confidante and lunch companion of various luminaries, artists, musicians, and thinkers. For example, he was a longstanding friend of Francis Bacon (who painted his portrait, as did Picasso, Giacometti, and Masson) and of Jean-Paul Sartre, and he married the stepdaughter of Picasso's art dealer. Yet at the same time as spending intimate time with the cream of the Left Bank in-crowd he was also a deeply respectful student of Mauss who cared about the organization of social life beyond Paris. Indeed Leiris was for much of his life a systematic ethnographer and ethnologist of African societies, who worked diligently at the *Musée de l'Homme* and took part in scientific data-collection expeditions in the French colonies. Perhaps the most notable feature of his writings, such as *L'Afrique fantôme* (1934) and "The Sacred in Everyday Life," was a concern for autobiography, and in a sense with these and other autobiographical works he anticipated the reflexive, anti-positivist, literary turn to be found in much later ethnography and ethnographic theory (see Clifford 1981). In "The Sacred in Everyday Life," a paper first read to the *Collège* in 1938, Leiris remembers his childhood in a

110

Proustian way. He conjures memories of objects in his boyhood, the household and its environs. Invoking the ambiguity of the sacred he asks at the outset of the essay:

> What for me is the sacred? To be more exact what does *my* sacred consist of? What objects, places or occasions awake in me that mixture of fear and attachment, that ambiguous attitude caused by the approach of something simultaneously attractive and dangerous, prestigious and outcast – that combination of respect, desire and terror that we take as the psychological sign of the sacred. (1988: 24)

His highly personal, biographically encoded version of the sacred included his father's top hat, revolver, and money box, these representing power and wealth. The parental bedroom, complete with portraits of grandparents and a clock, was also the "right sacred," as it was connected to legitimate authority. Contrasting to this was the "left sacred" of the bathroom, where Leiris and his brother would lock themselves away and tell stories or speculate about sex, "as if in a men's house in some island of Oceania – the place where initiates gather and where from mouth to mouth and generation to generation secrets and myths are passed on" (1988: 26). Equally sacred were the bushy area of the park surrounded, his mother told him, by stranger danger, and the racecourse, associated with the risk of riding accidents and the wastefulness of problem gambling. So secrecy, danger, risk, and thrill were the qualities of the left sacred, generating a huge sense of excitement and awe in the young Leiris. The right sacred was associated with feelings of security, power, and order.

In sum, Leiris showed that an existential biography of personal experiences with objects, people, and places during childhood made up a kind of symbol system with its unique sacred topography that was perhaps shared only with siblings. Even the very young self was embedded in a sacred world. This is a really important step. In academic scholarship the sacred tends to be associated with the collective, public, and shared. Leiris opens up the possibility for layered expressions that include a kind of micro-sacred – something that Halbwachs had also gestured toward in his writing on collective memory. Before writing "The Sacred in Everyday Life" Leiris had in fact already moved toward this sort of stance on personal cosmologies in *L'Afrique fantôme* (1934). Here he tried to record everything that was happening to him or going through his head when he was part of a major scientific anthropological expedition lumbering around Africa. He saw this kind of self-reckoning, which was years ahead of its time, as a way to allow readers to correct for

111

the subjective elements present in interpretation and data collection in the field.

Intellectually Leiris picks at a thread that is modestly latent in Durkheim or Lévi-Strauss, is more pronounced in Mauss, and even emerges somewhat with Mary Douglas's defense of the "Bog Irish" (see chapter 4). This is an appreciation of the wisdom of traditional or "primitive thought," and of myth and ritual. Leiris gives most of the credit for this realization to the ethnologist Lucien Lévy-Bruhl (1857–1939). This element of Leiris's thinking was no doubt boosted by surrealism's critique of modernity and reason (after all, these had resulted in World War I) and by an appreciation for African art among his friends in the Parisian avant-garde (for example, Picasso was notably obsessed with tribal masks). As Leiris stated in an interview given a couple of years before his death:

> We stood firmly against the West. And this was evident in a fairly blatant way in the surrealist statements and manifestos. What was going on was a rebellion against Western civilization, plain and simple. (in Price and Jamin 1988: 159)

As we noted a few pages ago, the scholars of the *Collège de sociologie* have never been easy to work with. Let's return to that theme. While adaptable to the humanities, notably art and film criticism, and recognized as brilliant, the literary style of their academic output and resistance to formal, generalizable, propositional knowledge claims has seen them neglected by most social scientists. Another issue limiting impact was that although highly productive, these hardworking individuals spent only a fraction of their time on writing we might think of as scholarly in any conventional sense. Indeed the efforts made on poetry, criticism, novels, and autobiography seem to have been more important to the self-concept of Leiris and Caillois than their academic contributions.

Yet a vision remains to this day. The humanistic and philosophical effort to get at deep meanings and personal emotional experiences through looking at sacrifice, death, and sex has continued in France. Although he has a focus on themes of desire and imitation, René Girard (2005) would seem to be squarely in the Durkheimian tradition, filtered via Bataille, when he speaks about the sacred, about the ritual sacrifice of the scapegoat, and about violence as the foundation of the social order. According to Alexander Riley (2005) the pathway from Durkheim also led through Bataille and the *Collège* and on to critical poststructuralism. Scholars touted as speaking about power and as deeply opposed to functionalism are in fact carriers of a particular Durkheimian legacy looking at experiences of the extreme or at rule-breaking behaviors as constitutive of the social order. One does not have to scratch much beyond the topics of Foucault's books or Kristeva's interest in abjection to see the connection runs deep. In mainstream sociology that is less influenced by French avant-garde tendencies, however, one senses that nobody quite knows what to do with Bataille, Caillois, and Leiris. This is especially the case in the United States. Their thinking is too impressionistic and literary to be easily assimilated to the routine sociological endeavor, even for those working on the cultural meanings of sexuality or the body. The theory is elusive when it comes to bullet points, and positive knowledge is hard to find amid the polemics and injunctions. What is clear, however, is that Bataille somehow intuited – or conjured – the most dramatic and least positivistic thoughts in the *Elementary Forms* and took them to a remarkable place on the frontiers of knowledge or the knowable.

The general impression we have from France for the period 1917 to 1950 is of scattered contributions of great insight and originality from brilliant minds. Yet as a dynamic intellectual movement the Durkheimian paradigm had underperformed. It moved into the intellectual background, with the curtain finally falling in an official way with Davy's retirement in 1955. As Victor Karady (1981) points out, figures like Claude Lévi-Strauss and Georges Gurvitch were influenced by Durkheim but would pay homage in somewhat oblique ways. They combined him with a far wider range of ideas. Many of the best thinkers of the next generation – those born in the 1920s and entering professional life in the 1950s – explicitly looked elsewhere. Michel Crozier, Raymond Aron, and Alain Touraine, for example, all spent time in the United States. Influences included Marx, Weber, existentialism, and political and bureaucratic theory. Elements of Durkheim's thinking persisted here and there, but not within a visible tradition of card-carrying advocates. Rather the impact was often, as Mike Gane (1988: 183) put it, "heavily disguised and indirect." It persisted not so much as concepts and models but rather as the echo of a ghost of a thought style that considered society as a structure, social agents as unaware of social mechanisms or the power of social facts, and the objective analyst as having epistemological privilege. Gane mentions specifically Bachelard, Koyré, Canguilhem, Foucault, Bourdieu, and Passeron as carriers of this legacy of sociology as a robust and theoretically inflected science. But none of this was very visible at the time. So Armand Cuvillier (1953) was able to ask a question in the title of his book: *Où va la sociologie française?* Here he indicated the neglect of Durkheimian ideas, theory, and methodological training, lamented the teaching of sociology by philosophers, and called, not unlike C. Wright Mills in a more famous essay a few years later, for social research that would

> avoid at the same time empiricism lacking in inspiration that is nothing but a collection of facts, and arbitrary speculations that replace the testing and patient analysis of reality with pure conceptual structures, which was the merit of the sociological works of the Durkheimian school. (1953: i)

If France was to become a dead end for a visible empirical-theoretical tradition building on Durkheim, the survival and extension of Durkheim's scientific program for a generalizing, explanatory social science would have to take place elsewhere. But this "elsewhere" could not be just anywhere. As Collins (2005) points out, the French case showed that the Durkheimian intellectual agenda had to be decoupled from nationalism and politics if it was to move forward in creative ways. This requirement ruled out some otherwise promising possibilities. For example, in the case of Turkey there were strong affinities between Durkheim's ideas about *laïcité*, solidarity, and the sacred nation, on the one hand, and the agendas of the Kemalists trying to build a modern, competitive state with minimal or compartmentalized Islamic influences, on the other. It is no accident that Durkheim's (1957) manuscript lectures on ethics, morals, and the state were, as we rather deliberately noted in chapter 2, collected from Mauss and from a deposit at the *Musée de l'Homme* by a Turkish sociologist, Hüseyin Kubalı, and first published in Turkey (see chapter 2). And leading scholars like Ziya Gökalp made a serious study of Durkheim's thought with an eye to themes of social reform and social stability. So the interest was there. But the story in Turkey was the same as in France between the wars. Moral homilies about the nation and duty, and tributes to Durkheim's genius, do not make for serious progress in research on society itself.

In the Anglophone world things were very different. Relatively speaking, universities were decoupled from the task of reproducing administrative elites (they did so through Oxbridge, but as a latent function rather than a manifest one as was the case with the *grandes écoles*). There were global flows of scholars and ideas. Here lasting systematic contributions were made because Durkheim's analytic capacities as a theorist of social order and the social system were at the forefront of reception dynamics. We find the first great extension of the Durkheimian program beyond the *Année sociologique* group, developing a new paradigm even before the *Collège de sociologie*, was to occur in a somewhat unlikely place – the British social anthropology of the 1920s.

British Structural Functionalism

In the early twentieth century, British anthropology was just emerging from a Victorian era in which biological and cultural evolutionary ideas, race theory, historical accounts of tribes and customs, and speculations about the origins of peoples were the dominant forms of analysis. Loosely associated were also elements of folkloric studies and comparative ethnology, some of these tethered to nationalist efforts to reconstruct an authentic folk culture. Scholars and missionaries collected accounts of superstitions, rituals, kinship systems, ways of life, and myths so as to understand the evolution of society from savagery to civilization. Notable as a paradigm was the huge triumph of linguistics in tracing the Sanskrit roots of the Indo-European languages. This suggested that an appropriate method was to try to reconstruct cultural and geographic pathways ("diffusion") and find remote historical social origins in scattered clues. Similarities in cultural "survivals" (anachronistic and/or enduring myths, customs, and folkways) hinted at past connections much as root similarities in words for water or bread could indicate a common ancestor for two different languages. Leading names associated with this kind of work included E. B. Tylor, R. R. Marett, Lewis Henry Morgan, and James Frazer. Frazer's multi-volume magnum opus *The Golden Bough*, first published in 1890, reconstructed a vast web of religious and mythical connections in a magnificently erudite but ultimately speculative cross-cultural and historical panorama (Frazer 1940). Durkheim's own group was caught up in the some of the dying moments of this intellectual tradition. Totemism, magic, myth, and ritual were all topics on which Durkheim's team expended effort as they attempted to be visible in ongoing, international debates of the 1890s and early 1900s.

The transition of British anthropology into a modern discipline ready to engage with more contemporary cultural and social theory was in no small part the accomplishment of **Bronisław Malinowski** (1884–1942). He had invented intensive, long-term fieldwork when, with the outbreak of World War I, he had been forced to remain on the Trobriand Islands in the South Pacific. Malinowski was a high-output, high-impact scholar. He was something of an academic celebrity in his day but at the same time managed to produce work of real quality. Although not a Durkheimian, he did try to generate theory and he did emphasize the significance of social organization for explanation. In a sense, then, Malinowski was an unwitting midwife for the later Durkheimian structural functionalist moment.

In Malinowski's view a society should be studied in a synchronic, comprehensive, or holistic way as a field of interacting institutions, beliefs, customs, and individuals. Each of these could only be properly understood with reference to the totality within which it was situated. The triumph of this approach, which was signaled with the publication of one monograph after another on Trobriand society, eventually brought an end to the Victorian mode of ethnology with its historical and evolutionary speculations.

Malinowski's books, most famously *Argonauts of the Western Pacific* and *The Sexual Lives of Savages* from the 1920s and, in 1935, the magnificent *Coral Gardens and Their Magic*, were a revelation (Malinowski 1966; 1962; 1965). They showed great sensitivity to the meaningful Trobriand social world, which Malinowski reconstructed and reported in unparalleled detail when writing on both daily life and special events. His data on the *kula* ring, in which ceremonial objects were passed between chiefs on different islands over large distances in a pattern of perpetual circulation, was perhaps his greatest direct contribution to the Durkheimian tradition insofar as it was pivotal as a data source and inspiration for Mauss's thoughts on *The Gift*. However, Malinowski's work lacked a theoretical center of gravity and tended to consist of scattered insights and arguments. It was also somewhat individualistic, with his brand of functionalism arguing that social and cultural arrangements came about to meet the needs of social actors. Rituals, he once said, existed to reduce anxiety. Very importantly, Malinowski trained up Evans-Pritchard and Meyer Fortes, figures to whom we will turn later in this chapter. Moreover, Malinowski's seminar at the London School of Economics operated as a kind of intellectual clearinghouse. People passed through, met, and exchanged thoughts and books. This centralized rather than dispersed network structure would facilitate the dissemination of Durkheim's ideas through the anthropological community.

For all Malinowski's charisma and output it was **A. R. Radcliffe-Brown** (1881–1955) who was to become the pivotal figure in translating Durkheim's most general functionalist precepts into a methodology that could make sense of the institutions, organizations, and beliefs encountered in fieldwork and ethnological texts. Radcliffe-Brown might fairly be characterized, unlike Malinowski, as

116

a low-output scholar. However, his best work had terrific density and high impact. As such, he formed the major alternative to Malinowski during the interwar years. Radcliffe-Brown was particularly significant in the anthropological community of the British Empire because he traveled and worked widely. Before taking up the Chair at Oxford in 1937, he had faculty positions in Sydney and Cape Town during the 1920s. At these locations he was able to influence top-notch local scholarship very directly, very immediately, and free from Malinowski's long shadow. Durkheim followed in his wake. Hilda Kuper (1984), for example, reports receiving a "heavy dose" of Durkheim that included *Suicide*, the *Elementary Forms*, and *The Rules of Sociological Method* during her years as an undergraduate at Witwatersrand in the late 1920s. Radcliffe-Brown's global movements also had impact in the United States. As Nisbet (1976: 4) remarks, Radcliffe-Brown's "coming to the University of Chicago in 1931" helped rescue Durkheim from neglect. His work demonstrated the "operational utility" (Nisbet 1976: 4) of Durkheim's ideas and made him respectable with both anthropologists and sociologists.

Radcliffe-Brown was a somewhat pretentious individual who, at least early in his career, liked to parade around campus with a cape and a monocle. His work was anything but superficially flamboyant. In contrast to Malinowski he was a second-rate ethnographer who had scrabbled somewhat half-heartedly at fieldwork, frequently with displaced individuals in institutional settings (missions, clinics) in the Andaman Islands in the Indian Ocean, and in the deserts of Australia. Yet Radcliffe-Brown had a first-rate analytic brain and was a master essayist who could craft emphatic and confident generalizing analyses that did not want for ethnological detail. The scattered papers from the 1920s, 1930s, and 1940s collected by E. E. Evans-Pritchard and Fred Eggan, and published in 1952 as *Structure and Function in Primitive Society*, offer an effective and time-efficient summary of his thought (Radcliffe-Brown 1952). There we find Durkheim is mentioned repeatedly and always positively.

The Durkheimian influence on Radcliffe-Brown took hold as he approached thirty years of age. True enough, he wrote to Marcel Mauss in 1924, but this was not due to a sudden moment of conversion. As early as 1910 his lectures demonstrate Durkheimian moments (Stocking 1984). He was an early reader of Durkheim's *Elementary Forms*, referring to this in a positive way as soon after publication as 1913. In the summer of that year he decisively stepped away from the diachronic perspective of his mentor W. H. R. Rivers as the two corresponded over complex ethnological issues. A letter of

Radcliffe-Brown's to Rivers from around this time features a reference to "the needs of the Andaman collective conscience" (in Stocking 1984: 151), and by Fall of that year he was arguing against the idea of survivals and calling for a study of social functions and the ways that customs and institutions worked to ensure social equilibrium. These ideas did not emerge in print until the 1920s, hence the illusion that he came to Durkheim quite late in his career.

Harking back to Durkheim's positivism and functionalism we find in Radcliffe-Brown a vigorous argument for nomothetic inquiry and robust theory building. This was to see him eventually take over from Malinowski as the leading anthropologist of his day. As Raymond Firth (1957: 1) put it, as the twentieth century progressed there was a "growing realization" in the discipline "of the need for a clearer structural approach to give precision to many anthropological generalizations." Malinowski, however, was "not a structuralist in the narrow sense, and appreciation of his work suffered by comparison." By contrast Radcliffe-Brown's writings somewhat mimic the tone and authorial subject position of the *Rules of Sociological Method*. In contrast to today's emphasis on reflexive ethnography or politics-sensitive, participant-inclusive methodologies (or for that matter Leiris's *L'Afrique fantôme* from the same period; see above), this was a confident, authoritative approach in which the anthropologist seeks scientific knowledge and to identify general laws in social life relating to the functioning of society. The people actually in the society may have some understanding of what is going on, but this should never be taken too seriously. Their beliefs and explanations should be better understood as a form of data or as a non-material social fact. The anthropologist, after all, knows best.

Radcliffe-Brown himself provided a very readable "Introduction" to *Structure and Function* that pulls his thoughts under a single theoretical umbrella. Generalizations are to be founded on observable social process, not conjecture about historical origins. Special attention needs to be given to "culture and to cultural tradition" (1952: 5), thought of as "art, knowledge, skill, ideas, beliefs, tastes, sentiments" as these are distinctive of human social organization in contrast to that of animals. Explicitly claiming to have built upon ancestors such as Durkheim, Montesquieu, Spencer, and Comte, Radcliffe-Brown argues there is a "total social system" and that we should investigate the "interconnections amongst features of social life" (1952: 6). These can be thought of in a layered way as adaptations to the environment, as institutional arrangements that bring social order, and as the "habits and mental characteristics" (1952: 9) of the individual that enable them to participate. The social system consists of interconnected institutions with associated norms for conduct, and organizations with roles that persist over time. The term "function" is commonly found in these writings. Drawing (like Durkheim, but actually expressing the issue more clearly than he did) on the organic analogy, Radcliffe-Brown argues for mutual interdependence between structure, function, and process as they solve the problem of social order:

> In reference to social systems and their theoretical understanding one way of using the concept of function is the same as its scientific use in physiology. It can be used to refer to the interconnection between the social structure and the process of social life . . . The three concepts of process, structure and function are thus components of a single theory as a scheme of interpretation of human social systems . . . the procedure has to be the examination of the connection between the structural features of the social life and the corresponding social process as both involved in a continuing social system. (1952: 12)

The last words are important here: for Radcliffe-Brown there needed to be "a certain degree of functional consistency amongst the constituent parts of the social system" (1952: 43) if it were to endure. Put another way, almost by definition a poorly coordinated society or subsystem would need to adapt or else it would go extinct – it would not be "continuing." Hence we would not see it, it would not be observable, we would not be able to write about it – it could not in fact exist. Pivotal in stability and continuity were the role played by "rights and duties in a social structure consisting of a network of relations between individuals and groups of individuals" (1952: 43). Equally important, as Radcliffe-Brown explained in his essay on taboo, was "a measure of agreement about values" (1952: 140) and shared interests. Whatever needed to be explained, its social function was the key to explanation: "Following Durkheim and others, I would define the social function of a socially standardized mode of activity, or mode of thought, as its relation to the social structure to the existence and continuity of which it makes some contribution" (1952: 140).

This all sounds rather abstract and dry. In the essays of *Structure and Function*, however, Radcliffe-Brown displays formidable ethnological erudition as he sets about explaining various aspects of life in what were called "primitive societies" at the time. Here we see what was to become a familiar hallmark of British structural functional anthropology. The theoretical armature of functionalism is used to explain the puzzling tradition or to decode a complex kinship system.

Once it is realized that everything contributes to stability, to the permanence of the whole, and to social integration, then an account can be constructed or, better, "retrofitted," looking back from the organization of the totality to the function of the part.

Perhaps the most famous analysis is of the relationship of the mother's brother to the sister's son in South Africa. This is a special tie characterized by warmth and affection, joking, and the ability of the sister's son to inherit property and take food without asking. This is decoded by Radcliffe-Brown neither as a quirk of personality, nor as a puzzling survival hinting at some prior form of social organization or custom that has mysteriously lingered on, but rather as a more-or-less inevitable product of a patriarchal, patrilineal kinship system. Authority, respect, and obedience go to the father and his side of the family. The behavior toward the mother's brother reflects the larger organizing principle of the kinship system, which in turn determines general patterns of behavior. Radcliffe-Brown notes that joking relationships are common in many cultures. These are marked by simultaneous friendship and perpetual disrespect (1952: 95). This in turn reinforces the "conjunctive and disjunctive" elements in any alliance between clans, tribes, and relatives by marriage. The joking relationship "keeps the parties conjoined" (1952: 103) and heads off conflict while at the same time maintaining some social distance. So the kinship system, which provides the basic social structure, determines the nature of customary behaviors, feelings, and norms. The method is to work from the whole to the part and, with the assistance of a comparative method (e.g. accounts from other tribes that have similar or different kinship systems and similar or different interaction dynamics), thence to explain the emotional and behavioral complex.

> The scientific explanation of the institution in the particular form in which it occurs in a given society can only be reached by an intensive study which enables us to see it as a particular example of a widespread phenomenon of a definite class. This means that the whole social structure has to be thoroughly examined in order that the particular form and incidence of the joking relationships can be understood as part of a consistent system. (1952: 104)

With functionalism so central to the theory package, it is no surprise to see Radcliffe-Brown, in another essay, endorsing Durkheim's theory of totemism and his view of the sacred as central to collective identity: "The most valuable part of Durkheim's analysis . . . [is] the recognition that the function of the ritual relation of the group to its totem is to express and so to maintain in existence the solidarity of the group" (1952: 128). Yet Radcliffe-Brown tethers culture to the practical circumstances of existence more than does Durkheim. Whereas Durkheim had seen the selection of the totem as arbitrary and its sacred value as emerging from an act of social projection, for Radcliffe-Brown totemic species' sacrality was at least partially derived from utility or centrality to the survival of a way of life. British anthropology always paid more attention to economic life and subsistence than we might think. Still, like Durkheim's, Radcliffe-Brown's functionalism saw him disposed toward explanations that sidelined the interpretations of actors. While we could learn something from talking to real people, for the anthropologist the meaning of a ritual lay in its contribution to the maintenance of the social order. Almost echoing the *Division of Labor* and the *Elementary Forms*, Radcliffe-Brown says that rites "are part of the mechanism by which an orderly society maintains itself in existence, serving as they do to establish certain fundamental social values" (1952: 152) and that they "transmit from one generation to another sentiments on which the constitution of society depends" (1952: 157).

True enough, Radcliffe-Brown recognized cultural variation, like any good social anthropologist. Yet he pushed back against the influential cultural relativism of the German-American anthropologist Franz Boas (1858–1942). He was also not fully ready for the more semiotically inflected cultural turn that would flower after his death. Culture for Radcliffe-Brown is seen as a "way of life" or pattern of organization and association more than as a set of codes, narratives, and symbols. Moreover, culture is never really seen as expressive or aesthetic in the way taken by Victor Turner or Clifford Geertz. Rather gestures and emotions are related to the functional needs of the system for stability. That said, Radcliffe-Brown can be a surprisingly subtle theorist. It is all too easy to caricature him as carving out cleanly chiseled statements on stable social systems. Yet in fact his theory talks about emotions. He also considers dynamic patterns of association as an aspect of social structure rather in the manner of a contemporary network theorist ("A society consists of a number of individuals bound together in a network of social relations" [1952: 140]), and repeatedly engages with themes relating to social tensions, disputes, and dispute resolution.

Radcliffe-Brown was responsible more so than any other person for institutionalizing Durkheim as a revered or totemic ancestral figure of nearly unquestioned intellectual authority in British anthropology. In 1945 he stepped down as Professor of Anthropology at Oxford and was succeeded by **E. E. Evans-Pritchard** (1902–73). The group assembled around Evans-Pritchard, specifically in Oxford but also in the UK more generally, was to continue the legacy of synchronic functionalist analysis with a focus on the problem of social order. Important figures included Meyer Fortes, Max Gluckman, Godfrey Lienhardt, M. N. Srinivas, and Franz Steiner. The tools pioneered by Radcliffe-Brown were variously adapted, and enabled these scholars to deal in particular with the puzzle of how societies with few formal social control mechanisms, no written legal codes, and often little hierarchical authority managed not only to persist but to do so in a peaceful and orderly way. Evans-Pritchard and Lienhardt themselves denied there was a collective identity to what we might call the Oxford group (see Fardon 1999: 33). But it is clear with hindsight that here was a corps of scholars in geographical proximity (if not at Oxford then just a short train ride away in London, Manchester, or Cambridge), armed with ethnographic field notes and a shared ethnological erudition, engaged in a hothouse of productive intellectual exchange, publishing at a good clip, and speaking the same paradigm language. The stars were aligned.

According to Mary Douglas (1980) Evans-Pritchard had first set out his stall in the 1930s while working at Faud 1 University in Egypt. The so-called Cairo essays, in her view, established an ambitious agenda for his lifework. They argued for anthropological cultural relativism and drew upon Durkheim and his group for intellectual authority. Aspects of primitive thought, Evans-Pritchard stated in these papers, could be found also in everyday life in modernity. There are collective representations in all societies that need to be scientifically studied and taken seriously regardless of how irrational or false they might seem. Analysis needs to connect beliefs and collective representations to institutions, groups, and social systems. That said, in his own scholarly monographs Evans-Pritchard generally cites Durkheim (and other theorists) lightly or not at all. The convention in anthropological texts of the time was to give an accurate and comprehensive god's-eye account of the tribe, not to engage in academic debates. Ethnographic authority was established through a kind of matter-of-fact description of general patterns on the ground rather than appeal to higher intellectual authority. To the knowledgeable reader, Durkheim sits in the background of what we might think of as these "descriptive analyses" organized around implicit visions of a unified social system, differentiated but interlocking functions, and moral-cultural-cognitive integration. Contra Douglas's account with its focus on collective representations, Evans-Pritchard's works may also surprise as they give a lot of attention to economic and political aspects of social organization. In sum, his work displays the spirit of the *Division of Labor* filtered through Radcliffe-Brown, but you need to know where to look or how to read to see this.

We do find some explicit acknowledgment of Durkheim's legacy in lectures that Evans-Pritchard gave on BBC Radio in 1950. This kind of product for a general audience has the advantage of spelling out what was taken for granted in the knowledge base of the professional community, hence not always visible in the publications of the research frontier. Here Evans-Pritchard contrasts the speculative and evolutionary anthropology of the nineteenth century with functionalism in the social anthropology of his day, wherein it is axiomatic that "societies are natural systems of which all the parts are interdependent, each serving in a complex of necessary relations to maintain the whole, and that social life can be reduced to scientific laws which allow prediction" (1951a: 49). Evans-Pritchard recognizes Spencer and Durkheim as making major contributions to this paradigm transformation. But whereas Spencer had been forgotten, Durkheim "had a greater and more direct influence on social anthropology ... both on account of his general sociological theories and because he and a band of talented colleagues and pupils applied them with remarkable insight to the study of primitive societies" (1951a: 51). Evans-Pritchard cites Durkheim's major works in a footnote, and significantly refers there to the "many articles and review articles in *L'Année Sociologique* from 1898 onward, and those by Hubert, Mauss, and others in the same journal" (1951a: 52). He was ahead of the curve in seeing that a substantial body of work existed beyond the big monographs by Durkheim, and he was to be instrumental in having much of the output of the *Année sociologique* translated and published in English. These translations were to improve the visibility of the first-generation Durkheimian scholarship that became assimilated to the cultural turn in anthropology through the 1960s and 1970s. In the radio talks Evans-Pritchard also recognized the work of Radcliffe-Brown. He was described as "following Durkheim" (1951a: 54) and as decisive in making Durkheim's influence greater in the United Kingdom and its Dominions than it was in American anthropology of the time. These detailed expressions of debt to and respect for Durkheim and his group, along with a recognition of their impact on British social anthropology, can also be found in the introductions to those translations of works by Durkheim, Mauss and Hertz that Evans-Pritchard encouraged and commissioned (e.g. Evans-Pritchard 1954; 1960). "I am convinced that no field study of totemism has excelled Durkheim's analysis" (1960: 24), Evans-Pritchard writes.

123

We might have expected resentment against so-called armchair anthropology. But what more impressive or generous statement could come from an ethnographer who had paid his dues toiling in the field?

Returning to Evans-Pritchard's own pioneering work, the theme of how cosmology and thought were socially constructed and linked to action and order were explored in a 1937 monograph, *Witchcraft, Oracles and Magic Among the Azande*. Dealing with a tribe in Sudan where he had conducted fieldwork in the 1920s, the book investigated how a set of beliefs we might think of as crazy or politically destabilizing constituted a meaningful, intersecting whole that generated social cohesion and ended conflict (Evans-Pritchard 1937). The Zande (or Azande – the two terms are used interchangeably in the literature) believed that misfortune, say illness or a crop failure or a small granary falling off its posts and onto a person's head, was often the result of witchcraft. Witches responsible for negative outcomes could be located using an oracular method. One involved rubbing pieces of wood together while asking questions. If the wood stuck or slid, this was an answer. Another oracle involved feeding poison to baby chickens while asking questions. In this case the survival or death of the chick provided information.

Evans-Pritchard shows that this system worked well as a means for dispute resolution, event explanation, and blame allocation within the community. Because everyone agreed on the reality of supernatural forces and on the justice of the oracular method used to identify witches, cognitive horizons were aligned. Nobody was complaining that witches did not exist or that the oracle was just a matter of chance. Systems for removing witchcraft from the body and for redress enabled social life to be restored to normal. A raft of **"secondary elaborations"** enabled seemingly contradictory evidence or puzzling results from the oracle to be explained away. These are modifications to a theory, excuses and explanations that help the core beliefs remain intact. If the person denies being a witch and we know that they are a good member of the community, well, perhaps the witch was acting unconsciously. If the misfortune does not stop, maybe there was another witch as well. If the oracle's answers are all over the place and are not logical, then it is signaling with these contradictions that the wrong questions are being asked.

In accord with the Durkheimian tradition's belief in validating the wisdom of "primitive thought," Evans-Pritchard asserts that the Zande are fundamentally rational. They were scrupulous about the preparation of the poison for the poison oracle and giving just the right amount such that the outcome of a question was uncertain.

Questions followed sequences in logical progressions as in a legal cross-examination. Like any good lawyer, the Zande were skeptical and worked hard to get to the bottom of causal chains. Famously, they were reluctant to say that any misfortune was due to "accident" and in this sense were more obsessed with tracking down culpability and causality than westerners would be in everyday life. Whereas we would be happy enough to say that the granary fell because of termites, the Zande would want to know why the termite damage to the posts would lead to a collapse just at the very moment a particular person was sitting under it.

The Zande reason perfectly well, only within the bounds of their own set of fundamental beliefs. Indeed Evans-Pritchard remarks that he tried living his own life according to these beliefs and practices and found it to be an eminently workable system. There were clear ground rules and practical solutions so long as you believed in the reality of witchcraft and the infallibility of the oracular method – put another way, so long as you shared the collective representations, then society would be stable and tensions could be managed. He summed up the book a few years later: "what at first sight seems no more than an absurd superstition is discovered by anthropological investigation to be the integrative principle of a system of thought and morals and to have an important role in the social structure" (1951a: 102).

Witchcraft, Oracles and Magic has been a hugely significant book within and outside of anthropology. In philosophy and science studies it has provided an exemplar for thinking through questions related to hypothesis falsification, the nature of reason, the circularity of belief systems, and the limits of cultural relativism (e.g. Wilson 1979). For example, scientific theories have been shown to generate their own secondary elaborations when challenged by awkward evidence from the laboratory. In sociology the book was to provide the backbone of Melvin Pollner's (1987) explorations of "mundane reason." Situated in the ethnomethodology tradition, Pollner explored how fundamental beliefs about time, space, causality, or unitary identity of the self are never questioned in everyday life in our own society. Seemingly discrediting information is discounted so that these core beliefs can be upheld. In a traffic court, for example, one driver in a collision might argue that a light at a junction was green and another driver that it was red. The court has an *a priori* belief that only one of them can be right and will find reasons (drink, bad eyesight, lying) that enables it to make a ruling. The idea that the light can be both green and red at the same time, or that one or another of the drivers momentarily passed into a parallel reality, is never entertained. It would literally be laughed out of court, just as the possibility that witchcraft does not exist never crosses the mind of the Zande.

Insofar as collective representations involve deeply fundamental ontological presuppositions as to the nature of reality (and I believe Evans-Pritchard demonstrated this to be a fact), Durkheim can be thought of as an ancestor of traditions looking for a cognitive foundation to solutions to the problem of social order. Regardless of levels of moral integration, if we agree on what is real we can align actions, expectations, and accounts such that we are all on the same page. Of course the line of descent here is not always clearly seen or acknowledged. The case for messy connections from Durkheim to ethnomethodology has been most powerfully made by Anne Rawls (2001), who suggests that Harold Garfinkel was drawing on both Parsons and Durkheim in trying to generate a solution to the problem of social order that looked to interaction, cognition, and shared sense-making. Such an interpretation may or may not be accurate, but if we bring collective representations into the frame it complicates the standard lecture course vision of micro-sociology rebelling against macro-sociology, using a cognitive rather than normative understanding of everyday social life (Heritage 1984).

The other masterpiece from Evans-Pritchard from before World War II was *The Nuer*, perhaps the single most important structural functionalist ethnography. It concerned a cattle-herding tribe in the south of Sudan. The big issue for Evans-Pritchard was how the problem of social order could be solved in such a dispersed society that lacked a permanent authority structure. Here is a short statement of the puzzle and the answer:

> The lack of governmental organs among the Nuer, the absence of legal institutions, of developed leadership, and, generally, of organized political life is remarkable. Their state is an acephalous kinship state and it is only by a study of the kinship system that it can be well understood how order is maintained and social relations over wide areas established and kept up. (1940: 181)

The structural push to explore kinship organization indicated in the quotation was matched by one concerning collective representations. Here Evans-Pritchard (1940) continues in the tradition of Durkheim and Mauss's *Primitive Classification*. In a dedicated chapter of great interest, he reflects on how concepts of time and space mirror social organization. The Nuer are organized by a kinship system consisting of patrilineal kinship groups (descent along the male line). Evans-Pritchard shows how memory of genealogies is selective. Ancestors

126

drop out, or come back into play, or are invented as groups split or unite. The process of remembering, forgetting, and creating reflects current groups and residential arrangements, with genealogies lined up so as to be consistent with contemporary social organization. Genealogical history, spatial distributions (say in villages), and social groups are coordinated. The analysis is consistent with that of Halbwachs (see above), although I could not find him cited. As Mary Douglas observed in a footnote unfortunately buried in her introduction to *Collective Memory* (Halbwachs 1980), Evans-Pritchard got to just the same insight from a completely different path. Consider:

> Beyond the annual cycle, time reckoning is a conceptualization of the social structure, and the points of reference are a projection into the past of actual relations between groups of persons. It is less a means of coordinating events than of coordinating relationships, and is therefore mainly a looking-backwards, since relationships must be explained in terms of the past. (Evans-Pritchard 1940: 108)

Such ideas on connections between organization, classification, and knowledge were to prove fundamental to the later work of Mary Douglas, perhaps Evans-Pritchard's most celebrated student, whose ideas we turn to in the next chapter. A companion volume published a few years later, *Kinship and Marriage Among the Nuer* (Evans-Pritchard 1951b), looked more to social structure and, significantly, was dedicated to Radcliffe-Brown as "friend and teacher . . . whose vast knowledge and illuminating analyses of primitive kinship systems have placed all students of the subject in his debt" (1951b: vii). Never as popular as its predecessors, this is in truth a book for the true connoisseur of British structural functionalism. It explores in a satisfying way the dense nexus of closely interlocking institutions relating to lineages, kinship, village formations, cattle camps, bridewealth, incest taboos, and marriages. These are revealed in structural functionalist fashion to be sources of social order:

> The internal network of kinship links gives the local community the cohesion necessary for it to function as a political unity . . . The whole society can be regarded as a network of strands of relationship which regulates relations between persons throughout Nuerland . . . In seeking to understand Nuer society, abstractions from behavior have been related to one another in order that it may be seen as a whole in the patterns which emerged from the confusion of actualities. (Evans-Pritchard 1951b: 178, 180)

We see in this single quotation the very essence of the Oxford tradition – a concern with social connections, with system integration, and with a kind of totalizing vision of an isolated society. The motto being, one supposes, "Only Connect."

Although we have focused on Evans-Pritchard in the preceding paragraphs, the anthropological community also considers as classics many other monographs from the structural functionalist group that surrounded him. **Godfrey Lienhardt**'s (1921–93) work *Divinity and Experience*, on religion among the Dinka (neighbors of the Nuer), stands out for its nuance (Lienhardt 1961). He comes much closer to cultural relativism than many of his peers in arguing for the near-untranslatable nature of some concepts, but at the same time has a broadly Durkheimian understanding of religion as an institution in a wider social context, not just as a set of beliefs. The book sits nicely alongside Evans-Pritchard's own *Nuer Religion* (see next chapter). **Meyer Fortes** (1906–83) was a prominent Africanist, best known for his work on Talensi religion and kinship systems. Never a star of the same magnitude as Evans-Pritchard, he was deeply knowledgeable about African society, a strong anthropological theorist, and institutionally important as incumbent of a Chair at Cambridge until as late as 1973. Along with Evans-Pritchard, Fortes was responsible for the edited volume *African Political Systems* (Evans-Pritchard and Fortes 1940), which, rather like the *Année sociologique*, stands as a collective monument to a coherent intellectual paradigm and a deep bench of talent. A focus here – yet again – was on the capacity of African society to be self-regulating, with kinship and residential groups realigning on a regular basis in response to circumstances and often without the need for authority structures.

Another member of the Oxford group was **M. N. Srinivas** (1906–99), who became the foremost anthropologist of India, especially village India. His studies of the caste system (e.g. Srinivas 1952; 1962) were couched in the structural functionalist idiom and paid close attention to connections through the social system. For example, he writes: "The introduction of any single tool or institution will have repercussions not only in the field of techniques but also in the social and religious fields. The peasant's traditional culture is a highly integrated one, and the removal or substitution of even a single item will be followed by changes in other spheres" (1962: 11). But for all this attention to linked institutions, technologies, and folkways, his works were also concerned with change, stratification, and inequality – themes that were far less visible in the African ethnographies of the time. His most notable concept was "Sanskritization," which refers to a ritual strategy in which castes attempt to remove pollution and move up the social hierarchy of respectability by adopting lifestyles and activities recommended in ancient sacred (Sanskrit) texts. For example, a lower caste might become vegetarian. This was an early, but today somewhat unsung, example exploring how ritual could be connected to stratification and cultural pragmatics. Sanskritization was "the process of social mobility as well as the idiom in which mobility expresses itself" (1962: 9).

Srinivas also noticed that villages tended to have a dominant caste that controlled land and access to scarce resources, in effect adding a more materialist and realist edge to the vision that had been assembled by Bouglé. In recognizing this deep village inequality – and on top of this the impact of colonialism in adding complexity to stratification – Srinivas's work displays a certain critical and normative moment that was generally lacking in the work of his Africanist colleagues.

As Chair at the London School of Economics from 1944, **Raymond Firth** (1901–2002) exercised both institutional and intellectual power. His ethnographic work on the tiny, remote island of Tikopia (Firth 1936) remains a classic of Polynesian ethnography that is reputed to be used by the islanders today as a valued source of information on their traditional customs and lifestyle. Firth had trained with Malinowski, but was also influenced by Radcliffe-Brown. An open-minded and flexible intellectual, he opened up the field of economic anthropology and placed a greater emphasis on personality and choice than we usually find in British structural functionalism. Like Mary Douglas, Firth was to remain influential through to the late twentieth century, although his output was more scattered and lacked the intellectual center of gravity we find in her sustained, deep, relentless efforts to connect culture, thought, and structure.

The United States

Durkheim was adopted surprisingly early in Russia. Indeed before the Revolution several of his works were translated into Russian and his emphasis on social facts, social problems, and moderate reform was appreciated. *Suicide* in particular had a favorable reception (Gofman 2000). The Revolution, of course, put an end to such auspicious beginnings. One notable early advocate was Pitirim Sorokin (1889–1968), who translated large selections from the *Elementary Forms*. Although Sorokin later moved to the United States and became an influential figure in American sociology it was his rival at Harvard, Talcott Parsons, who eventually did the most to publicize Durkheim's contributions. Sorokin gave Durkheim only seventeen out of seven hundred and sixty pages in his work *Contemporary Sociological Theories* (Collins 2005: 123). Parsons elevated him to his current status of "founding father." Credit for getting the name out in the United States might also be given to **Harry Alpert** (1912–77), who for his PhD at Columbia wrote on Durkheim and then had the thesis published in 1939 (Alpert 1961). Alpert described the biographical component of the book as "a temporary stop gap." The English-speaking world would have to wait another three decades for the "more thorough and more searching biography" he hoped would supersede his early attempt (1961: 13). Alpert also provided an extended, if not unduly profound, discussion of Durkheim's vision of sociology and society. By being a dedicated and full-length book this study did much to establish Durkheim as a major figure worthy of careful attention. Alpert was to remain probably the leading Durkheim specialist in the United States until Robert Nisbet. A glance at the sources cited by Alpert on Durkheim and his sociology (1961: 225–8) is instructive in giving a sense of the field in 1939. It is dominated by accounts from the *Année* group in French. We have already explained how Bouglé, Davy, and Fauconnet devoted themselves to textbook-style summaries of Durkheimian thinking. Sources in English devoted to the topic are few and far between, indicating the limited penetration of Durkheimian thinking into the Anglophone world at this time. It is notable, though, that Alpert lists items by Parsons and Merton that have since proven highly influential. We turn to these below.

Talcott Parsons (1902–79) was probably introduced to Durkheim's thought during his spell in Malinowski's group at the London School of Economics in the early 1930s. The work of Radcliffe-Brown had made Durkheim's influence unavoidable in British anthropology, even in the seminar of Radcliffe-Brown's competitor. Parsons had as his mission a desire to build sociology as an independent, high-status, deeply academic discipline in the United States. Durkheim provided a resource for this as he had faced the same challenge forty years before in France. Parsons saw in Durkheim's earlier call for a generalizing, all-encompassing, theoretically rigorous social science of sociology something he could identify with and build upon. What was needed was to mark out a territory.

We first see Parsons's Durkheim clearly in the one hundred and forty or so dedicated pages within his masterwork of the 1930s, *The Structure of Social Action* (Parsons 1949). Here his chapters on Durkheim are the "analytic core" of the project (Collins 2005: 122). Taking a philosophical approach, Parsons positioned himself against deterministic theories that saw people as controlled by social laws.

Yet he also highlighted the problem of social order as a fundamental issue that sociology had to address. Like Durkheim before him writing on the necessity for precontractual solidarity, he attacked utilitarian theory with its vision of individual maximizing actors, suggesting this could not explain the emergence of social order. Parsons also argued that rational actor models had an unwanted deterministic endgame. Action could be read off or predicted from the distribution of rewards, sanctions, and opportunities in the environment. So what had to be present for an action to take place that was non-random, hence solving the problem of social order, but also the product of free will? Using the method of close reading, Parsons engaged in an analytic reconstruction of the thought of four leading social theorists: Marshall, Pareto, Durkheim, and Weber. At the time Durkheim and Weber were probably the least well known of the four, but they were the most central to Parsons's solution.

Durkheim was enlisted by Parsons not so much for his positivist belief in social facts – which, as we have seen, had a rather determinist cast as externally constraining – but rather as the carrier of ideas about internalized normative motivation and as the master theorist of a kind of collective socio-cultural voluntarism that also took the problem of social order seriously. Parsons argued that Durkheim had worked toward this enlightenment slowly and inconsistently in his career. Empiricism, positivism, and social realism, visible in *Suicide* and the *Rules* with their talk of social facts, had prevented a clear vision from forming. Yet at the end of the day Durkheim had been able to arrive at an account of the subjective sources of social order. Parsons concluded:

> Thus in following out the problems of control Durkheim has progressed through the conception of control as subjection to naturalistic causation and that of avoidance of sanctions, to laying primary emphasis on the "subjective" sense of moral obligation. The element of constraint persists with a changed meaning, in the sense of obligation. In so far as he has that sense the actor is not free to do as he likes, he is "bound," but it is a totally different mode of being bound from either of the other two . . . The normal concrete individual is a morally disciplined personality. This means above all that the normative elements have become "internal," "subjective" to him. He becomes in a sense "identified" with them." (1949: 385–6)

For Parsons, nobody, except perhaps Weber, had expressed so well the possibilities for action to be meaningfully motivated rather than externally compelled and/or rationally maximizing. And Durkheim outdid Weber when it came to explaining social stability and the moral alignments that organized social action in coordinated, cooperative patterns. Parsons's proposition in *The Structure of Social Action* was that in a hypothetical "unit act" the individual would strive to attain an end of action within a specific situation. Drawing on Durkheim and Weber, he argued that norms and values in the wider society would shape both the chosen ends and the means used to attain these. In this way individual-level action was inherently "social," coordinated, and non-random and yet also motivated from within the self.

It is worth giving a paragraph over to Parsons's treatment of the *Elementary Forms* in *The Structure of Social Action*. He was a perceptive reader and, long before the "cultural turn," observed differences in tone and theoretical logic between the late masterpiece and Durkheim's earlier works. As was discussed in chapter 1, the first three major books had been tinged with determinism thanks to the emphasis on social facts as external and constraining on the individual. The *Elementary Forms*, however, in Parsons's reading had a stronger vision of dynamic actors motivated by internalized emotional and symbolic forces. Parsons clearly sees it as the culmination of Durkheim's intellectual development:

> Durkheim is found explicitly stating that society exists only in the minds of individuals. This represents the logical outcome of his whole development and also the final abandonment of his objectivist bias. It is of especial interest here because it represents a close approach to Weber's doctrine of "*verstehen*." (1949: 442)

So the two founding fathers had converged on a similar set of profound insights from different starting points (Gerhardt 2002). After writing *The Structure of Social Action*, Parsons moved from a consideration of social action toward more macro-level thoughts on system coordination and integration. In a sense he began to take up the sorts of issues that concerned Radcliffe-Brown, such as the relationship of culture to institutions and social organization. We turn to this work in the next chapter.

Aside from Parsons, the other important figure in the United States influenced by Durkheim was **Robert K. Merton** (1910–2003). While one senses that Durkheim was pivotal in the evolution of Parsons's thought, in the case of Merton he was just one of many influences on a long list. In Merton's 600-page *Social Theory and Social Structure* Durkheim appears on 23 pages, according to the index. Lazarsfeld has 30 entries, Parsons 24, and Weber 24. We find similarly stable numbers for Mannheim, Scheler, and Sorokin (Merton 1957c). It is clear that Merton drinks from more than one stream, and that he drinks, or would like to appear to drink, lightly and evenly from each. Merton's general tendency to think about social groups, to look for cultural explanations, and to have a sociological angle of vision is often seen as evidence of a Durkheimian shadow (e.g. Fuchs Epstein 2010). But then again one could make the case that Merton was not much impressed by what he saw. In a review essay published in 1934 he chided "recent French sociology." There was too much concern with the primitive mentality, too many philosophical position statements, and not enough attention given to contemporary statistical approaches and the analysis of contemporary society (Merton 1934). These comments are almost certainly directed at the Durkheimian legacy as it stood at the time (see chapter 2).

If the French sociology of his own day was not up to scratch, Merton's somewhat lengthy review of the first English translation of the *Division of Labor*, published in the *American Journal of Sociology* (also) in 1934, demonstrates deep respect (Merton 1976) and helped establish the book in the United States. He interprets the *Division* as demonstrating "the current of positivistic thought which stemmed from Comte" in its efforts to identify laws akin to those of the natural sciences, and praises its joined-up model of "social process and its structural correlates" (1976: 112). However, he also faults it for sweeping conclusions and problems of method. One senses that for Merton, unlike Parsons, Durkheim's big-picture visions were always a little *de trop* and that small points of insight or analytic leverage were of more value.

This reading is consistent with the fact that in a now famous essay, "Social Structure and Anomie" published in 1938, Merton (1957a) came to popularize the idea of anomie in American sociology. Yet he did more for the concept than for Durkheim, dragging the master along in the word's wake. In so doing Merton had obscured Durkheim's wider potentials as a resource for empirical sociology. Hence Nisbet wrote in 1965 that Durkheim was "par excellence the sociologist of anomie" (1976: 6) – the sort of statement that we would be unlikely to see today as defining his legacy. In his classic paper, Merton adapted Durkheim's key but often somewhat vague idea and made it much more specific. As Kenneth Thompson indicates, the critical element of Durkheim's concept relating to a systematic societal malaise associated with the transition to modernity drops out. Merton "gave the impression that he was only concerned with problems of non-conformity" (Thompson 2002: 121). Further, Merton transformed a concept relating to weak cultural regulation into one

133

relating to the problem of goals that were too strongly defined. He suggested that anomie resulted when there was a disjunction between the emphatically endorsed value system of a society, with its associated stratification system, and the opportunity structures open to a person. After looking at the prevalence of unrealistic aspirations for financial and social success in modern America he writes: "The social structure we have examined produces a strain toward anomie and deviant behavior. The pressure of such a social order is upon outdoing one's competitors" (1957a: 157). Deviance, Merton said, was a creative solution that could be described as "innovation" in which individuals tried to bridge the gap. Crime, cheating, and unethical behavior arise as actors try to improvise their way to success by using illegitimate means to reach valued ends.

In the years since, this essay has come to be seen as the origin moment for what is known as strain theory, one of the core paradigms in contemporary criminology. Merton's close specification of strain was in effect the identification of a hypothesis that is ripe for testing. It has generated a vast, largely positivistic and statistical literature in which efforts are made to test whether the gap between aspiration and reality ("strain") is a good predictor of criminality in individuals after controlling for the impact of other factors (say, inequality). Criminology tends to be much cited, and if we were to evaluate Durkheim's legacy in terms of citations Merton would be one of the most influential figures for intergenerational transmission (see Smith 2008b for a wider discussion of Durkheim and criminology). It is somewhat surprising, therefore, to see that although this essay has done so much to put Durkheim on the map in criminology, he is mentioned in it only twice. We find him noted in passing in the text: "there develops what Durkheim called 'anomie' or (normlessness)" (1957a: 135). He also pops up beneath this nod in a footnote. We are told the term "anomie" went back to the sixteenth century and had been resurrected by Durkheim. The reason for this resurrection would itself make a good research question, Merton suggests. There is no sustained discussion nor analytic page-by-page dissection of Durkheim's theory of anomie as we would expect given how intellectual history has bound Merton, Durkheim, and anomie into a thought bundle.

Evidence for Merton's substantial impact even before the rise of contemporary quantitative criminology can be found in a second essay on anomie he wrote for the revised edition of *Social Theory and Social Structure*, published in 1957 (Merton 1957c) some twenty years after the appearance of the first article. Here he notes that "recent years have seen the appearance of a sizeable literature that bears upon one or another aspect of anomie" (1957b: 161) and complains that the concept has become vulgarized. Nevertheless he is able to document a large number of published studies – many influenced by his own prior conceptual work – demonstrating how anomie plays out in diverse environments and contexts such as delinquency, prisons, class systems, and bureaucracies. The paper notably makes occasional use of the functionalist vocabulary and house style dominant in the 1950s (see next chapter) to crystallize his now consolidated vision:

> Anomie is then conceived as a breakdown in the cultural structure, occurring particularly when there is an acute disjunction between the cultural norms and goals and the socially structured capacities of members of the group to act in accord with them. In this conception, cultural values may help to produce behavior which is at odds with the mandates of the values themselves. (1957b: 162)

In this follow-up, too, Durkheim is somewhat buried, with most attention going to recent social science in the United States.

Let's end this chapter thirty-three years on from its start, in the year 1950. In France, the Durkheimian legacy seems about to expire. Mauss will die this year. The *Collège de sociologie* is peripheral and arguably past its peak. In the United Kingdom, Durkheim dominates the discipline of social anthropology as a kind of shadowy background of common sense theory regarding social organization and social integration. He has inspired a highly productive paradigm group centered on Oxford. But how long can it last? In the United States, Durkheim is acknowledged as a significant founding figure but only Parsons has really tried hard to understand and build upon him in a creative way. The next chapter looks at the period through to 1985. It encompasses, among other things, Durkheimian elements in structuralism, the rise of systems theory, and early efforts at a neo-Durkheimian understanding of ritual and the sacred in modernity.

Chapter 4
Through the Cultural Turn, 1950–1985

*Parsons and systems theory – the fall of Parsons –
Germany – Lévi-Strauss – British anthropology – Mary
Douglas – Durkheimian empirical sociology in the
United States.*

The title of this chapter is somewhat ironic, as the full potentials of connecting the cultural turn with the Durkheimian tradition were not to be adequately realized until the 1990s. With a handful of exceptions we might say that scholars failed to see the turn coming as they ploughed merrily along and neglected to change course. They went "through" the cultural turn, not round it. Durkheim himself was for the most part drawn upon by theorists lightly and was not comprehensively reworked or re-read. Many thinkers had other concerns foremost in their minds. Still, Durkheim's ideas remained influential and alive in significant ways that we can capture here.

Parsons and Systems Theory

Picking up where we left the last chapter, in America, let's start with Talcott Parsons, who from the 1940s onward moved away from theorizing action directly and became involved in what is generally called **systems theory**. For the purposes of this book, systems theory can be thought of as an elaboration of Durkheim's ideas about integration, functional interdependence, coordination, and adaptation as these are best expressed in *The Division of Labor*. Radcliffe-Brown had also been impressed by those themes in that book. But whereas his work offers an ethnologically dense but theoretically intuitive and accessible version of structural functionalism derived largely from Durkheim, systems theory proper is a more abstract, formal, and widely influenced approach that can make for very tough reading.

Parsons had a grand ambition in his systems theory. This was to unite or, better, actively synthesize knowledge from multiple disciplines and paradigms. From the 1940s onward his Department of Social Relations at Harvard was a kind of intellectual hub for this activity, bringing in talented students and collaborators and taking ideas from all kinds of fields, psychology and cybernetics visible among them. Parsons wanted to build a theory that would encompass various levels of social analysis, from the personality of the individual, through action, encounters, and institutions, to the entire social system. He understood that figuring out how coordination was achieved within and between these levels was fundamental to explaining society. So was accounting for social integration in a context of potential tension over goals and resource allocation. Durkheimian thinking about morals and solidarity was to play a crucial role, transformed in this case into vocabularies about values and norms, latent functions and need dispositions.

In *Toward a General Theory of Action* (Parsons and Shils 1962) and *The Social System* (Parsons 1952), both published at the very start of the 1950s, the argument was made that society found a general sense of direction through overarching social values. Parsons drew somewhat upon Ferdinand Tönnies (1855–1936) and his famous *Gemeinschaft* and *Gesellschaft* typology, elaborated in the 1880s. This distinguished informal and solidaristic groups like community and family (*Gemeinschaft*) that were held together by sentiments and moral bonds from those based upon more formal, legal, and instrumentally driven collective arrangements (*Gesellschaft*). Tönnies argued that the movement toward modernity involved a general shift in social organization from *Gemeinschaft* to *Gesellschaft*. Parsons combined this set of insights with Durkheim's elaborated visions of social evolution, individual–society relations, and functional interdependence. Institutions, Parsons said, were steered and judged by their shared values within a differentiated social system. At the level of the interaction order, people came to internalize and learn cultural values and norms through a process of socialization. These shaped their desires and their expectations about ends and means. Cultural components attached to institutionalized roles aligned actions in social situations. This was particularly important in contexts of double contingency when two actors needed to interpret an encounter in a similar way and know how to act appropriately. Parsons argued that norms associated with the roles at play allowed actors to accomplish this end.

Broadly speaking, for Parsons, Durkheim's focus on solidarity, morality, and symbolic life offered ways to find solutions to problems of coordination and integration. Although not considered as closely in these later texts as in *The Structure of Social Action*, he is noted in the Preface to *The Social System* as a pervasive background figure of "immense influence" (Parsons 1952: xi). Taking an example from Durkheim, Parsons reflects later in that book on how the ritual and symbolic aspects of punishment are linked to stigmatizing the social role of the deviant, thus making it unattractive. This signification would also help uphold institutionalized moral values. Likewise Parsons points to the role of religion and belief systems in the task of the moral integration of the social system: "These types of expressive symbols may be considered as manifesting and regulating the common moral sentiments or need-dispositions of the members of the collectivity. It is this type which Durkheim so clearly illuminated in his analysis of religious ritual in its symbolic aspects" (Parsons 1952: 395–6).

Whereas the two texts mentioned above have a flexible and somewhat provisional feel (*The Social System* is at times a little like a collection of creative essays or placeholding thoughts), the culmination of Parsonian systems theory was far more rigid. The so-called AGIL model (we explain the acronym a little below) was first set out in his book *Economy and Society*, co-authored with one of his most talented students, Neil Smelser (Parsons and Smelser 1956). Once again Durkheim gets a nod alongside other foundational thinkers at the start of the book, as one of the three thinkers who had contributed most to a "general theory of action" (1956: 2). He is joined by Radcliffe-Brown, Firth, and Lévi-Strauss in the annotated bibliography at the end of the volume. There are also two mentions for Evans-Pritchard in the text. Clearly there was wide reading of anthropology going on. Sadly missing, however, are Mauss, Halbwachs, and Simiand – figures in the Durkheimian tradition that can in fact be used to reconstruct a comprehensive sociological vision of modern economic social life (see Steiner 2011). We can only assume that they were somewhat unknown and off the radar for economic sociology in the United States at the time.

In the text itself we see Durkheim singled out for his identification of the non-contractual or precontractual bases of contract (i.e.

138

norms, beliefs, customs, solidarities) and for realizing that economic expansion was not driven by a pre-social need for goods or happiness. Rather "the primary wants of individuals are not independently given outside social interaction process (including the economic) but are the products of that process" (Parsons and Smelser 1956: 291). We see here an intimation of what was to be a core theme in cultural economic sociology decades later: desire, production, and consumption are all social. But above all else Durkheim lurks in the shadows playing his customary, uncited role in systems theory – offering a deep understanding of the moral and cultural origins of integration and coordination.

Parsons and Smelser argued that every social system or subsystem had to adapt (A) to its external environment; achieve some goals (G) linked to its social function; maintain internal coordination (I for "integration"); and have underlying beliefs that sustain motivation and prevent conflict (L for "latent pattern maintenance and tension management"). Hence the term AGIL. In this formulation, culture tended to shape the I and L subsystems. There is a shadow of Durkheim here, with culture involved in ensuring internal stability (via solidarity, integration) and emotional investments in the collective enterprise rather than being caught up in the pragmatics and materiality of adaptive task performance. The L subsystem in particular is somewhat elusive and seems to echo Durkheim's thoughts about the collective conscience as a kind of invisible bedrock on which society is built. Parsons had a concept in some of his other work, "societal community," that also had this everywhere-and-nowhere quality. The relegation of culture to the somewhat passive role of ensuring system stability was to come back to haunt the Parsonian systems paradigm in future. Ironically enough its own "A" subsystem failed to adapt to the changed intellectual environment that came with the cultural turn in the 1960s and 1970s. Something could have been done much earlier had ideas from Lévi-Strauss and others about the information-processing capacities of cultural forms (ideas that were quite available from the 1950s onward) been folded into thinking about the tasks (A, G) that culture performed within the social system.

Durkheim was to influence Parsons (1968) one last time in his discussions of societal evolution and the social system during the 1960s. Here the *Division of Labor* could be lauded as a foundational text that had theorized long-term transformations in social structure. These could be described as differentiation with corresponding changes in the collective conscience toward value generalization (Parsons 1968). Parsons specified the shift from mechanical to organic solidarity a little more precisely using his pattern variables, which had made a debut in *The Social System*. These mapped out shifts from ascription to achievement, from particularism to universalism, and so forth, as characteristics of the arrival of modernity. The point was to suggest that attachments and beliefs became more abstract as a way of allowing inclusion in a situation of pluralism, complexity, and de-traditionalization. Although this growing generality would encounter pushback or be weaker in some settings than others (e.g. the family versus the research university) it was still, Parsons claimed, the master trend associated with modernity.

The high-water mark for this structural functionalist systems theory, both as a working paradigm and as a Promised Land for social thought to navigate toward, was around 1960. Parsons was beset by headwinds thereafter. One of the more significant and theoretically informed early interventions was from David Lockwood in a conceptual critique of *The Social System* published as early as 1963. The essay was entitled "Social Integration and System Integration" and much later expanded upon in his book *Solidarity and Schism* (1992, where the original essay is reproduced). Drawing on comments from Alvin Gouldner, Ralf Dahrendorf, and other theorists of class and conflict in industrial modernity, Lockwood argued that what he called "normative functionalism" was over-invested in prior beliefs about "social integration" through norms. It underestimated possibilities for "system integration" (i.e. a stable and functional social system with predictable behaviors) to be developed through other means, such as force (e.g. punishments for non-compliance, the use of the police and army in a dictatorship) or atomized utilitarian calculus (e.g. "I need to pay the rent. Therefore I will go to work today like everyone else even though I hate my job"). The over-integrated model also did not fully understand possibilities for social dysfunction and poor coordination between norms, values, institutions, and interests. Lockwood demonstrated how the problems of functionalism became particularly acute when it came to explaining social change: "The propensity to social change arising from the functional incompatibility between an institutional order and its material base has been ignored by normative functionalists because of their concentration on the moral aspects of social integration" (1992: 412). In other words, the model had assumed and theorized integration to the point where it had lost the intellectual flexibility needed to explain or perhaps even imagine other outcomes in the real world.

Lockwood wrote those words in the early 1960s. Probably even he did not foresee the precipitous decline of Parsonian systems theory, especially in the United States. The narrative is familiar but needs repeating because Durkheim, to a certain extent, was dragged down with him and remained somewhat discredited for two decades. Parsons was said to downplay power and conflict, to be conservative, to overplay value integration (Gouldner 1970), and to propose abstract and static models of social life that squeeze out agency and vitality both analytically and normatively – and for that matter descriptively (Habermas 1987; Heritage 1984). Perhaps most important of all, for all his attention to strain and to societal evolution Parsons's work seemed radically out of touch during the era of the Vietnam War. In this geopolitical context, ideas from Marxism and world systems theory seemed more tractable when it came to dealing not only with armed conflict but also global flows, domestic militarism, colonialism, and struggles for political power.

For those resisting this materialism there were new, "structural" readings of Weber now on tap. These downplayed hermeneutics, meaningful action, and his religious sociology and focused instead on his thoughts about the economy, capitalism, and the emergence of the modern state. If you wanted more meaning and intersubjectivity, well, micro-sociology was on the rise. This saw the origins of social order emerging from the everyday heroism of interaction accomplishment. In contrast to a passionless systems theory, symbolic interactionism appealed to humanists and ethnographers with its focus on real groups and situations. It stressed the role of radically local norms, situational contexts, and knowledge in producing local forms of order. **Symbolic interactionism** had long been associated with Chicago, but by the 1960s expertise was widespread around the United States. There was no shortage of talent, with figures like Herbert Blumer, Howard Becker, and Anselm Strauss leading by example with fine, lively, empirical studies. A more cerebral and theoretically dense challenge that could appeal to the same intellectual demographic as systems theory came from **ethnomethodology**, itself inspired by the equally cerebral and dense European tradition of **phenomenology**. These both emphasized how individuals made sense of the world and coordinated mutually intelligible lines of action. Conversation analysis, a rigorous empirical spin-off from ethnomethodology, enabled the amazing fine detail of social order to be made visible in everyday talk and soon racked up an impressive corpus of discoveries about how such talk works.

The founder of ethnomethodology was **Harold Garfinkel** (1917–2011), a formidable theorist and writer and a onetime student of Parsons at Harvard. The conventional narrative is that Garfinkel rebelled against Parsons as he sought the origins of social order in micro-level interactions, where situated cognitive processes (making sense and producing accountable lines of action) took priority over the internalized norms that had been pivotal to systems theory (Heritage 1984). An alternative reading, however, is to suggest that Garfinkel worked to specify more fully the issue of double contingency (i.e. two people interacting and trying to do so in a coordinated way, as opposed to, say, a person interacting with a rock) that Parsons had highlighted as a central action problem back in the 1940s and 1950s (Rawls 2001). Certainly the problem of social order was always pivotal to Garfinkel's thinking, and in this sense he was a distant heir to Durkheim, busy, as Anne Rawls puts it, working through "Durkheim's aphorism" (Garfinkel 2002). The case for a connection of Garfinkel to Durkheim has also been made by Richard Hilbert (1992). Hilbert argues that ethnomethodology is all about the ways in which a collective conscience is constructed from the ground up in everyday life.

So Parsonian thought was subject to critique from all sides. Yet from the perspective of the Durkheimian tradition, Parsons can be viewed positively. He was the figure who went by far the deepest in elaborating themes concerning functional integration in a differenti-ated social system. Yet in speaking of culture as abstract norms (e.g. "deference") and values (e.g. "egalitarianism," "universalism") that could be captured in one word, and in thinking of society as an abstract system, he somehow drained the lifeblood from the study of meaning and, indeed, from the study of society itself. Although Parsons was writing well into the 1970s the cultural turn passed him by, or he passed it by, and his tendency toward thinning out and pruning by abstraction never left him. It was an eventual return to Durkheim seen through the lens of the cultural turn and without the Parsonian filter that was pivotal to building cultural sociology in the United States. We discuss this story in chapter 5.

If America turned against systems theory in the 1960s and 1970s, this was never quite the case in Germany, where there has always been a stronger bond between social theory and philosophy. Before we move to consider German systems theory we should first take the opportunity to say something about Durkheim in Germany. He had been well known at least since George Marica's remarkably early overview of his life and works (Marica 1932) and was taught as part of the theoretical canon along with Tönnies, Sorokin, and Sombart, for example. Yet Durkheim had never been seen as belonging in the first rank. The *Handwörterbuch der Soziologie* (pocket dictionary or handy guide to sociology) from 1931 was an early collaborative attempt at a systematic overview of German sociology (Vierkandt 1931). It provides a sense of Durkheim's relative importance. The index shows him mentioned on 10 pages. Weber is present on 40, Marx on 27, Simmel 23, Scheler 19, and Sorokin 5. So he is an important middle-ranking figure, which was a level of visibility above his ranking in the United States at this time.

Durkheim's reputation did not really improve after World War II. His most important advocate for many years was René König, who helped introduce German readers to Durkheim's works with summaries of texts, positive readings of their implications, and expositions of the intellectual development of Durkheim and his school (see König 2013 for a collection). Much of this work was published in the journal that König controlled, the *Kölner Zeitschrift für Soziologie und Sozialpsychologie*. With his detailed knowledge and scholarly appreciations of forgotten figures and texts, König was in many ways a *Durkheimian Studies/Études Durkheimiennes* figure *avant la lettre*. Beyond this, he used Durkheim as a springboard to advocate for an empirical, international sociology in contrast to the inward-looking ideology critique widely found in German at the time. There was also a constructive intellectual contribution. According to Hans Joas, König (1976) developed a distinctive reading of Durkheim not as a moralist but as a thinker "concerned above all with the conditions for the formation of a new morality" (Joas 1993: 230), and as thinking through "the creativity of collective and individual action as well as the linking of creativity and responsibility or normativity" (Joas 1993: 231).

These ideas arguably had little impact until Joas himself took them up decades later (see chapter 5). Durkheim's reputation and influence in Germany remained modest for decades. It was not helpful that Theodor Adorno (1967), who was a towering rival to König in the German sociology field, wrote a negative appraisal in his introduction to a German translation of Durkheim's *Sociology and Philosophy*. For Adorno, Durkheim could be read as having controlling and authoritarian tendencies (a complaint also made by Bauman; see chapters 1 and 5). In addition, Adorno claimed that Durkheim's treatment of the collective conscience, understood in this case perhaps naïvely as society's self-image, failed to come to terms with the issue of false consciousness. For the most part, though, Durkheim was crowded out by the two main foci of creative German social thought: phenomenology and critical theory. It was in such a context of neglect that systems theory came at least partly to the rescue.

Jürgen Habermas (1929–) was perhaps the greatest social theorist both active and creative in the 1970s. Despite the fact that he was to criticize Parsons for creating an overly systemic vision, his own intellectual style was in many ways similar. His mentors, the Frankfurt School duo of Adorno and Horkheimer, had drawn upon Weber and Marx to argue that instrumental rationality in modernity was associated with negative social outcomes such as domination in the industrial workplace, bureaucratic control, manipulative culture industries, totalitarianism, and a meaningless existence. They argued that history had falsified an Enlightenment project that had worshipped "reason" as an antidote to power and prejudice. Yet they did not seem to have much idea what to do about this situation other than to engage in the skeptical, wary, and retreatist posture of a "negative dialectic." Habermas, however, set out to recover reason in a positive way by thinking of it as a communicative process and by arguing that society was not all bad. What he called the "lifeworld" consisted of meaningful human action and association. This was contrasted to the more instrumental and controlling "system world." Putting this in a Parsonian idiom, we could say that he argued the A and G subsystems had taken over. We needed to find ways for I and L to regain their autonomy and influence.

In his masterwork, *The Theory of Communicative Action* from 1981, Habermas (1987) engages in the activity of reading, analytic reconstruction, and synthesis in the manner of Parsons in his *Structure of Social Action*. For example, there are protracted discussions of foundational statements by Marx and Weber. These are used to trace out the negative impacts of rationality in industrial capitalism and state functioning. And in thinking through the lifeworld, Habermas drew not only on phenomenology, ethnomethodology, and interactionism (George Herbert Mead, Thomas Luckmann, Harold Garfinkel, etc.) but also on Durkheim. Parsons had used Durkheim as the carrier of ideas about voluntaristic action and normative social integration. Habermas deployed him in a kindred way, but tended to recast him as an emblematic theorist of meaningful solidarity. In Habermas's thinking, the integrative force of the sacred had shifted location from ritual to language with growing social differentiation and value generalization in the condition of modernity. Language use in free and fair, undistorted exchange could become the source of primal solidarity and a resource for re-enchanting social life. Habermas called this "communicative rationality." Durkheim offered a stepping-stone for the task of connecting rationality back to freedom via a normative, solidaristic conception of language pragmatics and function. For example, in his discussions of law Durkheim had shown a communal religious impetus (solidaristic feelings, emotions about the sacred) being converted over time into legal codes (writing, discourse). Habermas writes:

> in his later writings, particularly in his studies of the sociology of religion and law. Durkheim came close to the idea of the linguistification of a basic religious consensus that has been set communicatively aflow. From this perspective I shall attempt to defend the changes in the form of social integration described by Durkheim as indicators of the process of rationalization ... The rationality potential in action oriented to mutual understanding can be released and translated into the rationalization of the lifeworlds of social groups to the extent that language fulfills functions of reaching understanding, coordinating actions, and socializing individuals; it thereby becomes a medium through which cultural reproduction, social integration, and socialization take place. (1987: 86)

The potential contributions of Durkheim to systems theory were mined more indirectly and with less utopian force in the scholarship of **Niklas Luhmann** (1927–98). He is one of the few thinkers in social theory capable of writing and thought that is more abstract than that of Parsons or Habermas, or indeed Durkheim when at his least empirically anchored. And so Luhmann critiqued Durkheim because "his concepts and the facts he studied now seem too densely aggregated" (1982: 18). Put another way, for Luhmann, Durkheim was not abstract enough, not conceptual enough, did not differentiate enough, and was too tied up with explaining the world immediately around him.

Generally speaking, Luhmann's output displays a relentless concern with functional coordination and system complexity. This reflects the tradition that emerged from Durkheim's thoughts on social order and modernity and was continued through Parsons as he meditated on social cybernetics. Luhmann contributed an introduction to the first German translation of Durkheim's *Division of Labor* in 1977. This is both a sign of respect and the most significant source for his views on Durkheim. In a way the item perhaps tells us more about Luhmann's thinking than Durkheim's (Debray 2017). Luhmann tends to judge Durkheim by his own Luhmannian standards, praising him when he intuits a general analytic problem, faulting him for muddled or insufficiently differentiated thinking. Luhmann recognizes Durkheim's text as a classic, particularly as it placed the problem of social order center stage and was an important step toward complexity theory. But in his view Durkheim's work was also characterized by some conceptual confusion. Essentially, it failed to fully differentiate the analytic capacities of explanatory concepts and decouple them from assumptions about their functional role. In addition, the problem of the relation of the individual to society was too jumbled up with the matter of how social order was possible. The two should be separated, Luhmann said. Durkheim had underestimated potentials for conflict arising from complexity and placed too much mono-dimensional weight on morality and solidarity (instead of, say, money and pricing in the case of markets) as being the solution to the problem of social order. This is a critique somewhat similar to one made by Lockwood as discussed above – not particularly cultural or moral things can also hold society together or stabilize interaction, and symptoms of societal complexity are not necessarily evolutionary solutions to the problem of social integration in modernity.

So the biggest problem was a lack of differentiation in the theory itself. Concepts were locked together prematurely. Luhmann writes that "Durkheim's concept of the division of labor was preharmonized with his concepts of solidarity and morality . . . the concepts were geared to correlate, and this theoretical design determined their elasticity and their limitations" (1982: 7). Put another way, splitting apart solidarity, morality, and the division of labor would offer more analytic power and more explanatory options in contexts where the three did not line up. The themes exposed in this introduction to the *Division of Labor* were to occupy much of Luhmann's own creative work during the 1980s, as he attempted to explain how modernity handled complexity and how the increasingly autonomous self related to society.

Lévi-Strauss and Structuralism

When we left France in the last chapter, the Durkheimian tradition was effectively moribund. It was to be revived in a covert way by structural anthropology. In France, **Claude Lévi-Strauss** (1908–2009) came to carry the Durkheimian legacy after the death of Mauss in 1950. When exiled to New York during World War II, he had become a friend of the linguist Roman Jakobson, to whom he was to dedicate his late collection of miscellaneous, beautifully crafted essays *The View from Afar* (1985). From Jakobson he learned to think deeply about the work of Saussure. A giant in the field of linguistics, **Ferdinand de Saussure** (1857–1913), had argued that language should be studied as a series of acoustic images attached in an arbitrary way to the things and concepts they denoted. Patterns of presence and absence in phonemes (units of sound) made up words, and words made sense due to the presence or absence of other words, which keyed in turn to concepts. The structure of language could be studied synchronically through an exploration of its structure, known as *langue* (language) rather than *parole* (speech, particular uses of language). The push was toward a formal analysis of contextually abstracted and organized sign systems, rather than reconstructing the evolution of languages in the Victorian manner or studying linguistic pragmatics (motivated speech in real-world situations). It is of great significance that Saussure explicitly saw language as just one aspect of a more general cultural trait in humans to create sign systems. He suggested that a new science of **semiology** be developed to study the various ways signs and their grammars were constituted by society. Despite Saussure's influence, today the term **"semiotics"** is far more commonly used than "semiology."

There is a mythologically satisfying line of thinking that argues Saussure attended the lectures of Durkheim at the Sorbonne, was exposed to Durkheim's thinking about arbitrary classifications and the binary opposition of the sacred and profane, and was inspired to develop the first articulations of structural linguistics (e.g. Alexander and Smith 2005: 9; Collins 2005: 131). The linguist Witold Doroszewski (1933) reported in the 1930s that an informant had told him Saussure had been closely following the Durkheim/Tarde debate. Doroszewski asserted that Saussure's ideas about *langue* came from Durkheim. The idea of a deep influence is attractive, but the evidence for this pleasing possibility is in the case of Doroszewski "hearsay" and otherwise mostly circumstantial. True enough, Saussure and Durkheim were both in the same place at the same time, and Durkheim's binary of the sacred and the profane does seem rather Saussurian. But none of this would get a conviction in a court of law. Moreover, Durkheim was very junior when Saussure was in Paris and was certainly not lecturing on religion.

A better-documented connection between Durkheim and Saussure is in fact via the linguist and philologist Antoine Meillet (1857–1939). A former student of Saussure, he was briefly a teacher of Mauss and a minor figure in the *Année* group. Meillet took over many of Saussure's academic responsibilities after Saussure returned to Geneva from Paris. Meillet's contributions to the *Année*, however, do not have a Saussurian flavor, and he was later to influence folkloric studies into the mnemonic practices of epic storytelling. Put another way, his contributions to the study of myth were to be about the diachronic and pragmatic and not the synchronic and grammatical dimension that Saussure had advocated.

So the impact of Durkheim on Saussure (or the converse) remains a tantalizing intellectual possibility of the kind that we wish were true. What is clear, regardless, is that there are coherent intimations of a structuralist path in Durkheim's own work on classification, totemism, and kinship (see chapters 1 and 2) as formal cultural systems, and that Lévi-Strauss saw this with great clarity. It is equally clear that Lévi-Strauss picked up ideas from structural linguistics about the possibility for a general science of signs. He pushed these ideas hard such that they demonstrate what Durkheim might have achieved had he lived longer and maintained his direction of travel after the *Elementary Forms*. In conducting such ambitious work on social signs and making it empirically plausible, it helped that Lévi-Strauss was one of the few figures in the history of anthropology to exceed Marcel Mauss when it came to encyclopedic ethnological knowledge. He combined this with Durkheim's capacity for abstract thought and mental gymnastics. Lévi-Strauss probably exceeded both Saussure and Durkheim when it came to intellectual panache. His essays are laden with declarative authority and sparkle with brilliant insights from left field. Combined with his prodigious output, this quality of mind made Lévi-Strauss the flagship intellectual of the wider structuralist movement.

Although this book is about Durkheim and his tradition, we would probably have to rank Saussure as the larger influence of the two giants for Lévi-Strauss. He was being entirely honest when said he had made his anthropological journey "in good faith" and had "claimed that domain of semiology that linguistics has not already claimed for its own" (Lévi-Strauss 1966a: 114). The status of Saussure is clear:

> What then is social anthropology? No one, it seems to me, was closer to defining it if only by omission than Ferdinand de Saussure, when, presenting linguistics as one part of a science yet to be born, he reserved for this science the name semiology and attributed to it as its object the life of signs at the heart of social life. (1966a: 114)

For Lévi-Strauss, semiology, this "life of signs," was an all-encompassing expression of the social. Far from being disembodied and abstract, in the manner of a language grammar, it could incorporate all aspects of the social world, including behaviors and material culture that expressed and communicated.

> In admitting the symbolic nature of its object social anthropology does not cut itself off from *realia*. How could it do this when art, in

148

which all is a sign, utilizes material media? One cannot study the gods without knowing their images; rites without analyzing the objects and the substances which the officiant makes or manipulates; or social rules independently of the things which correspond to them. (1966a: 115)

Second in line behind Saussure as an influence upon Lévi-Strauss was the Durkheimian tradition. After all, the master structuralist's task was to explain the social, to get at how society worked, not to explain language. Saussure had provided tools but not the research questions, or the objects of study. Lévi-Strauss's admiration for Durkheim and Mauss arrives full-blown in the magisterial lecture we have been quoting: "The Scope of Anthropology." This was given in 1960 on the occasion of taking up a Chair in Social Anthropology at the *Collège de France*. Here Lévi-Strauss (1966a) laments the fact that the centenary of Durkheim's birth had not been adequately celebrated. This was remiss, as Durkheim was one of the "chief engineers . . . of anthropology as we know it today," a person who "incarnates the essence of France's contribution to social anthropology" (1966a: 112). Lévi-Strauss goes on to praise Durkheim as "the first to introduce the requirement of specificity into the sciences of man" (1966a: 113), or in other words to understand human variation and history, the relationship of the universal to the particular (arguably praising Durkheim for all the things Luhmann, above, did not like). However, in Lévi-Strauss's view Durkheim was inconsistent, notably in the *Rules*, and often moved toward a disembodied, metaphysical, and polemical sociology. He was prone to "automatic explanation" on the basis of theoretical precepts rather than a study of facts and details (see chapter 2 for a similar comment from Evans-Pritchard). It took Mauss, Lévi-Strauss says, to "simplify and soften the doctrine of his great predecessor" (1966a: 113) and to bring home the full importance of ethnographic variation or situated action. This comment lines up precisely with the view of Louis Dumont on Mauss we quoted in chapter 2 when introducing *Primitive Classification*.

It was not only here in the public lecture that the debt was expressed. We might look also to Lévi-Strauss's (1987) hundred-page-long introduction to Mauss's (1950) first volume of collected essays, *Sociologie et anthropologie*, or to the dedication of one of his masterworks, *Structural Anthropology* to the memory of Durkheim (Lévi-Strauss 1963b). The take-home lesson is that Lévi-Strauss saw Durkheim and Mauss as trailblazers who had lacked access to the insights of linguistics and who had chained culture to social structure too closely. They had, however, taken primitive thought seriously in their works, refused to see it as inferior, and placed matters of

149

classification center stage. Both had rightly insisted on fundamental similarities between primitive and modern thinking. For Lévi-Strauss, Durkheim's thoughts on totemism, primitive classification, myth, ritual, and religion were foundational as a source of influence as he went on this journey.

All that said, the Durkheimian qualities of Lévi-Strauss's thought are rather buried in many of his core texts. Often when Durkheim appears it is only so that Lévi-Strauss can take issue with him. There is a revealing passage in *Totemism* (Lévi-Strauss 1963a). Here he suggests that Durkheim's sociologism affirmed "the primacy of the social over the intellect" (1963a: 97) a problematic stance for Lévi-Strauss insofar as the social expresses the intellect in his universe. Equally troubling for him was the issue of having conceptual resources adequate to the task of capturing cultural content: "When Durkheim claims to derive categories and abstract ideas from the social order . . . he finds at his disposal no more than sentiments, affective values, or vague ideas such as contagion and contamination" (1963a: 97). Unexpectedly but hardly accidentally Lévi-Strauss praises Durkheim's rival, the idealist and metaphysical philosopher Henri Bergson, for better intuiting the free-floating nature of classifications. These impose something discontinuous on a nature that is continuous, like "the impress of a foot which instantaneously causes thousands of grains of sand to contrive to form a pattern" (Bergson quoted in Lévi-Strauss 1963a: 98). Put another way, for Lévi-Strauss Durkheim did not fully come to terms with the fact that classification was an arbitrary operation through which culture was bootstrapped into being. Content, accuracy, and ontological thing-ness were less important than a pure binary distinction between absence and presence, like the zeros and ones of sand and footsteps – it really did not matter where the foot fell. Likewise in *The Savage Mind* (Lévi-Strauss 1966b), which first appeared in 1962, Durkheim is critiqued for seeking too hard to explain the sacred status of the Arunta *churinga* in terms of general principles, rather than just accepting that its sacred status as an object was because it had endured through time and materially connected a people to their mythical past (1966b: 238–42). The sacrality was in a sense *sui generis*, the object chosen and consecrated just the result of chance. Ever the deep diver, Lévi-Strauss (1966b: 117) also takes issue with Saussure, Durkheim, and Radcliffe-Brown for having a focus on the visible and witnessable, on the conscious, and on what is empirically present to the observer of social life. They were in a sense too positivist, too empiricist, too concerned with what could be described that was marked on the surface. From structural linguistics

Lévi-Strauss had learned that elements that were not present (the phonemes not heard, the words not spoken) could play a determinant role in systems of classification and signification. None of these other scholars, Lévi-Strauss instructs us, fully understood the depth and layering of cultural systems.

Of course, we need not take what Lévi-Strauss openly acknowledged or his comments as the end of the matter when it comes to influence. Stephan Moebius and Frithjof Nungesser (2013) show in a detailed account that although Lévi-Strauss tended to play up the influence of Jakobson and Saussure and to portray himself as a solitary outsider or "born structuralist," his early agendas in the 1930s were decisively shaped by Mauss. The questions he asked at that time remained pivotal throughout his career. Meanwhile his opposition to utilitarian explanation and his totalizing methodology with its search for deep social facts always had a strongly Durkheimian feel. The river from Durkheim to Lévi-Strauss ran deep and it ran through Mauss. As we have seen this was partly acknowledged with generous praise, partly masked by little points of critique, asides, and footnotes. In this sense the case of Lévi-Strauss demonstrates what Jeffrey Alexander (1988b) sees as a wider pattern with regard to Durkheim: under-recognition and sins of omission in works by leading figures in the cultural turn or in cultural anthropology. The causes of this may be political or personal, may reflect visions of Durkheim as a positivist, or may disclose the attractions of a robust self-image when living in the shadow of the anxiety of influence. With deep readings or close readings, with attention to vocabulary or ways of arguing, with expertise in cultural theory, it is possible to see Durkheim is everywhere, albeit with varying levels of intensity. He set agendas, moved culture to the foreground, and developed a new way of seeing society. Yet often all we find that visible are cursory quotes, carping pushback comments, and sparse index entries in the works of, for example, Geertz or Turner; unacknowledged and partial, weak but perhaps deep parallels in, say, Barthes or Foucault.

We have talked around Lévi-Strauss and explored his intellectual origins. Readers may be impatient. What did Lévi-Strauss actually contribute himself? We have not addressed this yet. Early in his career Lévi-Strauss was a specialist in kinship theory and addressed the same kind of issues about social morphology that concerned Radcliffe-Brown, and indeed Durkheim: kinship groups, kinship descent, patterns of marriage determined by kinship structures and strictures, and kinship terminology (see chapters 2 and 3). Exposure to the example of structural linguistics enabled Lévi-Strauss to shift a field that had improved incrementally since the Victorian works of Lewis Henry Morgan on the Iroquois into a phase of exponential analytic progress. Lévi-Strauss discovered there was a natural affinity between the logics or thought styles of structural linguistics and those of dense kinship theory. Both have formalist mathematical tendencies, tending to arrange things in patterns of presence and absence and to seek deeply buried "grammars" that the analyst should grasp. Lévi-Strauss's (1969b) first great masterwork from 1949, *The Elementary Structures of Kinship*, is laden with terminology borrowed from linguistics. He argued that all known kinship systems were derived via a system of permutations and exchanges from a single "atom of kinship." The pivotal idea was that there was a hidden logic of operation, and that humans had ingeniously but unconsciously figured out a variety of creative ways of designing kinship structures following these hidden codes and rules. The book is full of technical-looking diagrams marking out kinship systems with plus and minus symbols – an analytic or stylistic feature that was later adapted to Lévi-Strauss's analyses of myths and that speaks to his formal and "scientific" ambitions. These symbols might mark out a positive or negative social sentiment, the presence or absence of a particular ritual gift, a place of residence, a line of inheritance, belonging in a totemic group or marriage class, an item of kinship terminology. Lévi-Strauss masterfully worked over all these levels of analysis to assemble the codes that made up the miraculous diversity of human kinship systems and associated rules of behavior in traditional societies.

In the field of linguistics today, even in laboratories and with experiments and not just in theories, language structure and language use are often seen as a way to study thought more generally. They are a kind of mirror of the mind. As his career developed, Lévi-Strauss repeatedly endorsed this theme. Much as Durkheim and Mauss had done in *Primitive Classification*, he took collective social products to offer information on the organization of (individual and collective) mental operations. As the years went by, Lévi-Strauss wrote less about kinship and more on myth, ritual, and classification, asserting that these best illustrated the binary organization of thought and the human capacity to arrange concepts/signifiers in structured relations to each other so as to make up arbitrary but deeply meaningful cultural systems. Pivotal in his method was a consistent belief that cultures were systems built from permutations.

Even the simplest techniques of any primitive society have hidden in them the character of a system, analyzable in terms of a more general

152

system. The manner in which some elements of the system have been retained and others excluded permits of conceiving of the local system as a totality of choices. (1966a: 115)

Although Lévi-Strauss was influenced by Mauss and Durkheim, he took things further than they did when it came to the strength of collective representations and deep cultural patterns. His was not a world of functional interdependence and equivalence between the ideal and the social. Rather it was a world in which people and social structure alike danced to the tune of the cultural system's operative logics. Such are the themes that marked out such major mid-period works as the two volumes of *Structural Anthropology* (1963b, 1973), *Totemism* (1963a), *The Savage Mind* (1966b), and his detailed four-book examination of South American myth that began with *The Raw and the Cooked* (1969a). Broadly speaking, there is a contraction of academic interests as we move through these volumes and from essays of the 1950s to those of the 1980s. Whereas the first volume of *Structural Anthropology,* which appeared in 1958, considered myth alongside behavioral issues like ritual and village residential patterns, *Totemism* and *The Savage Mind* from the 1960s were mostly concerned with classification. The final major works are devoted to tracing permutations of themes through a vast number of myths in an entire Amazonian culture area – in a way, a strange return to the hermetic universe of Frazer's (1940) *The Golden Bough,* which was a brilliant last hurrah of Victorian armchair ethnology. Lévi-Strauss seemed to be giving up on trying to explain society and to content himself with explaining creative cultural systems. In a sense he became less interesting for an explanatory social science as he went down a rabbit hole of increasingly arcane personal interests.

How are we to think about Lévi-Strauss? Clearly he took one strand from the Durkheimain tradition and pushed it to its limits. This was the strand of Durkheim that was inspired by the problem of primitive thought and by the generic process of symbolic classification and collective cognition. Yet Lévi-Strauss ends up in a very different position from Mary Douglas (discussed below). Whereas she wanted to tether cultural forms and ways of thinking to social structure (and in so doing risks a kind of sociological determinism), Lévi-Strauss had more decisively made the cultural turn, but risked the matching accusation of idealism. Culture floats free and has no master other than the semiotic logics of operation and permutation to which it is beholden. It is also important to see that with Lévi-Strauss

153

many things are lost along the way, making him into an inconsistent and selective heir to Durkheim:

- There is almost no sense of the sacred, and no awareness of the motivational force of religion, or of the morally evaluative aspects of classifications. Douglas, by contrast, retains something of these vital elements found in the work of Durkheim and Mauss.
- There is little concern with ritual action as a social motor. While Lévi-Strauss mentions ritual from time to time, he is far more interested in myth and in knowledge. He tends to see ritual as an expression of myth and not as generative for myth. Yet we saw that for Durkheim times of intense collective activity, such as the French Revolution, could generate new ideas.
- Relatedly, there is no sociology of emotion or of dynamogenic effects. There is precious little sense of agency and motivation in Lévi-Strauss. He admires primitive thought, but we glimpse this through the collective and somewhat static product of culture. The impression we have is of culture and society as rather "mathematical."
- A large number of Durkheimian themes relating to morality and moral regulation, education, modernity, anomie, the professions, etc. are all missing. Lévi-Strauss took a single thread and followed it to where it led, but in the process he left entire sets of ideas on the bookshelf.

As a pivotal figure in the cultural turn, Lévi-Strauss was to transmit the Durkheimian tradition to many who were unwitting of the legacy and who were simply attracted by structuralism and semiotics. The circle was to be closed again in the American cultural sociology of recent years. Here Lévi-Strauss's sociological translation of Saussure and his arguments about the significance of binary codes and cultural grammars were to be reunited with Durkheimian thinking, and play a major role in efforts to establish forms of cultural sociology such as the Strong Program (see chapter 5). But the recent revival of neo-Durkheimian cultural sociology did not come from Lévi-Strauss alone. Within American sociology there had been occasional nods and gestures toward Durkheim from the 1950s onward. We look at these at the end of this chapter. First we need to go back to the United Kingdom.

British Anthropology and Mary Douglas

We left the British structural functionalist anthropologists in the prior chapter around the year 1950. They were institutionally powerful, and had a coherent paradigm and a talent pool. Evans-Pritchard was to produce his last masterwork some time after *Witchcraft, Oracles and Magic* and *The Nuer*. This was to be *Nuer Religion* (1956). The book shows greater cultural sensitivity than the other two texts and has an intellectually modest, humanistic feel that marks it out as distinct from his pre-war output, not to mention the muscular essays of Radcliffe-Brown, who had died the year before its publication. *Nuer Religion* has a slightly theological mood and displays Nuer beliefs as a deeply meaningful, somewhat poetic system rather than as a source of morality contributing to social stability. It has been argued that the text is influenced by Evans-Pritchard's own conversion to Catholicism and a closer reading of the *Elementary Forms*. It might also reflect years of everyday exposure to Oxford's Tractarian ("High Church") version of Anglicanism.

The rise of structuralism led to *Nuer Religion* soon becoming something of a false trail with its humanistic and theory-light approach. It seemed to be trying to understand a set of beliefs somewhat in its own terms, rather than deploying the structural functionalist tool kit in re-descriptions, or engaging in Lévi-Straussian translations into semiotics. Consider Evans-Pritchard on sacrifice:

> It is only in a mystical, and not in a material, sense that Nuer sacrifice might be called a communion, in the sense that through sacrifice man communicates with God, who is invoked in the present (*in-vocare*) to receive the life of the consecrated victim and to hear what it is that those who make the sacrifice desire of him. (1956: 275)

For Evans-Pritchard, Nuer religion provides self-standing justifications for action and belief. These look somewhat like those of the Christian faith although they are not identical with Christianity. So it is really not much of a surprise when later in the book Evans-Pritchard pushes back against the assertion that God was a symbol for society: "This postulate of sociologistic metaphysic seems to me to be an assertion for which evidence is totally lacking. It was Durkheim and not the savage who made society into a god" (1956: 313). It would seem that Evans-Pritchard has made a decisive cultural turn that was not present in his earlier books with their morphological concerns. Yet he was not armed with the theory that would allow him

155

to establish a legacy for this study. Rejecting Durkheim's "sociologistic" approach in such a high-handed way arguably did not help. The world would have to wait a decade or so for Clifford Geertz to make the case more concisely and powerfully that things make sense in their own terms, and that the interpretation of a meaningful world can be a valid anthropological explanation of that world.

For all its "dead-end" qualities, *Nuer Religion* continued – like *Witchcraft, Oracles and Magic* – to play a role in debates over faith, belief, and rationality as a paradigm exemplar. Most notably, scholars just could not stop scrutinizing the claim that in a Nuer ritual substitution a cucumber really *was* an ox and not merely *representing or standing in place of* an ox during a sacrifice (see Wilson 1979). The pertinent phrase:

> When a cucumber is used as a sacrificial victim Nuer speak of it as an ox. In doing so they are asserting something rather more than that it takes the place of an ox ... The resemblance is conceptual, not perceptual. The "is" rests on qualitative analogy. And the expression is asymmetrical, a cucumber is an ox, but an ox is not a cucumber. (1956: 128)

It does not require much familiarity with linguistic philosophy or ontological theory to see this as a paradigm case that scholars could get their teeth into as a shared object for deep analytic thought. Resulting discussions veered from considerations of transubstantiation, to entity identity theory, to semiotics, to communicative pragmatics. From our point of view what is interesting is that Evans-Pritchard is more concerned to get the deep meanings and semantics of sacrifice right than to isolate social functions or move into the world of philosophical rationality theory. There was a change in thought style taking place, but it was too late in his career to have impact. Evans-Pritchard was to retain intellectual authority at Oxford well into the 1960s and even 1970s. However, with the publication of *Nuer Religion* his most important work was now behind him. Although he was still productive the man known as "EP" gradually slipped into the role of doyen, facilitator (notably of tremendously important translations from the *Année* scholars – a very significant unsung achievement – and by supervising the doctoral work of Steven Lukes on Durkheim), and pub storyteller of the anthropological community's collective memory (Fardon 1999). Other figures like Edmund Leach and Mary Douglas took over as leaders of British anthropology, generating the most creative ideas as EP took a back seat.

As the generation of Evans-Pritchard, Firth, Fortes, and Lienhardt retired, slowed down, or became mired in administrative duties, their neo-Durkheimian structural functionalism began to be replaced by three developments. One approach focused on individual action. Influenced by exchange theory, this worked with visions of the person as a goal-oriented maximizer and emphasized how individuals and groups transacted with each other in order to get what they wanted. This perspective was especially important for studies of nomads, traders, and political entrepreneurs and for situations where the community did not seem particularly bounded and isolated (e.g. Barth 1954). A second movement was to give more attention to social conflict or to social instability. Edmund Leach, for example, wrote of oscillations in the political organization of highland Burma, while Max Gluckman's "Manchester School" developed a "conflict" approach to tribal life in South Africa that retained elements of structural functionalism as it discussed what it called "rituals of rebellion" (Gluckman 1954; Leach 1954). The third outcome was to turn to structuralism, most notably but not exclusively that of Lévi-Strauss. This path was to appeal to a greater or lesser extent to Rodney Needham and to Leach. Needham translated Lévi-Strauss (and some *Année* Durkheimians), but later fell out with him in a dispute that reached deep into the complexities of kinship theory. Leach changed his theoretical hat many times during his career but by 1970 was enthusiastically decoding the Bible and revealing a wealth of Lévi-Straussian binary oppositions behind the story of Adam and Eve, or expositing on the semiotics of traffic lights (Leach 1970; 1983).

Although some devotees were more committed than others, for much of British cultural anthropology in the 1960s and 1970s structuralism proved to be a pick-and-mix option. It did not require a wholesale epistemological conversion or a deep capacity for abstraction for Lévi-Strauss to be useful from time to time. Rather, structuralism could be drawn upon to make sense of certain items of anthropological data where binary codes seemed to be at work. In this sense a pattern emerged that would later be replicated in American cultural sociology. An example is the volume *Right and Left: Essays on Dual Symbolic Classification*, edited by Rodney Needham (1973). Dedicated to the memory of Robert Hertz, this contained no fewer than eighteen essays from eighteen contributors, most from the 1960s and 1970s but some from before this time, looking at the symbolism of right and left in various cultures (mostly African) and how these were linked to wider binary classification systems. Some of the chapters feature technical diagrams and lists of binaries, but many don't. Structuralism had become a niche tool embedded in a wider tradition of ethnological expertise, not a vision of society as a whole. Needham's own editorial introduction equivocated on the issue of universality and ruminated on problems of methodology. We get much of the mood when we read Needham himself admitting that "the ordering of ethnographic evidence by logical criteria does not prove that these are intrinsic to collective representations. In these regards the comparative study of dual symbolic classification, as expressed especially through the values of lateral symbolics, constitutes a paradigm of the difficulties that must beset any attempt to arrive empirically at a theory of thought and action" (1973: xxxiv–xxxv). Prudence, pragmatism, and modesty were the order of the day.

So the Durkheimian structural functionalist paradigm in anthropology was withering away and by the 1960s there were a number of options on the table. Perhaps it is a good thing that there was now a marketplace of ideas. But for the structural functionalists, worse was to follow. In a turn remarkably reminiscent of Paul Nizan's *Chiens de garde* (see chapter 3), by the 1970s New Left scholars had emerged arguing that structural functionalism was in fact a conservative ideology with evil consequences. While all anthropology was the "handmaiden of colonialism" (a common sound bite of the era), structural functionalism was *primus entre pares* in obscuring power and domination both within traditional societies and in the colonial process, and in gazing down from a position of privilege. By about 1975 even those older scholars who were not attracted to critical theory agreed that the study of bounded "tribes" and the conventional ethnographic monograph, with its imagery of functionally baked-in stability, had had its day. An approach that had seen tribes or societies as closed systems was replaced with one looking at flows, movement, trade, and communication as well as at interactions between traditional societies and modernity (followed soon after by a systematic dismantling of the distinction – everybody was modern, just in different ways). With the emergence of a highly reflexive poststructuralism in the mid-1980s, any breezy confidence in scholarly authority, positivism, social facts, and empirical research findings was gone.

This does not mean the Durkheimian tradition was dead in British anthropology. It was kept alive in a very interesting way and almost single handed by the brilliant **Mary Douglas** (1921–2007). In many ways she was a direct descendant of the British structural functionalist anthropological tradition. A student of Evans-Pritchard and Srinivas, Douglas had been present in Oxford during its heyday from the 1940s into the 1950s and had taken on board its core knowledge base concerning kinship, marriage, religion, the primitive economy, social organization, and the functional relations between them. Her PhD fieldwork was on the Lele people of the Belgian Congo. Although the resulting book (Douglas 1963) was only a modest success when it came to visibility, it met the high professional standards of its day. There was a broadly structural functionalist account of intersecting institutions, beliefs, and practices that was perhaps a little dated even for its time but nevertheless nicely done. Importantly, the ethnographic material from her fieldwork was not only to inform the ethnographic monograph but also to furnish a wealth of more or less bite-sized examples for the rest of her career, especially those concerning beliefs in witchcraft, magic, and pollution that seemed to loom large in Lele culture.

As her career went on, Mary Douglas developed a rare capacity for making the familiar strange through exemplar comparison and juxtaposition. Durkheim generally held to an evolutionary view of society. In his understanding we had moved slowly from mechanical to organic solidarity over time. Albeit at the cost of some anomie, now there was more universalism, value generalization, and scientific reason than in prior stages of social life. And this was a good thing. A hallmark of Douglas's thinking, however, was the argument that in every society we could find the full variety of socio-cultural types. Entrepreneurs in New Guinea were like market traders in London. Environmentalist groups in California were like certain villages in Africa. Pollution fears and ritualistic cultural activities were everywhere in all societies. For this reason Douglas tends to focus on local social contexts, networks, and groups as the relevant environment for determining cultural bias and worldview, not big-picture motifs such as the transition to modernity or the scientific revolution.

Yet if Douglas was skeptical about our own society being fundamentally different from those typically studied by anthropologists, she was far from making a critique of the modernist knowledge project. In combination Douglas's key works mark out an attempt at systematic, cumulative, and expansive theory where the anthropologist "knows best," at just the time when anthropology as a discipline was heading in postmodern directions. Scholars influenced by Lyotard or the "writing culture" movement of Clifford and Marcus (1986) made modest claims for research findings, had high levels of reflexivity, were opposed to totality, and denied the possibility of perspective-free truth. In this sense, from the late 1970s onward Douglas was a holdout of the epistemological mindset of Oxford anthropology of the 1940s. But even as she asserted her authority, her work was not completely bloodless and bookish. There was a sense of play, eclecticism, and provocation that indicated something of the sprit of the age. One dimension of this was that, like Roland Barthes, Eric Hobsbawm, or Terry Eagleton, she wrote popular articles and reviews designed to provoke or amuse, josh or joust. These public interest items were published in highbrow newspapers and magazines. In many cases they were to have lasting significance because they contributed to the evolution of ideas that were later worked up in monographs.

A lively reception awaited *Purity and Danger* (Douglas 1966), which was a far less buttoned-down product than her Lele study. It is often listed when attempts are made to identify the most influential books in anthropology or in cultural theory. One gets the sense upon reading it of a person finally set free from the challenge of completing first the PhD and then publishing the "thesis book" as a ticket to the profession. *Purity and Danger* was an eclectic work that drew upon the Durkheimian tradition regarding classification, but pushed it in new directions. It was the start of a remarkable twenty-year period of intellectual productivity and creativity that reached well beyond anthropology to touch sociology, economics, material culture studies, political science, and science studies.

Purity and Danger has many dimensions and often has a quirky and essayistic tone. Nevertheless, reception dynamics have been less scattered and more focused. The argument that has become by far the most cited over time, the one that features in nearly every introductory course in cultural anthropology, concerns the ways that classification systems generate anomalies. All societies have a belief in the need for order, Douglas says. Dirt and symbolic **pollution** are also something that every society has to control. Ironically the root of the problem lies in systems of classification that societies set up to understand the world and bring order. Things that "don't fit in," that are in the wrong place, and that confound or challenge those attempts at systematization are problematic or dangerous, dirty, defiling, and polluting. Much of this is captured in the three famous quotes that follow:

In short, our pollution behavior is the reaction which condemns any object or idea likely to confuse or contradict cherished classifications. (1966: 45)

To conclude, if uncleanliness is matter out of place, we must approach it through order. Uncleanliness or dirt is that which must not be included if a pattern is to be maintained. (1966: 50)

160

Defilement is never an isolated event. It cannot occur except in view of a systematic ordering of ideas. (1966: 51)

Such polluted and dangerous things need to be dealt with through special prohibitions or spatial arrangements, although in some circumstances they may contain magical properties that can be used in beneficial ways. Douglas famously gives her much-cited example of the dietary rules in Leviticus. These set out things that the Ancient Hebrews could and could not eat. Creatures that were defiled and prohibited tended to be outlying singletons, or had some but not all the features of a major classificatory category. In Lele culture, by contrast, the pangolin was not anathema. As a scaly mammal that climbed trees it was odd. It looked a bit like a lizard. But in this case it had therapeutic and spiritual potentials and was at the center of a cult that answered deep existential needs (unfortunately these special qualities are also recognized in traditional Chinese medicine, and the pangolin is now endangered as a result).

Quite a few further words are needed about this text. One is that its reception was influenced by the rise of structuralism as a dominant paradigm in the 1960s, with associated visions of culture unchained. The book arrived just about at high water of that particular tide. The timing was spot on. Here was a book showing that arbitrary classifications made a real difference to belief and ritual, that meaning somehow trumped the social, and that puzzling things could be explained using the tool kit of cultural theory. In a sense, though, the book was atypical of Douglas's output over the next few years. Her wider scholarship generally tried to show how social structure and collective belief lined up into coherent patterns with neither determinant.

It is generally noted that the model of pollution in *Purity and Danger* is within the Durkheimian tradition. Let's reflect on this. Although Durkheim is cited, he is not in fact given as much dedicated attention as William Robertson Smith. Arguably Douglas is not as truly "Durkheimian" here as we might imagine. Some confusions remain that have never been properly explored and organized by scholarship. In the *Elementary Forms* Durkheim emphasizes that the profane needs to be kept away from the sacred by taboos, prohibitions, and spatial divisions. By the profane he means the mundane or everyday or humdrum. Douglas, however, draws attention to something else. In her writings the sources of pollution are themselves highly charged. They are magical, disgusting, contaminated, or contagious. They seem to have special powers and to be themselves outside of the ordinary. In fact they are a bit like the "left sacred," but, then again, sometimes they just have an "ick factor." There does not always (if at all) seem to be the sense of supercharged, transcendent wrath and vengeance that Durkheim spoke about when dealing with the left sacred.

This question of whether what Douglas identifies is or is not the same as Durkheim's left sacred and/or his profane is not the end of the confusion. That which is polluted can be (i) matter out of place (dirt in a kitchen, not a farmer's field – we know what the thing is but don't like its social or spatial location); or (ii) a thing that does not fit a single classification but that seems solid and bounded enough and has determinate properties we can identify and name (the pangolin); or (iii) that which resists and defies classification, that is vague or unbounded (goo, slime, blood). These all have logics that are slightly out of alignment with each other. Yet most citations to the book are rote or formulaic and do not notice there might be (at least) three *different* things going on. Further, Douglas shows – again somewhat *en passant* and without real analytic effort – that there is a range of emotional responses possible to the classification problem, such as awe, enchantment, disgust, humor, and unease. Of these, disgust has been given by far the most attention. It is never fully explained why we have some responses and not others in particular cases. Douglas seems implicitly aware of a lingering set of problems requiring disambiguation and analytic effort at differentiation, but rather blithely she leaves it for another day. She boils the residuals down to the far simpler theme of anomaly versus ambiguity, which is then pushed aside.

> I apologise for using anomaly and ambiguity as if they were synonymous. Strictly they are not: an anomaly is an element which does not fit a given set or series; ambiguity is a characteristic of statements capable of two interpretations. But reflection on examples shows that there is very little advantage in distinguishing between these two terms in their practical application. (1966: 47)

This claim that there is "little advantage" in further efforts at understanding may well be mistaken. Provisional, stylized, and essayistic, her work has, in fact, contributed both an amplification of the Durkheimian paradigm by bringing in the concept of symbolic pollution and connecting this to classification (widely noticed), and a (less noticed but potentially productive if examined further) set of confusions and elisions about the relationships between the sacred, profane, polluted, evil and sacred evil, and mundane that still to this day need a lot of sorting out (for attempts see Kurakin 2015; Smith 2014a). Many of these confusions rest upon ordinary language usages in the Franglais of academic life, but some seem to have substantive or ontological origins relating to the nature of things and the nature of classification violations. Regardless of the complexities that can emerge at high levels of analytic resolution, it is of the greatest significance that ideas about negative valuation, pollution, magic, and mystery were connected once more to classifications in her work. These were of no central interest to Lévi-Strauss, with his mathematical visions of logical operations in the collective human mind. Yet such themes were centrally present in the thought of Durkheim and his group. When dialed back a little these issues were to be of real significance in making structuralism a tractable resource for later cultural sociology (arguably anthropology was less in need of a fix). They allowed distinction, boundaries and hierarchies, ritual exclusions, and positive and negative valuations to come into the analytic frame.

In what follows, space constraints dictate that we can only briefly trace Douglas's remarkable sequence of influential books. These essentially flesh out a Durkheimian sociology of knowledge showing how social structure determines culture and thought and then behavior. The books are in a way the heirs to *Primitive Classification*, and also to the *Division of Labor* with its morphological moral determinism. *Natural Symbols: Explorations in Cosmology* (Douglas 1970) was written somewhat quickly. It is something of a messy, dense cornucopia of brilliant ideas that arguably has too many moving parts and travels too fast for most readers. For all that, it is perhaps even more deeply intellectual in feel than *Purity and Danger* and may well be her most important or revolutionary book. Douglas herself realized it needed tidying up and published a revised or rewritten edition only three years after initial publication. It is in *Natural Symbols* that Douglas, drawing initially on Basil Bernstein's vision of restricted and elaborated linguistic codes, begins to develop the influential **grid/ group model** that would later sometimes become known as "Cultural Theory" (an imperialistic term coined by certain devotees that has long annoyed everybody doing other kinds of cultural theory). In the process she also mounts a normative defense of ritual, which she sees as unfairly maligned: "Ritual has become a bad word signifying empty conformity," she writes (1970: 1). With reference not only to Africa but also – famously – to the "Bog Irish" (unquestioning rural Catholic peasants who did not understand the Latin Mass but nevertheless got a lot of meaning out of going to church), she suggests that there was nothing necessarily inferior about tradition or about a less thought-through, less reflexive, and less symbolically coherent approach to religious life. Their so-called "empty ritual" (1970: 3) was just as valid as a more studied, abstract, and intellectual approach to faith. This argument is generally agreed to reflect her own attitudes to Catholicism and opposition to the Vatican-led reforms of the 1960s. Such personal religious convictions sit inside a wider worldview. Douglas was in many ways a conservative and traditionalist who thought that much comfort and enjoyment could be found in everyday conventions and customs, such as housework, gardening, or shopping for groceries.

From the point of view of cultural theory the most interesting element of *Natural Symbols* concerns the grid/group model, which it introduced. She claims that each society or social organization within it has two dimensions. "Group" refers to how well it has a clear and strong boundary around itself, or at least thinks it has. "Grid" has proven to be more problematic to define over the years. Something of a movable feast, it is variously seen as rules, internal hierarchies, distinctions, regulation, perhaps networks or restraints. Together, grid and group generate a social space that can be mapped onto a two-by-two table or a graph with two axes. This can then be filled with cultural attributes that are said to correlate with each social form. The core argument is essentially a magnificent elaboration of *Primitive Classification* and its assertion that social structure determines classifications and thought. *Natural Symbols* also follows the classic Durkheimian move of using scattered ethnological examples to anchor core claims, although notably Douglas draws examples from modernity as well as from the anthropological corpus.

What is truly innovative is the way that the grid/group model goes beyond the anthropological study of classification as we might usually think of it. The old warhorses are things like totemism, myth, ethno-taxonomy, kinship nomenclature, and so forth. The work of Douglas and her followers is far more expansive and ambitious. It considers how social structure might be systematically related to cosmology, risk and blame perceptions, attitudes to social problems, visions of how to fix what is wrong with society, voting behavior, political moves, responses to anomalous scientific and mathematical findings . . . the list goes on. It is a methodological tool for comparative cultural analysis that, for Douglas at least, would allow anthropology to have more productive efforts toward general theory. She writes:

164

One way to solve the comparative problem is to limit the predictions of a hypothesis to any given social environment . . . The hypothesis which I will propose about concordance between symbolic and social experience will always have to be tested within a given social environment . . . The more limited the cultural ranges within which the comparison is made, the more significant the results. (1970: 64)

The upshot of grid/group was a method that might allow for appropriate comparisons and contrasts to be made within and between cultures with some sense of the methodological ground rules.

Returning to *Natural Symbols*, here Douglas elaborates the grid/group argument with reference to sin, ideas about evil, luck, and other cosmological beliefs. Yet the argument that is most developed with regard to the grid/group model is that embodied experience and body symbolism are shaped by social structure. Douglas writes:

The social body constrains the way the physical body is perceived. The physical experience of the body, always modified by the social categories through which it is known, sustains a particular view of society . . . As a result of this interaction the body itself is a highly restricted medium of expression. The forms it adopts in movement and repose express social pressures in manifold ways. (1970: 65)

When translated into her model, the body is seen as/experienced as bounded and internally differentiated in a high-grid, high-group setting (think about modern western biomedicine in a modern hospital setting); as bounded but vulnerable to witchcraft and moral contagion in high-group/low-grid settings (the egalitarian African village); and as not apparently significant for symbolic activity in societies with high grid but low group (an image here, not one given by Douglas, might be uniformed droids in some futuristic warehouse – she always struggled with examples for this cell).

The ideas from *Natural Symbols* were further elaborated a few years later in *Cultural Bias* (1978). The title tells us what grid/group social structure explains in this book. It sets understandings about what is normal, what fits, and what is right. She later wrote of group thoughts running in grooves. In *Natural Symbols* and in *Purity and Danger* Douglas had made frequent reference to examples from the modernity. In the 1970s we find this concern with explaining developed economies and societies intensifying, and with it her claims on the attention of the disciplines of economics, politics, and sociology. In a sense Douglas was becoming a breakout scholar, one of the few anthropologists – like Bronisław Malinowski (see chapter 3), Margaret Mead, and Claude Lévi-Strauss – to have wider

165

intellectual visibility and influence. A decisive signal was sent at the end of the 1970s in her collaboration with Baron Isherwood: *The World of Goods*. Here Douglas and her co-author (Douglas and Isherwood 1979) push back against economics, with its models of profit-maximizing individuals armed with pencils and utility curves. The book not only analyzes but actively defends the ritualistic and "irrational" elements of consumption – those that are not immediately practical, economical, or efficient but that are communicative, expressive, and solidaristic.

The book shows how consumer goods and household activities are resources with which people construct a social world and self-identity and – in the spirit of *The Gift* – build connections to others. And so it is that as a subtext the book makes a general defense of welfare and sharing as aspects of a good society. An agenda-setting work, *The World of Goods* is seen as a pivotal precursor of what would become the anthropology and sociology of consumption. This field, associated with figures like anthropologist Daniel Miller and sociologists such as Ian Woodward or Alan Warde, really got moving more than a decade later. It went on to explore the meanings of shopping, home decoration, everyday domestic objects, and rituals in ordinary households, often using ethnographic and interview methods. More recently, Douglas's text has also impacted on studies of material culture and iconic consciousness due to its early demonstration that objects are invested with social meanings (Woodward 2007). Perhaps the most remarkable or ambitious text to emerge in this tradition is Daniel Miller's *A Theory of Shopping* (1999). This cites Douglas and Isherwood only once. However, much of their spirit is there in an anthropological inquiry into an everyday activity in a north London high street. Miller argues that shopping has ritual elements shaped by love, care, devotion, and sacrifice. He draws on Bataille to suggest that shopping is a non-utilitarian activity surrounded by feelings of transgression and visions of excess, by dreams of perfecting self and others, by meaningful but not necessarily rational expenditures. Consumption is a deeply social act.

The uncanny ability of Mary Douglas to be ahead of the curve was also manifest in the next book, *Risk and Culture* (1982), which appeared around ten years before Ulrich Beck's (1992) equally influential, zeitgeist-grabbing *Risk Society*. Douglas's text was co-authored with US political scientist Aaron Wildavsky. Here the argument was made that grid/group logics determined (mostly cosmological) attitudes to environmental risks, dangers, and pollutions. Essentially, environmentalist opposition in the United States was due to "sect" organization in small, non-hierarchical groups such as anti-nuclear cells or Friends of the Earth. Like egalitarian villages with witchcraft cosmologies in Africa these groups see (the authors claimed "exaggerated") dangers everywhere. They also have low levels of trust in governments and experts. The historical narrative in *Risk and Culture* is of these groups and their worldview, which originated in 1960s Californian counterculture, gaining increasing power over time, especially as the United States emerged from the 1960s.

The book has raised more than a few hackles by starting from the belief that attitudes to risks such as nuclear power are overblown in the general population. Wildavsky was probably more responsible for this spin than Douglas, who would likely have taken a more anthropologically neutral stance if left to her own devices. In t/his view ordinary people are stubborn and refuse to believe the experts they really should trust. People were also allegedly foolish at times in refusing to rely on markets to find workable solutions to reduce risk and pollution. Regardless of who is right or wrong about objective risk levels and how to manage them, more troubling analytically is that much of the argument does not really conform to the grid/ group logic. Various contingent and historical factors (mail marketing, tax subsidies for non-profits, the expansion of higher education) are brought into play to account for the triumph of environmentalist thought in leafy suburbs, where people employed in modern corporations and state enterprises on good salaries could hardly be seen as living anti-technology sectarian group lifestyles in a radical hippy counterculture. In other words, risk perceptions seem to be uncoupled from group structure, and a cultural sociological approach looking to discourse might do better (Alexander and Smith 1996). Nonetheless this is a text that has done much to show that risk and danger are seen through cultural lenses. Less noticed but perhaps equally relevant methodologically is an argument, transposed from classic structural functionalist studies, on the patterns of witchcraft accusation in African villages. We might profitably analyze how actors allocate blame and where they look for solutions. Pointing the finger and suggesting a remedy are profoundly social acts, and by looking at these closely we can diagnose all kinds of social tensions.

The final book we will consider is entitled *How Institutions Think* (Douglas 1985). This brought Douglas's typological analysis of thought styles and worldviews down to the organizational level. It offered a clear signal indicating her interest in a local sociology of knowledge in contrast to a more expansive and cosmological, tribe-wide anthropological vision. Drawing in this case particularly on the sociology and history of science (for example on figures like Ian Hacking and Ludwig Fleck), she insists that thought is social and that knowledge is generated by collectivities, not by individuals. This is not exactly news for any sociological audience, of course, but the book has been impactful in management science. It helps that the title is extremely catchy and the content leads the reader to reflect closely on how members of organizations have a shared way of getting the job done, dealing with problems, or being creative. Institutional settings provide the basis for "thought worlds," each with its own classifications, sense of membership, and values. Douglas gives attention to the feedback loops between the organizational form, the everyday interaction order of daily experiences, and the thought style of the institution's members. These circulate, attending to issues of morality and motivation, helping in turn to overcome free-rider problems and offer a sense of justice.

The grid/group "Cultural Theory" model at its best is elegant and persuasive. It is perhaps the best model we have offering a systematic rather than *ad hoc* explanation of how social structure and culture/thought/belief/worldview might be related. Advocates Perri 6 and Paul Richards write: "Douglas's intellectual legacy matters because it represents the most ambitious attempt made in recent decades to demonstrate the explanatory potential of the Durkheimian pro-gramme" (2017: 211). They reiterate two pages later that it "offers the social sciences a rigorous body of theory of astonishing range, profundity, distinctiveness and philosophical merit to overcome the problems that bedevil the major frameworks dominating the social science debate" (2017: 213). If they are correct then clearly this is a remarkable achievement. This book is not the place for extended, detailed critique, but we should note that there are some rough edges and persistent problems (for a more systematic review of issues by sympathetic advocates see 6 and Richards 2017: 84–92; Fardon 1999). Here are some issues to consider:

- The model believes that thinking emerges from social organiza-tion. This is a legacy of middle-period Durkheimian thinking of a *Division of Labor* kind that is sometimes not noticed as Douglas uses post-cultural-turn vocabularies. There are problems when-ever a person has "the wrong" kind of thinking as predicted by their structural location. A vision of culture as decoupled from social groups and as involving circulating narratives, symbols, etc. is better able to deal with questions of social dispersal (for the issue of environmental risks as an example see Alexander and

Smith 1996). It is perhaps not surprising that some followers influenced by psychology have adapted the theory such that it captures worldviews and thought styles, but do not try too hard – if at all – to correlate these to social location or real groups. Dan Kahan in his influential "cultural cognition theory," for example, modifies Douglas such that individualism/solidarism and egalitarianism/hierarchy form the two-by-two table and these reflect worldviews revealed by attitudinal clusters in survey responses (Kahan, Jenkins-Smith, and Braman 2011). The worldviews in turn shape outcomes like attitudes to scientific expertise on climate change. The result is an "ideational and methodologically individualist theory" (6 and Richards 2017: 91). It manages to dodge the question of poor fit but at the price of doing away with "groupiness" as an explanatory factor.

- Close readers will encounter multiple ambiguities and shifts in the oeuvre concerning levels of analysis and causality and explanatory power. Does grid/group determine *subjective* experiences in the mind, or rather shape classification systems or knowledge that is *external* to the individual? Does social structure *cause or determine* cultural beliefs, or are they mutually reinforcing and symbiotic in so far as they *shape* one another? (See Fardon 1999.) Is the model the *only game in town*, or should it be used in combination with *other* explanatory resources that provide for a more complex, scumbled, and softened vision of social morphology? The strong form of the model – the one taking the first clause of each of the sentences above – is very explanatory, powerful, and parsimonious but risks poor fit and simplistic, deterministic overreach in the manner of the external and constraining Durkheimian social fact. The alternative idea set, drawing on the second clauses, might be too feeble and apologetic to offer a compelling narrative: for example, grid/group location explains much about X but does not really tell us how people themselves actually think, and it has impacts in conjunction with rational choices, exposure to the media, diffuse overlapping networks, and wider shifts in civil society.
- People belong to more than one group. They move about during their daily lives and during the life course. Do they think differently when at their high-tech job in a major corporation during the week than when at their orthodox Jewish synagogue on the Sabbath? Which level of analysis is more important and why and when? If people can "code switch" their thought styles according to their settings, how do they manage this? If they do code switch,

169

where does this leave underlying personality systems or the deep dispositions people carry around between settings? Some folks are just superstitious.

- Examples that go into cells can be nitpicked to death after looking at the specialist sociological literature on particular topics. This generally documents complexity, layering, and hybridity in groups, institutions, or elements of the social system. For example, "markets" are often given as an example of a low-grid, low-group social form. However, just reading the business pages of the newspaper tells us that markets are subject to legal oversight and are regulated. So are they high-grid too? Moreover, business associations promote market activity but are a locus of group solidarity replete with Durkheimian rituals (Spillman 2012). So now they are high-group too? This vulnerability to empirical challenge by experts is a generic problem with typologies proposed by theorists and also applies, for example, to Durkheim's examples for his forms of suicide (see chapter 1).

- The high-grid/low-group cell is a longstanding problem (Fardon 1999). Examples when shoehorned into this cell seem unsatisfying or hard to find (Kahan et al. 2011). The confusion is not helped by the idea of the "isolate" or hermit with which the cell sometimes overlaps and sometimes doesn't. It is interesting to note that this problem of a "dud cell" reflects those experienced by Durkheim's typology of suicide where fatalism (high regulation, low integration) also has a residual and uncomfortable status (see chapter 1; Besnard 1993; 2005).

- The "grid" dimension often does not seem to do much of the lifting, with group boundaries explaining most cultural shifts (Fardon 1999). Perhaps for this reason, "grid" has shifted around over time, variously referring to levels of hierarchy, networks, regulation, restraint, rules, and laws. The grid/group model itself has gone through various iterations as if to solve this and other issues (Spickard 1989). The problem here is somewhat reminiscent of that in Durkheim's *Suicide* where it seems all too easy to collapse the distinction between anomic and egoistic suicide, as empirically they tend to run together.

- As an anthropological relativist Douglas pushes back against ideas of cultural evolution or visions of societies moving toward modernity. Nevertheless, if we believe in unidirectional change, much of what is going on could be captured with some slight modifications to the conventional *Gemeinschaft/Gesellschaft* models of socio-cultural transition, with Parsons's pattern variables, or

170

with accounts of Weberian bureaucratization, marketization, and disenchantment.

Notwithstanding all these problems, the grid/group model remains very appealing in its ambition, generality, and flexibility. It remains an under-explored resource in cultural sociology, anthropology, and social theory today. While there may be reluctance to buy into the entire grid/group package, it should be remembered that Douglas's books are full of brilliant insights. There is no law saying that these cannot be taken up piecemeal as needed.

The United States: Empirical Studies in the Structural Functionalist Idiom

We looked at Parsons and functionalism at the start of this chapter in the context of systems theory. But there was more to the paradigm than just abstract, somewhat philosophical attempts to build the scaffolding with which to make sense of society. The structural functionalist movement in the United States also produced monographs and papers deploying its tool kit to explain modern institutions, contemporary society, and historical events in empirical detail. Such work often seemed more flexible, realistic, and persuasive, more connected to the "real world," than formal systems theory itself. Indeed the attractiveness and vitality of the scholarship often varied inversely with the proportion of systems theory in the account.

Take as an example **Neil Smelser**'s (1930–2017) study (1959) on social change during the industrial revolution in Lancashire, England. This employed the AGIL model complete with its signature box diagrams to look at shifts in technology, work, and industry on the one hand, and family life on the other. It is perhaps the single most important effort to demonstrate the utility of AGIL for macro-historical sociology, and probably for this reason the book is admired but never loved. Attention is given to the differentiation of functions, the tensions and problems these generated, and the solutions that were found during a turbulent historical epoch. The general picture is of a sequence of social responses that manage change:

> disturbances are brought into line by mechanisms of social control and their energy turned to the generation of more specific solutions for the original problems giving rise to the dissatisfactions. The social units which emerge, if the sequence is successful, constitute a structure more differentiated than the old. Finally after a period of extraordinary

171

progress, the new units are consolidated into the social system and thereby routinized. (1959: 402)

The book is detailed and scholarly, yet as the quote makes clear it underplays the hand of concrete class conflict in favor of a vision of the "system" facing trouble and in need of an adaptive upgrade. It is not clear whether the AGIL model is a help or a hindrance in the task of analysis, insofar as it generates a laborious architecture into which events and actors are shoehorned with necessarily minimal grace. The general vision in studies such as Smelser's *Social Change in the Industrial Revolution* was of culture holding things together (keywords: stability, balance, functional interdependence, tension management), but only up to a point. Eventually the "strain" of social change would be too much and there would be conflict and innovation.

Such analyses generated a much later polemic from Charles Tilly (1981). For Tilly, who was a noted historical sociologist interested in power, domination, class, and the state, these functionalist explanations of historical events – and indeed Durkheimian/Parsonian sociology more widely – were tautological or full of platitudes and truisms. What was needed was an account more attentive to power, one that identified concrete agents and mechanisms as well as speaking about abstract system dynamics as "causes," and that saw domination, not integration, as the most significant attribute of any social system. An indication of changing times came when there was an eventual pushback to Tilly from Mustafa Emirbayer (1996) some fifteen years later. This indicated that Durkheim had much to offer comparative and historical sociology when taken seriously and read more productively.

Far more musical toward culture than Smelser was **Kai Erikson**. He also had the unfair advantage of being a gifted writer. Erikson begins his pivotal book *Wayward Puritans* (1966) with direct reference to Durkheim. He reminds us that in *The Division of Labor* Durkheim had theorized that punishment was all about repairing a wound to the collective conscience. It was more about the community than the criminal. Durkheim had also reflected that crime might be functional insofar as it enabled values to be reaffirmed through outrage and punishment. This had led him to the suggestion in *The Rules of Sociological Method* that every society or social organization would have some kind of deviance. The bar was movable such that even a "society of saints" would have deviance by virtue of elevating minor transgressions. This would allow it to punish offenders and so affirm morality (we covered all this in chapter 1). These ideas were brilliantly adapted and pushed forward by Erikson. He pointed out that the kinds of deviance that people are upset about tell us a good deal about their values. He further suggests that "the amount of deviation a community encounters is apt to remain fairly constant over time" (1966: 23) but also that more deviance tends to be identified in times when community boundaries need to be rebuilt or better defined. This is the process known as **boundary maintenance**.

Erikson's historical inquiry looked at the Massachusetts Bay colony, which had been set up on a religious model by pioneer settlers from England back in the seventeenth century. Erikson identified three "'crime waves' which took place in the early years of the Bay colony . . . and helped settlers define the boundaries of their emerging society" (1966: 29). Confirming Durkheim's "society of saints" hypothesis, two of the "crime waves" involved religious persecution arising from hyper-sensitivity to small differences in doctrine or behavior – say, having long hair or holding a Bible study group where individuals could express their own interpretations of scripture. The other "crime wave" led to the witchcraft accusations by hysterical teenage girls being taken seriously in Salem. Individuals were prosecuted on the basis of circumstantial and spectral evidence, then tortured and killed.

Of course, Erikson says, the theological and sacred/profane/supernatural nature of the "crimes" reflected the religious self-image of the wider community. A different kind of society would have defined its boundaries with reference to a different kind of deviance. Erikson also argued that specific political and existential crises sat behind each of these identifications of "deviance" and the overly harsh, boundary-maintaining social responses that followed. The crises related to charismatic succession, loss of political autonomy, the migration of outsiders threatening the Puritan ethos and way of life of the community, and the loss of collective solidarity and mission. As might be expected the book has been critiqued for ignoring power (say, competition over land), much like other Durkheimian/Parsonian attempts at historical sociology such as Smelser's. Yet it remains an influential text. Partly thanks to Erikson, Durkheim's ideas remain much cited in the wider literature on the social construction of deviance (Smith 2008b). There is much common ground with other constructivist accounts and it is not uncommon to find Durkheim or Erikson mobilized in discussions by scholars of labeling theory or moral panics, even though these approaches had origins in other traditions.

Some other moves afoot in the United States were more anthropological than historical and were influenced by the *Elementary*

Forms more than *The Division of Labor*. An early adopter was the anthropologist **W. Lloyd Warner** (1898–1970), who studied a New England town in the manner of a tribe. In a series of studies Warner (Warner and Lunt 1941; Warner 1959; 1963) explored the groups that made up the city, each with its customary activities. Particularly noteworthy was his analysis of memorial parades and commemorative ceremonies. He interpreted these as a solidaristic ritual enterprise and made explicit reference to Durkheim's thinking.

Although Warner can at times read like a functionalist making simplistic analogies between tribal life and modernity (Lukes 1975), Randall Collins argues that there are important, subtle lessons to be learned. According to Collins (2005), Warner outlines a strongly hierarchical, stratified vision of "Yankee City," showing how dynamics of class and status surround gatherings and how in-group solidarity (through religious, voluntary, arts, or ethnic associations, for example) would involve excluding others. Conversely, participation in associations and their solidaristic, symbolically expressive rituals could sometimes provide risky opportunities for advancement. Hence Warner writes:

> Many people in the community, particularly those in the lower classes, use talent to help improve their stations in life and gain social recognition . . . They may be recognized economically and advance themselves accordingly . . . or . . . they may be recognized socially by more highly placed persons and participate at a higher level in the social system. Very often, to the observer, the efforts are pathetic, since they accomplish nothing for the participant and even evoke ridicule. (1963: 138)

Likewise Warner's study of the pivotal commemorative activities showed they were controlled by high-status families. There were prestige hierarchies. Deference was expected from lesser people who wanted to become involved. Collins saw a sociology of groups, situations, and ritual power buried deep inside Warner's work, upon which he could build. We return to Collins to see what he made of this insight in the next chapter.

Like Warner, **Edward Shils** (1910–95), who had worked with Parsons on the highly abstract *Toward a General Theory of Action*, was inspired to mobilize Durkheim more empirically to explain ritualized aspects of modern life. With Michael Young he authored a classic paper on the coronation of Britain's Queen Elizabeth II (Shils and Young 1953). It was argued that this was a national ritual of solidarity, a celebration of constitutional monarchy/democracy, and an affirmation of national values and British identity. Shils and Young

174

pointed not only to street parties and the ceremonial parade, but also to the role of television in bringing people together. The implications of this observation were only developed much later by Elihu Katz and Daniel Dayan (1992) with their study of festive viewing and media events. Although the paper displayed some ironies, the argument of Shils and Young was perhaps too deferential and so it inspired a later rebuke from noted Durkheim scholar **Steven Lukes** (1975). Taking aim also at Warner (who was exculpated by Collins, above – it would be a worthwhile project to look at how two major scholars can arrive at such different readings), Robert Bellah (on the Kennedy inaugural), and Sydney Verba (on the Kennedy assassination), Lukes noted that such work overlooked the cognitive or even ideological dimensions of political ritual in the "mobilization of bias." Ritual can anchor common sense or shape attitudes regarding the political order. Further, the Durkheimian scholars tended to assume that integration and solidarity result rather than demonstrating these ritual impacts. Lukes argues that more attention needed to be given to contestation, apathy, and ritual as a resource for motivation and exclusion. For example, the Orange Day parades in Northern Ireland were a ritual organized around sectarian politics, not national unity. This line of argument was extended by historian David Kertzer (1988) a decade or so later in a full-length monograph. He pointed to ritual as a political tool for domination and protest, and as a resource that could build solidarity in the absence of consensus.

Shils (1975) was to also deploy Durkheim (alongside Weber) elsewhere with his theories of the "sacred center." In his paper entitled "Center and Periphery" that was first published in 1961, he argued that every society has pivotal institutions that are endowed with a certain charisma. There is a "central zone" that is "the center of the order of symbols, of values and beliefs, which govern the society. It is the center because it is the ultimate and irreducible; and it is felt to be such by many who cannot give explicit articulation to its irreducibility. The central zone partakes of the nature of the sacred" (1975: 3), and this assisted social cohesion. Typically, aspects of the state associated with this center are seen to have special world-ordering powers and to have legitimate authority. In the United States these would be things like Congress and the Supreme Court. The upshot was that bureaucratic and legal-rational domination in modernity was perhaps not as barren of meaning as Max Weber had suggested. This was the case not only for awestruck citizens. Although secular power and authority were often reinforced by close contact with the sacred center or control over its resources, even members "of the elite tend to experience the 'transforming' transcendental overtones which are generated by incumbency in authoritative roles, or by proximity to 'fundamentally important things'" (1975: 12). Put another way, they feel the sacred obligations of office.

Another figure in this US milieu was **Robert Bellah** (1927–2013). In 1959 he wrote an essay on "Durkheim and History" for the *American Sociological Review* (Bellah 1959). Here he looks over Durkheim's body of work and notes just how often visions of social change or social evolution are present; comments on Durkheim's comparative method; and discusses the significance of the *Elementary Forms*, largely in terms of the concept of collective representations. The feel of this essay is, however, a little unpoetic and uptight. It was to be a few years later, in the 1960s proper, that Bellah was to breathe more deeply and in a relaxed way and develop a confident, strongly "religious" sociology of religion, arguing for the *sui generis* power of belief and the significance of non-rational forces in shaping social life. Along with Weber and Freud, Durkheim provided a key resource for this activity that worked at the interface of comparative religion, social theory, history, and theology. Bellah's most famous essay appeared in 1966 and was on **civil religion** in America (Bellah 1970a). The idea here, broadly consistent with Shils, Warner, and others, is that there is a set of beliefs and myths in the United States that stands beyond party affiliation and that is not tied to any particular faith community. Rather there is a sense of the sacred surrounding national institutions, histories, and memories that sets a higher standard for aspiration and evaluation. We often encounter this during state ceremonies or in political speeches when reference is made to iconic Presidents, to times of trial for the nation, to the sacrifice of soldiers, to the evils of slavery, or to the destiny of a people. Although Durkheim does not appear in the essay, his spirit runs through it. We find it indicated in the footnote tagged at the bottom of the first paragraph: "The Durkheimian notion that every group has a religious dimension, which would be seen as obvious in southern or eastern Asia, is foreign to us. This obscures the recognition of such dimensions in our society" (1970a: 187). A few years later Bellah was again using Durkheim (again along with Weber and Freud) to argue against the neglect of religion and irrationality in western thought. In his essay from 1969 "Between Religion and Social Science" (Bellah 1970b) he asserted that the idea of collective effervescence might play a role like that of Freud's unconscious, as it could "point to depths within human action that are not fully understood but do not fit into the convenient patterns of Enlightenment thought, focusing around the twin ideas of interest maximization and cognitive accuracy" (1970b: 239).

With Bellah it is often hard to isolate the precise Durkheimian credential. He drew on his wide reading and tended to use theory with a light touch. Indeed we see Tocqueville and not Durkheim leading the agenda in books such as the co-authored *Habits of the Heart* (Bellah et al. 1985), even though the book is about belonging and meaning in social life today and seems to be dripping with accounts of anomie. Nevertheless Bellah retained an interest in Durkheim throughout his life, turning late toward a more mechanistic or biologistic interest in how rituals work to produce first collective effervescence and then culture more generally through embodiment. For example, Bellah (2005) approvingly cites the work of William McNeil (1995) on how military drill, coordinated dance, and chanting build confidence and solidarity in groups. This move toward a kind of determinism, which meshes nicely with the neurocognitive turn in sociology, perhaps reflected his longstanding worry that the insights of Freud, Durkheim, and Weber "do not so much explain anything as point to dark recesses where powerful but poorly understood forces and processes seem to be affecting human action" (1970b: 240).

Erving Goffman (1922–82) had been a student of W. Lloyd Warner. We often forget that he was an anthropologist before he became a legendary sociologist. Like Garfinkel he is generally seen as opposed to the Durkheimian top-down vision of social order. The case has been made, again by Randall Collins (2005), that Goffman belongs in a kind of micro-conflict Durkheimian tradition in which stratification hierarchies are built up from encounters in everyday life (see chapter 5). In his treatments of everyday interaction, first formulated in the 1950s, Goffman (1967) made use of concepts of ritual and self in ways that indicate clear lines of influence, most notably from Durkheim's ideas about *homo duplex* and the cult of the individual (covered in chapters 1 and 2). These readings would certainly have been encountered during his formal anthropological training. For Goffman the self is surrounded by a sacred aura and requires careful protection. For example, interaction rituals, such as everyday greetings or polite gestures, ensure mutual respect. He writes of these:

> This secular world is not so irreligious as we might think. Many gods have been done away with, but the individual himself stubbornly remains a deity of considerable importance. He walks with some dignity and is the recipient of many little offerings. He is jealous of the worship due him, yet, approached in the right spirit, he is ready to forgive those who may have offended him. Because of their status relative to his,

some persons will find him contaminating while others will contaminate
him, in either case finding that they must treat him with ritual care.
(1967: 95)

With such words, which precisely echo in rhythm and tone those
from Durkheim's (1986c) essay "Individualism and the Intellectuals"
that I quoted in chapter 2, Goffman makes a connection between two
of Durkheim's major themes: ritual and the cult of the individual.
This is something that Durkheim himself did not quite manage to
accomplish in an explicit way.

Imperfect, gestural, and essayistic as these scattered empirical efforts may often have been, they indicate the ongoing force of
Durkheim's ideas. In a sense they planted a seed. But it would take
perhaps two decades before there were sprouts, three before there
were leaves, and four before a substantial tree could be seen. We turn
in the next chapter to look at this story. But before we get there, let's
summarize where we are around the year 1985. Parsons's systems
theory is no longer influential, but Durkheim lingers on somewhat in
work in this highly abstract genre in Germany. Critical Weberian and
Marxist approaches are dominant in more empirical macro-sociology
and have left historical studies by "normative functionalists" looking
dated, simplistic, and wooden.

Micro-sociology has been on the rise since about 1965 and is generally interpreted as standing against the Durkheim who advocated
social facts as external and constraining. Mary Douglas has been
highly productive for many years and has been carrying the flag. Yet
her work has become more influential in political science, science
studies, and organizational theory than in core anthropology and
sociology. Lévi-Strauss is a giant figure and universally acclaimed
as a towering intellect. However, he seems to have abandoned the
effort toward a general semiotic theory of social structure and social
organization, and has retreated under his own *Golden Bough* with
an abstruse analysis of interconnected Amazonian myths. Foucault,
Derrida, Althusser, Baudrillard, Lyotard, and Bourdieu have taken
his place as the most influential, exciting, and innovative French
thinkers.

Yet perhaps the rise of these powerful new theorists did not
necessarily mean the Durkheimian tradition was totally eclipsed.
To close this chapter on a positive note we can indulge in some
informed speculation that Durkheim was still at work, only in mysterious ways. Alexander Riley has traced a line of influence running
through Bataille, Mauss, and Caillois. This goes right through to the

178

poststructuralist tradition that was now dominant. Riley (2005; 2013) suggests that Foucault had a longstanding interest in Bataille, and notes that Foucault quoted Bataille when writing about transgression – a concept which for Foucault was central to his interest in madness, violence, death, and sexuality. When given a Durkheimian gloss, Foucault seems to valorize "unreason" and see in it a way to access sacred forms of knowledge that were stamped out in the transition to modernity. Today, he claims, we can access this mystery only through works of art or literature that press against the limits of language and rationality; or through seeking out scattered transgressive spaces and activities in which the uncontained sacred can be found.

Derrida's interest in Mauss is well known thanks to his famously difficult essay on *The Gift* (Derrida 1992; see also chapter 3). However, Derrida was also influenced by Bataille, and saw in him a writer who had realized early on that there was meaning beyond discourse (Derrida 1978). Derrida praised and was allegedly influenced by the surrealist poets who had been members of the *Collège de sociologie*. Jean Baudrillard used Bataille, along with Mauss's writings on potlatch, in his move away from neo-Marxism toward a theory of society and the economy as fundamentally irrational. He spoke of our society's obsession with death and car accidents, with terrorism, with seduction, and with pornography. These are all manifestations of destruction, negation, and play.

Riley intriguingly suggests that Durkheim was speaking as a member of a "modern secular intellectual class" (2005: 296) when he advocated that society be held together by a kind of abstract and rational moral/sacred glue. The postmodern turn was not away from the sacred but rather attempted to renew it through a different channel. It was more existential, embodied, personal, playful, and connected to pleasure and consumption. It was also informed by the dark experiences of the twentieth century with their evidence of the failure of reason. Durkheim had advocated for faith in the project of the Third Republic. History had taught a different lesson. Salvation lay in skepticism and an embrace of the abject, marginal, and unthinkable.

Chapter 5
Into the Twenty-First Century: Durkheim Revived, 1985–2020

Durkheim neglected – the rise of cultural sociology in the United States – Jeffrey Alexander and the Strong Program – Randall Collins and interaction ritual – other Durkheimian work in the United States – the Durkheimian Studies/Études Durkheimiennes group – Germany – adaptations of Mary Douglas on grid/group – evolutionary psychology– the return of normative Durkheimian theory.

The year is 1985. Durkheim is firmly entrenched as a "founding father" of sociology and anthropology. But he does not seem particularly interesting. It feels as if his ideas have been mined out. Not much has changed since 1965 when Nisbet (1976 :5) described his impact in the United States as being in the study of social problems such as "crime, suicide, family instability, and social strife" as well as in pinpointing "restless individualism" and anomie as the root causes of these. Introductory lecture courses routinely talk about social facts and illustrate this with reference to Durkheim's work on suicide. Textbooks contrast "conflict" with "consensus" theory. More specialized classes on Durkheim are rare and none of these seems to be where the action is. The Durkheimian positivist vision remains uncited but in the deep background of much quantitative work dealing with variables and outcomes, especially in criminology and health. The volume of this work is increasingly visible in journals due to the proliferation of university mainframe computers as well as statistical programs that dramatically reduce the financial costs and learning curves for doing multivariate analysis. Such progress, unfortunately, makes Durkheim's serial cross-tabulations in *Suicide* seem hopelessly out of date. Cultural anthropology at this point in time has nearly done with bashing structural functionalism, and was even winding down critique of the colonial enterprise. It is about to enter the peak of its "writing culture" phase dominated by guilt, doubt, and radical reflexivity with regard to the problems of knowledge and representation. In this iteration of postmodernism or poststructuralism, the cultural turn is becoming differentiated out from efforts toward a general explanatory social science. Mary Douglas is a holdout with her belief in the possibility of an integrated theory of structure and knowledge. She has just published *How Institutions Think*.

There is as yet not much sign of the "cultural Durkheim" who would rise to authority in the next few decades. And the Durkheim who wanted to talk about collective morality and normative integration is still on the ropes, taking blows by association with the Parsonian theoretical legacy. From the perspective of a vibrant microsociological community, his systems-level macro-explanations failed to account for creativity and agency. For these scholars Durkheim was a "positivist" who saw people as constrained by laws and social forces but who could not get at the nitty-gritty of social life. He seemed to be a lumbering giant, about to become fossilized and consigned to encyclopedia entries on the history of theory. Talented critical theorists, a second attack constituency, claimed the structural functionalist legacy could not explain violence and change. Indeed Durkheim was typecast as a conservative even among many of his supporters thanks to the enduring impact of interpretative efforts from one of the few visible experts in the United States, Robert Nisbet (1952). As we saw in the last chapter, early efforts to inject some vitality and relevance by theorizing ritual and solidaristic aspects of modernity had received pushback from Lukes, Lockwood, Tilly, and others. Modernity was understood as characterized by weak beliefs, fragmented audiences, and struggles for power. What use was a "conservative" theory talking about ritual, integration, and solidarity for explaining any of this?

Yet the early and mid-1980s were also a period when renewal was about to start. As the saying goes, the darkest hour is just before the dawn. The substantial biography by Lukes (1973) was widely available and had opened up new vistas by demonstrating the full range of Durkheim's thinking. Importantly, it offered a kind of one-stop shop that did away with the library detective skills previously needed to discover just how much Durkheim had written on so many varied topics. Jeffrey Alexander (1978) had recently published a substantial tome outlining Durkheim's shifting theoretical logic and, in the manner of Parsons in the 1930s, his contributions toward a voluntaristic theory of action. It is notable in retrospect that Alexander, soon to become a renowned theorist but at the time barely out of graduate school, was insisting this early, via a detailed reading and reconstruction, that the *Elementary Forms* did not quite fit with the other books as part of a set. There was more voluntarism, more semiotics, more culture unchained, and a vision of the origins of the social in the sacred. The full implications of this interpretative effort did not sink in with him or his audience for quite some time. This was in part because the central theme of Alexander's book was to display Marx and Durkheim as the "antinomies of classical thought." Readers were caught up in the external compare-and-contrast activity rather than looking for internal contradictions in Durkheim himself. Moreover, in this volume Alexander seemed more interested in uncovering and documenting the materialism buried in the *Division of Labor* than in identifying an epistemological break (Weiss 2019), and he did not follow up. He was still busy investing in Parsons as a vehicle for his project of neofunctionalism (below). One senses even he did not quite know the implications of what he had read and how he had read it.

In Europe the *Durkheimian Studies/Études Durkheimiennes* group had not yet started its journal – the debut was to wait another ten years, until 1995. However, the pool of students and scholars deeply interested in Durkheim as a theorist was starting to attain a critical mass as the 1980s progressed. With his detailed textual and archival research, Philippe Besnard had been first out of the gates and was leading by example from Paris. Still, this group was to eventually turn "inward" to the study of Durkheim and his group and so was involved in an exegetical history of theory activity. It was in the new field of American cultural sociology that innovative and generalizable theoretical efforts toward social explanation were to develop.

In the United States the most important context for Durkheim's revival was what was going on outside the Durkheimian camp, narrowly defined. There were changes in the wider intellectual and disciplinary environment. The cultural turn had taken place in the 1960s. In the humanities there was a push for more theoretical understandings of creative products and artistic movements, these replacing evaluative and normative appreciations of expressive excellence or idiographic accounts of lives, deeds, and works. Pivotal here were the inputs of structuralism, poststructuralism, hermeneutics, and narrative theory. In the social sciences such interpretative models and more general sensibilities were imported from the humanities, initially into history and anthropology. Sociology, however, was very slow on the uptake, thanks in part to the peculiar disciplinary dynamics we have reviewed. There were other fish to fry. Yet a number of sociologists were eventually, belatedly to be inspired by those kindred disciplines. Durkheim, especially the late Durkheim, was to become a point of connection, a node that linked the cultural turn back to the sociological tradition itself.

For our narrative it is especially notable that thinkers who had an elective affinity with Durkheimian social thought were highly significant in the anthropology of the 1960s and 1970s. Neither Victor Turner nor Clifford Geertz had a self-image as a Durkheimian. They bundled him in with positivism and an overly systemic, overly static vision of society. Yet in a sense these brilliant scholars paved the way for the more sensitive and meaning-centered form of Durkheimian sociology that was to come. The path is somewhat mazy. These thinkers turned their back on Durkheim only to develop ideas that seem to correspond to much of his thinking. They never really acknowledged this. Their work then provided an inspiration for a new interpretation of Durkheim that was to follow, wherein we can now read them as unwitting Durkheimians. Victor Turner (1969) was noted for arguments about "social drama" (see below) and for understanding the ritualistic, performative elements of social conflict and public disputes. He also spoke of "communitas" (essentially, solidarity and egalitarianism) and "liminality" (a creative and volatile context in which everyday rules are suspended). It would not take too much effort to show this is all prefigured in the *Elementary Forms*. Clifford Geertz (1973) called for "thick description," for treating social life as if it were a text to be subject to close reading and interpretation, and for social action as motivated and communicative. Well, that sounds a bit like the way Durkheim wrote about ritual and the sacred in the *Elementary Forms* too. We need also to think about the fate of rival theories (Parkin 1992). It is surprisingly easy to forget that communism collapsed in Russia and eastern Europe in 1989. This was a huge geopolitical and cultural event that inevitably sent shock waves through the social theory community. The event took much of the wind out of the sails of Marxist sociology: Marxism had failed, people protesting in the streets did not seem to want it, and somehow the ills of the political project contaminated the analytic intellectual project as well. Attention could shift to the alternative Durkheimian and Weberian visions of modernity.

But the presence of an opportunity structure provided by the cultural

183

turn and the fall of communism was still not enough. Something more local and specific had to happen for a cultural Durkheim to emerge. Both "Durkheim" and "culture" needed to be untethered from Parsons and from normative functionalism both in terms of analytic propositions and in perceptions. To repeat: culture was seen in 1985 as a disreputable, fuzzy concept when compared to power, networks, or the state. It was tied to integration, not conflict. It was notably undynamic. Part of the problem – although probably only Geertz (1973) managed to articulate this well at the time, in the chapter on "strain" in *The Interpretation of Cultures* – was that the vision of culture provided by Parsons, and extracted by him from Durkheim, was both too abstract and too stripped back (see Alexander and Smith 1993). Ideas about norms and values, best articulated in Parsons's brilliant work of the 1940s and 1950s, seemed unfortunately wooden, distant, and lifeless. They had in fact been passed by in the "cultural turn" in the humanities, including in anthropology in the 1960s where terms like code, ritual, narrative, and symbol were the lingua franca of diverse intellectual communities. Durkheim seemingly had nothing to offer because, at least at first glance, he looked, like Parsons, to be obsessed with high-floating abstractions and vague generalities.

So "culture" had been pinned in a corner by structural functionalism in general and the AGIL model in particular. It was charged with keeping a lid on things and aligning action paths. It was vague, overarching, and not amenable to institutional or ethnographic or case-study analysis. In a strange way it would need the creative destruction of Parsonian thought to be complete for a different spirit of Durkheim to be released, but this would take time. It is not at all facetious to posit a parallel with the situation Robert Hertz had described nearly a century before relating to burial customs (see chapter 2). The phase of intense pollution of Parsonian functionalist cultural explanation needed to be over. It needed to be both dead and buried for quite a while. When no longer a threat, it could rest in peace and something uncontaminated could rise from the grave.

Credit should be given where credit is due and our last variable in this protracted multivariate narrative is a slightly ironic one. Two figures who would later be thought of as in competition with Durkheimian ideas provided assistance in bringing the cultural turn to American sociology as a whole. Bourdieu and Foucault both spoke about the sociological ways in which culture was implicated in mechanisms of control and exclusion. In so doing they helped destigmatize theoretically informed cultural explanation among many mainstream sociologists. After all, they had uncovered with empirical work the ways that meanings were linked to consequential outcomes at the core of the macro-sociological agenda, such as class domination, state power, and social reproduction. They were an unwitting Trojan Horse for what was to follow.

Potential energy accumulated, the pendulum finally swung, and during the 1980s American sociology as a whole became more receptive to culture. The culture section of the American Sociological Association, once founded, became one of the largest almost overnight. A decade later an edited collection could be compiled announcing the arrival of "The New American Cultural Sociology." The volume signaled that a change in the wind had taken place and that something was going on that was very distinctive from both British Cultural Studies and European high theory (Smith 1998b). This American cultural sociology was a meaning-centered inquiry that was middle-range, non-ideological, and somewhat positivistic in that it looked to explain as well as interpret. Durkheim was a significant player and pivotal in initially tentative efforts to figure out what this cultural sociology might look like. Reanimated and set free from the Parsonian legacy, he was reinterpreted in light of the cultural turn as a flexible, dynamic, exciting scholar of myth, ritual, classification, and the sacred.

This new wave of Durkheimian theorizing drew in particular on the *Elementary Forms*. This was a text that previously had been neglected. In sociology in the United States, Durkheim had long been associated with the other three major texts. He was a positivist student of social facts who also wrote about morality and social change. As for the *Elementary Forms*, this had been left to anthropologists. When read by sociologists this had been generally understood as an excellent illustration of Durkheim's functionalist view of ritual. Much of this is captured by Alpert's analysis from 1939 identifying four functions of ritual (disciplining and preparing the individual, bringing cohesion, revitalizing the social group, generating euphoria and other solidaristic sentiments that help people cope with life). Tellingly, this typology was still present in a 1976 reprint of Nisbet's 1965 anthology of Durkheim commentary, suggesting that not much had changed interpretation-wise in four decades (Alpert 1976; Nisbet 1976). We can find many other indicators of the mooring in sleepy backwaters occupied by the *Elementary Forms*. Ernest Wallwork's (1972) book was dedicated to a study of morality in Durkheim's thought and mentions the *Elementary Forms* in passing on just eight pages. Three of these are footnotes. Nisbet's (1975) book-length guide to Durkheim has a chapter on "Religion," but amazingly devotes only twenty pages to the masterwork. A look at the footnotes here shows that *The Division of Labor* is the keynote text for Nisbet's understanding. The flip side of this neglect was that in the late 1980s a new package full of fresh ideas was on the table ready for unboxing.

To summarize the prior paragraphs: the rise of the *Elementary Forms* to centrality was in a sense historically over-determined. The cultural turn had arrived, Parsonian functionalism was gone, Marxism looked weak, the pendulum had swung. The arrival of a fresh new translation by Karen Fields in 1995 (Durkheim 1995) was to cement this newfound momentum and put the *Elementary Forms* really at the center of things. Still, it was a long process. We must be cautious not to overstate the extent or speed of Durkheim's revival. As late as 1992 Frank Parkin noted that "sociologists calling themselves Durkheimians are extremely difficult to find, whereas self-styled Marxists and Weberians are everywhere in evidence" (1992: 1).

Jeffrey Alexander and the Strong Program

A pioneer in identifying a Durkheim informed by the cultural turn and amenable to contemporary sociological inquiry was the prolific **Jeffrey C. Alexander**. We have already noted how his close reading in the 1970s had led to the beginning of a realization that the *Elementary Forms* was a special book. Yet in the mid-1980s Alexander was still most associated with **neofunctionalism**. This was an effort to revive the best of Parsons and to jettison what was not needed – for example, to eliminate functionalist assumptions about cooperative social institutions; correct ideas about the inevitable evolution of social forms; and rectify the lack of attention to power and domination. The good aspects of the Parsonian agenda were said to include efforts to bring micro- and macro-levels of analysis into the same picture (from the individual, to the encounter to the social system, etc.); a commitment to non-reductive, multidimensional theorizing; and a respect for the history and tradition of social theory (Alexander 1985). A problem was that once ideas about functional equilibrium and systems-level explanation were pushed aside, it was hard to see what exactly was "functionalist" about the paradigm other than a commitment to multidimensional, layered theorizing (Turner and Maryanski 1988) that encompassed levels from micro to macro and both structural and cultural variables. Those attracted to neofunctionalism tended to be scholars interested in the history of theory and in metatheory (theory of theory). Papers tended to critique, review, and suggest in programmatic ways. Nobody seemed to be engaged in empirical investigations that explained or challenged other scholarship. This was unfortunate insofar as the discipline of sociology in the United States has a certain "show me the money" quality. The payoff needs to be demonstrated, not argued in the abstract.

Crucially, it was Alexander's movement away from neofunctionalism and away from Parsons and toward a less metatheoretical and more middle-range empirical cultural sociology that made all the difference. Many did not notice this change, and indeed Alexander was to be thought of primarily as a neofunctionalist for a long time afterward. Yet even while publishing books with "neofunctionalism" in the title, he had already started to move in a more cultural direction in the mid-1980s (Mast 2017). A conference in Bad Homburg in 1983 on the later Durkheim provided an initial impetus, after which Alexander engaged in a creative re-reading of Durkheim's *Elementary Forms* that sought to liberate potentials buried within the text that were perhaps not even seen by Durkheim himself. The task was not unlike that of Lacan reading Freud, or Althusser reading "for Marx." The themes Alexander now saw had been obscured or downplayed in his own prior interpretations by his Parsonian interests and by the failure of the cultural turn to make it to sociology. For example, a post-Parsonian, neofunctionalist analytic concern with social order and internalized action provided a pair of spectacles that filtered out much of the color, vibrancy, and radical potential that Alexander was now finding in the *Elementary Forms* in the mid-1980s. A text that had previously been reported as capturing the internalized normative motivations for social life was now re-described as having a semiotic and religious vision of a clearly autonomous and structured cultural order.

By the late 1980s the *Elementary Forms* was firmly positioned by Alexander as a classical source of legitimacy for a wider agenda. This was to build a cultural sociology that would put symbol, classification, emotion, ritual, and meaning center stage (Weiss 2019). It was a point of origin and a meeting ground for lines of thinking that were expressed in outlying works by Bellah and Shils, and, Alexander also argued, many of the major figures of structuralism and poststructuralism. Whether the reading is correct is a moot point. We can still read the *Elementary Forms* with an eye to social realism, positivism, or functionalism. But the fact remains that this interpretation was motivational and was to become influential and widely shared in the next three decades. The signs of transition were first visible in scattered working papers, and a little later in papers and chapters that appeared not in major journals but rather in invited edited collections.

The first really major public signal of change was the release of just such an edited collection, *Durkheimian Sociology: Cultural Studies* (Alexander 1988a), that assembled several original papers by various authors, many of which took it as gospel that the *Elementary Forms* was a radically different major statement from the prior three books. Between them the chapters indicated a critical mass of excellent scholars with thinking shaped by Durkheim, although it is notable that at the time the numbers were made up by a few figures from outside of the sociological discipline. In his introductory chapter Alexander sets out the stall he was to stand behind for the next three decades. The first sentence tells us that the book was "designed to bring the analysis of symbolic phenomena more directly into the discourse of sociology" (1988b: 1). The second paragraph notes that the cultural turn had passed sociology by and that "researchers and theorists are still fighting the last war" (1988b: 1). The essay continues by claiming that Turner, Geertz, and others were all decisively influenced by Durkheim even if they didn't always show it. Next up we read that the *Elementary Forms* has cast a long shadow by demonstrating that the social order involved symbolic patterns, ritual, myth, and the sacred. Crucially, this text was now to be distinguished from the earlier "structural concerns" (1988b: 10) of the middle-period Durkheim as his thinking underwent a "decisive shift" (1988b: 11). The message is repeated in Alexander's own substantive contribution. In that chapter he notes that: "Although many interpreters have discussed this movement toward the sociology of religion, none have appreciated its full significance ... Only after the pervasiveness of this theoretical shift is understood can the challenge that Durkheim's legacy poses to contemporary social science be fully appreciated" (1988c: 188). Rising to this challenge, for Alexander, means coming to terms with the deeply emotive, ritualized, semiotic, and sacral elements of modernity.

Finding a compass bearing by revisiting a classic was just one task. Next up there was the really pivotal, detailed work of figuring out just how to do empirical Durkheimian cultural sociology in this new mode. For a while in the 1980s Alexander had considered writing a book on Watergate, an event that had been a defining moment in his graduate-school years. The book never appeared, but this was a fruitful dead-end typescript if ever there were one. Papers emerged here and there that contained the seeds of much that was to follow over the next four decades. An early analysis was firmly cast in the neofunctionalist idiom in seeking to retool functionalist theory to make sense of power and division. With ample reference to Parsons, Evans-Pritchard, and Smelser it considered themes of "schism," "conflict," and "integration" during Watergate and spoke about alignments of the cultural and social systems (Alexander 1984). But just a few short years afterwards we see a very different treatment of the same historical sequence (Alexander 1988c). It is an analysis very much in the contemporary cultural sociology mode. Alexander unpacks the performative and ritual aspects of the official hearings into President Richard Nixon's illegal activities (Alexander 1988c), shows that the inquiry involved sacred national symbols, and provides a gloss depicting a competitive ritual drama of purity and pollution. The analysis is highly attentive to narrative contestation and was to be the first of his many subsequent forays into explaining American politics as a battle to control meaning where the mass media play a crucial role in a symbolic process (e.g. Alexander and Jaworsky 2014), and where the major actors are the Presidency, Congress, organic intellectuals, and civil society organizations.

Another early paper tends to be overlooked but has been quietly influential (Alexander 1992). This investigated the social meanings of the computer as this technology emerged after World War II. Reconstructing the social imaginary, Alexander showed that the "information machine" was coded as sacred and profane. This paper was an early example of his technique of deep reading using popular or mass media texts as forms of primary data. The result of his interpretative activity is to identify enduring collective representations. In this case the early computers (room-sized research mainframes in universities and at major corporations such as IBM and Bell Labs during the 1950s and 1960s) were described in media accounts with religious imagery as objects of awe. The analysis of concepts and indicators lined up very neatly indeed with the characteristics of the sacred as described in the *Elementary Forms*. For example, the computers, like the *churinga*, were hidden, protected, and secret. They needed to be handled with care by skilled attendants. There was a strong binary. The computers were dangerous, but as well as having the potential to destroy the world (e.g. by recommending or initiating nuclear war, by designing new weapons) they could save it (e.g. by devising a way to end world hunger). They had unimaginable and mysterious powers of knowledge. Alongside the Watergate papers and typescripts, this study provided for Alexander's group a kind of working template for how to "do" empirical cultural sociology in a Durkheimian mode as a discourse analysis using textual materials. A paradigm could start moving.

Alexander's work on interpreting Watergate as a ritual involving symbolic process was partly inspired by Lévi-Strauss. Thoughts about binary opposition led Alexander to develop a more general understanding of the cultural codes that were at play in American political discourse (see 1988c for an early deployment). These have proven to be one of his most enduring and successful ideas. Tellingly, the codes were described in a Durkheimian move as "sacred" and "profane" (= "good" and "bad," not "good" and "mundane"; see Kurakin 2015) and they had a certain Douglasian quality insofar as the dynamics of interpretation and labeling were caught up with themes of purity and pollution. The codes had relative or "analytic" autonomy from the social system by virtue of their internal grammar – this made them what Alexander termed a **culture-structure**. Sacred actors, organizations, and relationship were rational, open, honest, democratic, and so forth. Profane actors were secretive, irrational, hierarchical, dishonest. Significantly, the binary codes connected the classical Durkheimian thematics of classification to the social semiotics of a pluralistic, linguistically mediated modern society. These codes – dubbed a little later the **discourse of civil society** (Alexander and Smith 1993) – were to be at the core of much of the early work of what became the "Strong Program" (Alexander and Smith 2001; 2010; 2019). This was an intellectual social movement initiated by Alexander a few years after his self-conversion to cultural sociology.

The **Strong Program** itself is worth our attention here for at least a moment, as this has become a major international carrier of the Durkheimian tradition and an effort at collective paradigm-building deliberately styled in the manner of Durkheim's own group. It consists of Alexander, his students, and a global community of supporters and fellow travelers, all of them conducting Durkheim-inflected sociology to a greater or lesser extent. Members of the group typically elaborated Alexander's ideas, developed them with him through co-authoring, or deployed them in different empirical fields where they had specific expertise that he did not. A few members contributed to developing original theoretical insights of their own. The pattern is remarkably similar to what we see with Durkheim and the *Année* group. The leader does most of the lifting but talented individuals like a Mauss, Hertz, or Halbwachs could sometimes come up with top-notch work as well. The center of operations for the Strong Program was initially a small group at the University of California, Los Angeles, but it was later more firmly institutionalized in the Center for Cultural Sociology at Yale. At a minimum, work by those associated with the group was about deep meanings and refused reductionism to structure or power. Maximally, those identifying tended to use Durkheimian concepts explicitly regarding the sacred, profane, and ritual. Viewed *in toto*, the output of the Strong Program core and its fellow travelers is an extremely large corpus that substantially magnified Alexander's own individual achievements and added considerable shelf-weight to the library of recent Durkheimian empirical sociology.

Alexander and Smith (1996; 2010; 2019) usefully identify a series of paradigms or research tools emerging from the Strong Program. The first of these was those binary codes we have just discussed that had emerged in Alexander's Watergate research. Their empirical relevance was repeatedly demonstrated and expanded. The codes were pushed back in time and shown as deeply entrenched in the United States. They could be found in over two hundred years of scandals and controversies (Alexander and Smith 1993). They were also pushed forward from Nixon and demonstrated to help interpret the struggles of Presidents Bush, Obama, and Trump (Alexander and Jaworsky 2014; Mast 2018; Smith 2005). Other work confirmed that they had explanatory traction in liberal democratic contexts outside the United States (Spain and France in the case of Smith 2005), underwent a system of Lévi-Straussian permutations to form the codes of fascism and communism (Smith 1998a), and played a role in city level politics as well as national debates (Jacobs 2000). Commentators noted that regulatory, evaluative codes seemed to be different elsewhere, particularly the Global South (Baiocchi 2006). More recent work involving Alexander and his collaborators has been responsive. It has explored multiple contending political codes in other parts of the world such as Latin America (Alexander and Tognato 2018). A frequent finding has been that a sacred code specifying a need for stability and order can be found competing with ones that give priority to democracy and liberty. Politics can involve struggles between groups holding different codes, each trying to have its worldview institutionalized and operationalized. This body of work has converged nicely with findings concerning populism and charisma. Coming out of a separate and more Weberian tradition, these were also documenting the existence of a religious aspect to modern politics and identified alternative cultural codes with differing understandings of just what was sacred or profane in social organization (e.g. Zúquete 2007).

The neo-Durkheimian move to look at codes, classification, and typification was augmented by developing understandings of how society could have a ritual dimension without there needing to be any rituals in the traditional sense of bodies co-present in time and space. Nor did there need to be a consensus. Rather there could be a heightened sense of living in important times when much was at stake – an idea taken somewhat from Victor Turner's (1969) thoughts about **social drama,** which had already been successfully applied in a cultural sociology mode by Robin Wagner-Pacifici (1986). Drawing on his African ethnographic materials, Turner had insisted that periods of crisis involved public contestation, communicative activity, and higher levels of emotional engagement. There was a sense that events were taking place of great significance, that these were a challenge to core beliefs and values, and that society needed to engage urgently in the activity of social or civic repair. This innovation essentially mirrored Durkheim's ideas about sacred time and renewal, and when combined with thinking about the public sphere and collective deliberation, could be applied widely to newsworthy crisis and scandal.

Durkheim's concept of collective representations and the collective conscience were also intuitively appealing but hard to make empirically tractable. Habermas's somewhat utopian writings on the **public sphere** became very visible in the early 1990s following the collapse of communism in eastern Europe and the Soviet Union (it seemed as if the "public sphere" or "civil society" had stood up to the state). For the Strong Program these thoughts offered a solution. The public sphere was a realm in which the sacred and profane discourses of civil society could be understood as playing their part in a public evaluative and ritual process involving circulating and contending collective representations.

Over time this attention to civil society, which had a somewhat concrete feel and included social movements and organizations, gave rise to a slightly separate stream of ideas about a **civil sphere** that provided a somewhat universalistic or "Hegelian" space for claims and moral evaluations (Alexander 2006). If "civil society" was hard to pin down, the civil sphere was everywhere and nowhere, a kind of abstract realm of virtue that was nevertheless potent. Agents in public life were evaluated as civil or uncivil and held to a higher standard – a process of benchmarking against ideals not unlike that to be found in Durkheim's writings on individualism (Cladis 1992) or Bellah's (1970a) on civil religion. The mass media, meanwhile, needed to be decoupled from prevalent understandings that they were an ideology engine or fact-finding institution (Alexander and Jacobs 1998). Rather the mass media were a sphere of activity associated with ritualized deliberation and bard-like narration – an element in a linguistically and symbolically mediated collective conscience. In this activity, agents were aligned with civil codes and public narratives.

192

The upshot of all this work was that by around the year 2000, a new and comprehensive Durkheimian paradigm had been established for interrogating and understanding political life in modernity as a ritual process of contested codings and stories, evaluations, and breaches and repairs. Of course Durkheim's *Elementary Forms* was not the only resource used by the Strong Program, and in a sense a capacity to match Durkheim's tradition with a wider universe of cultural theory was a major reason for adaptive success (Alexander and Smith 1996; 2010; 2019). The Strong Program was a paradigm in which a cultural Durkheim met the cultural turn.

Ideas about **narrative** came soon after an intensive phase of binary code publications. Influences were especially Paul Ricoeur, for hermeneutics, and Northrop Frye, for thoughts about the culture-structures of narrative genre. The turn to narrative not only captured the role of stories in social life but also allowed more flexibility and nuance to enter into interpretative activity. In the Strong Program, narratives were assimilated to the language of the sacred and profane and shown to be connected in turn to binary coding activity. Generally speaking, "inflated" narratives would frame events as a crisis, emergency, or moral disgrace. These were associated with strongly binary codings of protagonists and antagonists as sacred and profane (Jacobs 2000; Smith 2005) and would tend to launch social dramas.

Around two decades into the Strong Program, attention was given to material and visual culture in a new paradigm move labeled as the **iconic turn**. This was inspired in part by aspects of the *Elementary Forms* dealing with the role of props in ritual and the mention of sacred things in modernity (see the famous quote about the flag and blood in chapter 1). Also significant was the work of Roland Barthes on social mythologies as these attach to objects, and a more general body of theory in art and architecture criticism (see Alexander, Bartmanski, and Giesen 2012). There was a general sense that not all meaning could be about language. The basic argument was that "iconic power" was mobilized when a sensory experience at surface (a striking image, a cool piece of design) matched or encapsulated a deeper set of "background representations" such as collective beliefs, myths, or narratives.

Performance had been implicit right from the start in the Watergate papers but was theorized more systematically much later with borrowings from drama theory (Alexander 2004). Alexander drew on Durkheim's account of Aboriginal ritual in order to anchor this move, noting for example that outcomes were said by Durkheim to be contingent on the skill of the dancer. Performative power was said to depend on the capacity of actors (politicians, activists, etc.) to achieve "fusion" with deep sacred codes and positive narratives while performatively polluting their opponents (Alexander and Jaworsky 2014; Mast 2018). Put in another and more Saussurian, way, the surface *parole* was important as well as *langue*. It needed to mesh with deep structures and to mobilize and deploy these in convincing ways. This is a very dynamic kind of Durkheimian sociology that gives attention to a foreground of action and ongoing interpretation, to cultural pragmatics, rather than a background of values, norms, or social facts.

Over the years the Strong Program has been accused of idealism, of ignoring non-discursive meanings, of being unable to cope with irony, of inaccurate readings of Durkheim, of being overly reliant on textual data, and of needlessly picking fights with broadly cognate approaches that it dismissively dubs as Weak Programs (see Alexander and Smith 1996; 2010; 2019). To its credit, it has responded over the years to such critique in case studies specifically about violence and control, and with the evolution of new sub-paradigm elements. For example, power has been theorized more explicitly even if still in a cultural mode as belief, signification, and persuasion (e.g. Alexander 2004; Smith 2005; 2008a); there has been an interest in materiality and visuality thanks to the iconic move; scholars have increasingly turned to interview methods (McCormick 2015); and members have reached out toward conflict theory, especially neo-Weberian accounts in the comparative and historical sociological tradition (Norton 2014; Reed 2013). The Strong Program may not be a pure Durkheimianism, but it remains at the time of writing a very significant outpost of the cultural turn in the Durkheimian tradition that understands modernity as never fully rational.

Randall Collins and Interaction Ritual

The use of Durkheim in cultural sociology exemplified by the Strong Program is one in which attention is given to meanings embedded in semiotic systems, classifications, and codes. Taken from structuralist and poststructuralist understandings of discourse and myth, these approaches see culture as an independent realm of non-material social facts. The aim of analysis is to decode what is going on and to see how culture-structures shape motivations, legitimacy, and action options. **Randall Collins** describes this as the "code seeking" approach to Durkheim. He has proposed another model that has proven just as influential – the model of **interaction ritual chains** (Collins 2004). Built (like Alexander's) on a new reading of the *Elementary Forms*, Collins's theory moves ritual and social organization ahead of belief (unlike Alexander's). Meanings are still important but they emerge from encounters between embodied individuals. They are institutionalized and reinforced as a result of repeat encounters. Moreover, rituals and their associated symbols are elements of a stratification order. Hence in this vision the sociologist needs to start by looking at encounters in social settings and then move out to interpret a cultural system and its hierarchical consequences.

Although the interaction ritual model became highly visible only after the publication of Collins's book dedicated to the concept in 2004, the key ideas can be traced back to far earlier in his career and the 1970s. In his book *Conflict Sociology* (1975) Collins cites Durkheim heavily. A substantial section entitled "A Short History of Deference and Demeanor," which is co-authored with Joan Annett, considers the work of W. Lloyd Warner and Erving Goffman as a contribution to stratification sociology (see chapter 4). Collins notes that Goffman was important in "effecting a synthesis of Durkheimian theory with the Chicago School" (1975: 162) and that he "interprets the materials of organizational power relations in terms of the Durkheimian perspective of the ritual construction of moral realities" (1975: 162). Collins goes on to explain how individuals "seek out favorable contacts and evade unfavorable ones" (1975: 165) as a way to boost status, autonomy, and power.

Collins continues with an extended discussion on deference rituals and surveillance, on the uneven distribution of ritual resources, and on the role of courtesy in stratification and egalitarianism. He shows how norms changed during the transition to modernity (e.g. more informality) and how encounters were the basis for competitive efforts at inclusion and display (e.g. cliques, wit, conspicuous consumption). The essential picture is not unlike the one in the later *Interaction Ritual Chains* (Collins 2004), but, thanks to Weberian influences, more attention is given to exogenous macro-structures such as power or wealth or status groups, and also to the structural transition to modernity. The interaction order of micro-rituals is seen more as a phenomenological horizon for the experience of inequality and a local context for the reproduction of specific hierarchies rather than as a point of origin for those wider macro-structures. This treatment given to rituals and power in *Conflict Sociology* is likely to appeal to those who feel that Collins goes too far in *Interaction Ritual Chains* or that he leaves certain concerns off the table.

195

By 1988 Collins was starting to advocate explicitly for what he called a "Durkheimian tradition in conflict sociology" (Collins 1988), and the Weberian influences seemed to be diminishing. Collins sought to strip out functionalism and recover "an underground wing of the Durkheimian tradition which feeds very nicely into conflict theory" (1988: 108). He turned again to Goffman, Warner, and (in a rather neat "back to the future" move) Fustel de Coulanges on the *Ancient City* for a vision of competitive ritual organization, participation, and experience.

With the publication of *Interaction Ritual Chains*, Collins (2004) became yet more radical. Here he attempts to develop a model of stratification and competition that is almost fully Durkheimian and that gives maximum weight to the micro-order. He calls this inter-action ritual (IR) theory. Drawing on Goffman in particular (see chapter 4), Collins believes that the atom of social life is the encounter or situation, not the group, class, demographic category, or even the individual. Situations are in effect micro-rituals that give birth to culture. He writes:

> Culture is socially alive only when rituals are successful, that is, when the situational ingredients exist to make rituals emotionally intense and cognitively focused. IR theory gives a precise mechanism for showing when new symbols are generated, and when old symbols retain social commitments or fade away as no longer meaningful ... it is also a return to an older Durkheimian formulation in which social morphology shapes social symbols. Current IR theory differs from the classic version mainly in giving a radically micro-situational slant, stressing that the social morphology that counts is the patterns of micro-sociological interaction in local situations. (Collins 2004: 32)

In his talking-through of this approach Collins picks up not just on the *Elementary Forms* but also on a line of thinking in Durkheim that we see going back to remarks in the *Division of Labor* and *Suicide* concerning crowd behavior. If you look back to chapter 1, you will see two block quotes of the kind Collins uses to anchor his claim. One speaks to contagious collective emotion in a crowd and the other to the Aboriginal group falling into a rhythm and becoming ecstatic. Such material speaks to the organizational effects of currents swirling in the collective conscience, as well as to themes of dynamic density and coordinated action. In an ingenious reading of the *Elementary Forms* that builds on such themes, Collins elaborates and describes what he sees as the mechanics of ritual. He argues that Durkheim discovered how the sacred emerges from a process in which the group engages in coordinated action with a common focus of attention. The actions often involve rhythmic entrainment in activities such as singing or dancing. There is a barrier against outsiders. There is also a shared emotional mood and a shared focus of attention. Outcomes include symbols that are sacred or totemic for the group. These have been at the center of the ritual action. Durkheim showed this to be the case with the *churinga*. Such symbols are charged up by the group activity and operate rather like batteries to store energy and belief and memory from one ritual to the next. In addition there is solidarity and collective belonging, a sense of morality and a distribution of emotional energy that powers up participants for a while afterward.

Much of the attraction of Collins's work lies in his courageous efforts toward the application of his model to non-obvious, non-religious contexts. Generally this is accomplished through comprehensive, meticulous readings of the secondary literature. Clearly, events like Hitler's Nuremberg rallies, a Gospel church service, or the Woodstock Festival could be made to fit the model very well, but these highly charged collective events are a soft target for any cultural sociologist. As a rule of thumb Collins takes on more difficult material, with a turn to small-scale and low-key activities in everyday life. He talks through at length how smoking, carousing in bars and nightclubs, and even high- (or low-) quality sex can be explained using his model. These are all "micro-rituals" wherein the success or failure of the encounter depends on sustaining the conditions for a good interaction ritual. For Collins, the attractions of smoking, drinking, and sex have very little to do with pharmacology or biology. They are all about the emotional and solidaristic rewards of positive sociality.

A further ambitious push by Collins (2005) was to apply the model to intellectual production. Here he builds on his earlier work on the social origins of creative thinking in philosophy. He argues that original thinkers are not isolated individuals working by candlelight but have usually had the benefit of group interactions and networks. These fired them up, made them feel important, and gave them the energy needed to engage in creativity. With the resulting smart ideas and commitment to the enterprise, they could dominate others in the intellectual field. Usefully for our book he points out that Durkheim's own group had a collective identity and mission. Its members were successful in establishing a new paradigm thanks to intense, collective, ritual-like activity that made their task seem sacred. Things fell apart when Durkheim's death deprived the group of its totemic leader (his totemic status was the product of his group centrality) and Mauss could not take his place. The *Année sociologique* was revived, but without the intense frenzy of collaboration it had fed off before World War I (we looked into this history in chapters 2 and 3). The members had some situational power by virtue of office but increasingly lacked intellectual authority as thought leaders. A social context of regular ritual interaction had made all the difference to creativity.

Collins repeatedly highlights a crucial variable in interaction ritual: **"emotional energy."** This is commonly written as "EE." Successful interaction rituals generate a sustained positive mood and a sense of well-being. EE lets individuals "act with initiative and resolve, to set the direction of social situations rather than to be dominated by others" (2004: 134) – and so, Collins argues, it ties to stratification. Lower-status individuals are deferential, demoralized, and more emotionally disorganized. They are primed to fail by social process. Crucially, emotional energy and micro-rituals are joined together in establishing hierarchies through feedback loops. People who have access to interaction rituals feel powered up. They connect with others who have successful rituals and so form elite networks that are to their material and subjective advantage. They are cool and smart and become high-status. More important still, they think of themselves as cool, smart, and high-status and behave accordingly, working harder and dominating others. Next they derive yet more energy from being winners in the interaction rituals of deference and domination. Resources head their way, including those that enable them to stage yet more successful interaction rituals. Those who are excluded are losers who become depressed and mope about, perhaps even suffering physical or mental ill health as a result. They might try to establish their own counter-interaction rituals to bootstrap themselves out of their misery on the sidelines. If these fail, they may eventually resign themselves to second-class status and a lower place in the pecking order of life, consoled by bathing in the reflected glory of those they serve. This ritual/hierarchical system spreads itself out in chains through society and so comes to form a stratification system allocating rank, status, and mobility chances. Collins writes: "Thus high EE gives dominant persons a kind of micro-situational legitimacy ... The stratification EE thus makes other aspects of stratification particularly solid and hard to dislodge" (2004: 133).

The interaction ritual model has been widely applied and for many it is a nice compromise between cultural sociology, with its primary focus on meaning (after all, Collins does discuss totems, symbols, and rituals); pragmatism, with its view of practical situated actions and motivated actors; symbolic interactionism, with its insistence that the social world is made up of real encounters and real groups in real situations, not diffuse things like the public sphere, civil sphere, iconic consciousness, or "free-floating" codes; conflict sociology, with a vision of social competition and hierarchy; and even sociologies of the body and embodiment.

Aside from the pure intellectual merits of Collins's theory, this flexibility is one reason it has been so successful. Whereas the Strong Program is perceived as somewhat too idealist for many, with IR theory there is something for everyone to like. The nuts-and-bolts quality of the IR model in identifying the necessary factors for ritual success has also made a difference. Scholars can see just what they need to do to apply the model – "shared mood," "barrier to outsiders," "common focus of attention," etc. And so it has been widely used to explain outcomes and social dynamics in case studies about social encounters, such as qualitative historical accounts of transformative events or ethnographic materials on recurring everyday settings.

Yet the model is vulnerable to critique. There is a tendency toward ontological reduction to the material and concrete and visible – the interaction of bodies in settings. This is disturbing to those who like to think of society as having levels and layers and systems that have relative autonomy or emergent properties. Moreover, because the model highlights the embodied roots of cognition and emotion (rhythm, co-presence, shared attention) it can easily slide into biological determinism. Notwithstanding Collins's arguments against biological and pharmacological explanations for sex, drinking, smoking, and coffee consumption, theoretical possibilities exist for writing papers referring to the serotonin and frontal cortex. These are often problematic and speculative when written by sociologists who lack scientific training in the relevant disciplines. Still, opportunities perhaps exist also for connections through to the emerging field of neuro-cognitive cultural sociology associated with Vaisey, Lizardo, Levi-Martin, and others.

Another problematic issue is that Collins sees individuals relentlessly seeking ritual satisfaction. If emotional energy is a drug like cocaine, or, as Fine (2005) puts it, "cat nip," then the problem is in dealing with the diversity of associational forms and moods. We might ask: why do we not spend all our time at electronic dance music raves or participating in orgies? To his credit, Collins is aware of this issue and tries to address it in a sustained way. For example, intellectuals reading books or mystics engaging in meditation are, he says, having a kind of virtual interaction ritual with sacred ideas, enjoying energizing internal conversations with imagined others, or assuming socially approved identities (romantic outsider, rebel, thinker, artist). Often there are status rewards that come with being an acknowledged expert and center of attention. When coming out of the research library or monk's cell, actors can collect the ego-boosting EE benefits in "real" IR (Collins 2004: ch. 9; Benzecry and Collins 2014). Whether this discussion of solitary and quiet activities bolsters or undermines the collectivistic, realist premises of the model, or whether it is an Azande-style secondary elaboration (see chapter 3) that unwittingly demonstrates the joys and powers of a materially decoupled and context-free cultural system of signs and symbols, is something that readers will have to decide for themselves.

This necessary accommodation of the theory to low-key, slow-burn social realities and the extended time horizons of the stratification order has another risk. It means that emotional energy itself suddenly does not seem well defined – just when we thought we knew what it was. Most readers simply do not notice that in an effort to make his theory as general as possible, Collins rejects that idea that EE is simply "excitement, agitation, loudness" or "joy, shrieking or running" (2004: 133), although this takes him away from much of the discussion of collective effervescence in the *Elementary Forms*. It does not help that his most convincing empirical case studies in his book tend to focus on transient and high-intensity situations (e.g. carousing, sex), making casual readers think this is exactly what he is talking about with EE. When Collins says EE means having a long-term drive and direction, confidence, organizational capacity, and grit, we move toward the territory of the well-tempered personality system and to attributes of the self that do not seem particularly "emotional" or situational, but rather the product of entrenched reflexivity and discipline. Followers have generally not traveled with him in that direction, with most case studies being about immediate situations, strong emotions, and outcomes. Lastly, the discussion of how macro-structures, notably things like class, emerge in part out of micro-encounters, and of how truly consequential stratification systems (something more important than hanging out with the coolest people at a bar) have a large situational component, is not as developed as many would like. The specific connections of micro and macro are perhaps better made in his earlier book, *Conflict Sociology* (1975).

Other Durkheimian Work in Sociology in the United States

The Strong Program and interaction ritual theory are the two big explicitly Durkheimian paradigms to have emerged in American sociology. They have evolved thanks to a comprehensive, bottom-up reconstruction of Durkheim's work by noted theorists. Yet Alexander and Collins are not the only Durkheim-inflected scholars to be highly influential in the United States. There is a vague penumbra of Durkheimian work where the footprints are sparse but the spoor are visible to the knowledgeable tracker.

Durkheim's work was also to influence **Michèle Lamont**, although in a more diffuse and less theory-dense way. Lamont's keynote theme has been to demonstrate that meanings and moral boundaries are a pivotal dimension of social life. This echoes but also updates Durkheim's belief in collective morality and moral regulation, but splits away from his understandings of a general societal collective conscience. Lamont tends to work with demographic segments or occupational categories ("professors," "working men," "upper managers") and explore their members' personal (but as it turns out shared or socialized) attitudes. Using interview studies, she uncovers the underlying criteria or cultural codes through which the social category of interest attributes worth and with it status.

The key themes in Lamont's work are perhaps first visible in an influential collection that she co-edited with the noted Durkheim scholar and biographer Marcel Fournier (Lamont and Fournier 1992). The book, which helped put cultural sociology on the map in the early 1990s, consisted of case studies of **symbolic boundaries**. In their introduction to the volume, Lamont and Fournier highlight the tradition that ran from Durkheim and Mauss through Lévi-Strauss to Douglas and the ways that this opened up the questions of classification, belonging, knowledge, and exclusion that were later explored by more critical traditions investigating stratification. The pattern of looking at how solidarity and group identity were imbricated with hierarchy and stigma was to endure in Lamont's work. Hence in her first monograph, which came out in the same year, Lamont set out to:

> compare competing definitions of what it means to be a "worthy person" by analyzing symbolic boundaries, i.e. by looking at implicit definitions of purity present in the labels interviewees use to describe, abstractly and concretely, people with whom they don't want to associate, people to whom they consider themselves to be superior and inferior, and people who arouse hostility, indifference, and sympathy. (1992: xvii)

The findings indicated that morality, which was a goal and a value in itself, made a difference in the ways that middle-class people made judgments, especially in the United States. These allowed Lamont to directly challenge Bourdieu and his vision of distinctions and classifications as inherently competitive, hierarchical, and framed in terms of cultural capital, while at the same time agreeing with him that distinctions are pivotal in social life.

Lamont (2000) went on to consider how the working class saw itself as worthy and dignified rather than as oppressed or degraded. *The Dignity of Working Men* showed how workers in America and France drew distinctions through "boundary work" (2000: 3) with reference to virtue, to sharing, to thrift, discipline, and generosity. These were the "salient principles of classification and identification" (2000: 4). Although this book, like *Money, Morals, and Manners*, has a Durkheimian spirit, it is even more buried. For example, a reference in footnote seventeen records the influence of the methods of W. Lloyd Warner's Yankee City study. Quotations from informants, not screeds from *Primitive Classification* or the *Division of Labor*, dominate the main text. These are legitimate choices for framing the work and anchoring its significance. In this sense Lamont's work is a paradigm case for a more general methodological problem we face in this book. We are writing about the "Durkheimian tradition." Deciding where the edges of this task are to be drawn is a hermeneutic exercise that becomes increasingly a matter of opinion as textual evidence dries up. We are left with inferences based on research topics and questions, scholarly trajectories, styles of thought, and forms of explanation. With Lamont, it must be admitted that over time the Durkheimian inflection with regard to classification that we find most clearly in the early edited collection with Fournier has been attenuated. Lamont has generated an increasingly inclusive paradigm that makes use of French pragmatism, Bourdieu, and also ongoing American sociology on race, national identity, and ethnicity as this looks at social boundary construction. Durkheim has taken a back seat, but I like to think he plays a role in setting out the broad agenda with his profound understanding that morality, solidarity, and classification are at the core of social life and collective identity.

Just as important in field-building as Lamont was **Viviana Zelizer**. In the case of Zelizer the pivotal work for kick-starting a new paradigm was *Morals and Markets* (Zelizer 2017). This shows that there was early resistance to life insurance. It was seen in a way as gambling with God and as an improper way to think about or manage death. As Kieran Healy notes in his introduction to the 2017 edition, this book "begins with broadly Durkheimian questions about seemingly fundamental divides between the sacred and the profane, and a strong contrast between gift-based and market-based solutions to exchange problems" (Healy 2017: xvii). The result was a study that opened up

202

issues relating to the ways that culture impacts upon the economy, economic change, and economic institutions. This was a fundamental move insofar as economic life is widely held to be the most rational, utilitarian, and soulless sphere of the social system.

Morals and Markets was quickly followed by another high-impact work, *Pricing the Priceless Child* (1985). This demonstrated how children had once been seen in utilitarian terms as bodies for labor or as a family resource. During the nineteenth century they were suddenly sentimentalized and viewed as valued, vulnerable beings. Put another way, there was a movement from a profane to a sacred status. New discourses about nurturing, protecting, and developing were associated with this shift, as were legislative protections against child labor. Zelizer (1994) went on to write about the complex social meanings of money, suggesting that Simmel was wrong in treating it as homogenous and as flattening out meaning. Even Mary Douglas, she says, did not "go far enough with the cultural analysis of money" (1994: 23). For Zelizer, money was not all the same. She discusses how money might be set aside or used for special purposes according to where it came from – a process she dubs "earmarking." An inheritance from a grandparent or a birthday gift or a welfare check would be cases in point. There are differing expectations about where, when, and how money should be spent depending on the social relationships involved, the signals that needed to be sent, and the duties and obligations connected to social roles or personal histories. She writes: "As Marcel Mauss observed in 1914, money is 'essentially a social fact.' The earmarking of money is thus a social process: money is attached to a variety of social relations rather than to individuals" (1994: 25). This is a classic Durkheimian argument of a kind that would not be unfamiliar to a structural functionalist anthropologist from the Oxford group in looking at economic life in an African village. They had always insisted that social relations came first and that prestations and consumption reflected a cultural order made up of roles, rituals, rites, and obligations. Zelizer arrived at this point from a different origin and with the sensibilities of a widely read, sociologically informed cultural historian.

Zelizer's work has had a wide influence as an illustration of how (very loosely Durkheimian) historical and case-study work could be conducted in American sociology, and, equally noteworthy, that such work could get disciplinary recognition. It is important to remember that Zelizer was publishing such studies well before theorists like Alexander or Collins had fully embraced Durkheim. In a sense she was the true pioneer. How so? The explanation lies in Zelizer's longstanding interest in social history, a field that had been receptive to the cultural turn long before sociology in the United States. Indeed for many years cultural sociology was borrowing from or influenced by the examples set by culturally minded historical sociologists. Papers in the 1980s and early 1990s would routinely cite cultural historians like William Sewell Jr., Lynn Hunt, or Mona Ozouf. It is also instructive to reflect that in building a field of moral-economic-cultural sociology, Zelizer achieved where the *Année sociologique* in-house economic sociologist Simiand (see chapter 2) failed. His many volumes are a little too earnest and argue sometimes with data but often by assertion and abstraction. Like Alexander's much later neofunctionalism, they did not have an elective affinity with the style of the cultural turn. Zelizer's books make for a more attractive read and they show as well as tell. By dealing with questions relating to the economy, and by taking advantage of the cultural turn, Zelizer's work cut immediately right to the heart of materialist, rationalist sociology in a way that Simiand's could not. The field she started has become a large although not an exclusively Durkheimian one. Perhaps inevitably, influences from Bourdieu and Foucault arrived. Yet references to kindred spirits such as Mary Douglas or Daniel Miller are also commonplace in the literature. The field at present is one of the most substantial in cultural sociology as scholars write about meanings of markets, commodities, and prices, economic taboos, the role of narratives and codes in shaping value, branding and reputation, and the personal significance of particular items of material culture (see Wherry 2012; Woodward 2007).

The collective memory tradition initiated by Maurice Halbwachs gained strong momentum from the 1980s onward and remains one of the most impressive, visible, and active legacies of the Durkheimain tradition. **Barry Schwartz** was probably the most notable early adopter as far as American cultural sociology was concerned. Schwartz has become so well known for his work on collective memory that it is often forgotten that his Durkheimian influences and interests are diverse. For example, an early paper considered the social psychology of the gift (Schwartz 1967). A book on vertical classification (Schwartz 1981) makes use of Lévi-Strauss, Durkheim, and Needham and deploys structuralist binaries to look at how metaphors of "high" and "low" map almost universally onto inequality. In the early 1980s Schwartz started to take a greater interest in Presidential reputations. For example, a paper on the meaning of George Washington in his own times was framed around the Weberian idea of charisma (Schwartz 1983). It noted that Washington had enhanced his reputation and power by repeatedly turning down office. The interpretation of this act as anti-tyrannical consolidated his authority. By the early 1990s Schwartz was writing at full steam about issues of memory and commemoration. A keynote in his work during this period and afterward was to locate himself broadly in the Durkheimian tradition, but to push back against cultural relativism and the idea that the past was infinitely malleable. He thought that Halbwachs had gone too far. For example, Washington, a wealthy patrician landowner, was never quite able to shed his aristocratic image. Unlike Lincoln, who was born in a cabin, Washington could not be seen as a man of the people (Schwartz 1991). Swartz insists that he is following Durkheim when he argues that ritual carries the past into the present and that it is the weight and reality of past facts and historical experiences that to some extent consecrate the collectivity today.

Schwartz was also one of the first Durkheimian scholars to explore deeply problematic and contested memories. An influential paper with Robin Wagner-Pacifici investigated the Vietnam Veterans Memorial in Washington, seeing this as an example of "genre problem" (Wagner-Pacifici and Schwartz 1991). The paper marked a turning point in memory studies, shifting attention from how memory reinforces solidarity in a simple Durkheimian way toward reflecting more on how it is contested, complex, and ambivalent – what is now the common sense *problématique* for so many papers in the memory studies literature. The Vietnam War, which had been lost and which had caused great division in the nation, needed to be acknowledged as a tragic mistake and not celebrated as a victory. The soldiers needed to be seen as heroic patriots, not as losers, or as willing accomplices in a mistaken enterprise. How could these ends be accomplished? A complex and multivalent memorial emerged from a series of design decisions, protests, and bolt-on compromises. Names engraved on a black marble wall individualized sacrifice. A flagpole was added to signal patriotism and to align the dead with the national sacred. A sculpture of exhausted soldiers offered pathos. The analysis remains exemplary as a study of how material culture, narrative, and commemoration come together in a complex assemblage in the shadow of collective memory.

Moving on from George Washington and the Vietnam memorial, Schwartz (2000) went on to write a very substantial volume of work on Abraham Lincoln. This precisely delineated the way the President had been a flexible sacred symbol over the years in response to political and social exigencies. Schwartz demonstrates that Lincoln was variously seen as the champion of the ordinary man, a fighter against racism, or as a war leader depending on the circumstances within which the larger nation found itself over the hundred years following his assassination. These multiple personae were not conjured from nothing. Rather they drew in selective ways on various aspects of his real biography.

Written with meticulous attention to detail, much of Schwartz's work might be thought of as an accommodation of earlier Durkheimian ideas on memory (Halbwachs) and the nation (Bellah, Shils) to realism, the recognition of pluralism, and the decline of grand narratives, but without giving up entirely on the idea of sacred symbols and sacred nations. Something of this nature can also be found in Lyn Spillman's (1991) comparative account of centennial and bicentennial celebrations of the founding of Australia and the United States. Whereas the centennials could be understood in their time in a straightforward way as a celebration of a shared, triumphant narrative of nation building, the bicentennials were contested. Indigenous people, women, minorities, and other excluded groups challenged dominant narratives in the collective memory. The result was a move toward empty spectacle with which nobody could disagree. An example would be the ever-popular firework display. But, of course, none of this meant that the national identity itself was not meaningful. To the contrary, Spillman shows it remained something worth fighting over. Led by Schwartz, Jeffrey Olick, and others, memory studies became firmly institutionalized as a medium-sized field and was in 2008 to have its own journal. Today the legacy of Halbwachs stands alongside that of Mauss as the most significant of any immediate member of Durkheim's team.

Whereas Collins derives a situational stratification model from Durkheim via Goffman, and whereas Lamont looks at the meaningful boundaries members of classes set up, a more traditional class-based stratification sociology alternative emerged in the influential work of **David Grusky**. Trained in quantitative methods and intimately familiar with the stratification literature, Grusky comes to Durkheim from an unusual place. As this book has demonstrated, most scholars with an interest in Durkheim have background interests in culture and theory. Grusky, however, uses Durkheim to think through empirical issues in the largely positivist stratification field.

According to Grusky, Durkheim has been unfairly neglected as a class analyst and yet his thinking was prescient concerning the nature of solidarity or what some might term class-consciousness in the world today. Stratification research with regard to economic life has long been divided between two camps. Some are concerned

with the occupational status and prestige hierarchies and their consequences. The core patterns have been well documented and validated
through survey work. The findings here are empirically accurate but
treatments by scholars can be descriptive and theory-light. Others,
more influenced by Marx and by social theory, focus on large-scale
class categories ("proletariat," "workers," "owners," etc.) into which
many occupations can be subsumed. This latter group have claimed
to be able to account for macro-events like revolutions as well as
individual behaviors like voting. However, their explanations have
been plagued by a messy fit with reality and by behaviors that did
not follow theoretical predictions about class interests (for example,
workers voting for a right-of-center party). Moreover, class identification has proven stubbornly weak. When respondents are asked
how strongly they feel "working-class" they are often confused by the
question or rank class identity lower than other identities ("plumber,"
"sports fan," etc.). Grusky notes that class theory has moved the
goalposts in response to these failures. Initially conceived to explain
transformative world-historical events (revolution, democratic inclusion), such class theory increasingly makes more modest claims about
attitudes or lifestyles or has adjusted its definitions of "class." Grusky
characterizes this "tinkering, adapting and revising" as "the flailing
efforts of a subfield" (Grusky and Galescu 2005: 350). Nonetheless,
analysts clung to their core beliefs as a consequence of theoretical
or political commitments and on the basis that they explained some
patterns in the data. Grusky dubs such failures "big class" models
and insists that a return to Durkheim's vision of smaller occupational
solidarities offers a way to resolve many problems. It brings class
theory and more empirically accurate or mainstream stratification
theories into dialogue. It allows a better fit with observed behavior,
survey data, and the grand narrative of managed industrial conflict,
but does not give up on connections to more general social theory.

Grusky suggests that Durkheim's work provides insights into the
institutionalization of conflict that rendered big classes unviable in
the long run, and the ways that "small classes" (i.e. *gemeinschaftlich*
occupations) shape individual values, life chances, and lifestyles. In
this formulation, smaller organizations in the workplace fulfill at
least some of the activities that were supposed to be the province
of big class organizations, such as offering ethical guidance, resolv-
ing or initiating conflicts, and providing political representation (we
discussed these ideas in chapters 1 and 2). Occupations also provide
the foundation for attitudes and lifestyles thanks to processes of selective recruitment, socialization, and interaction, and the formation of

common political aims. This broad-brush characterization of what occupations do can be specified more precisely for diverse contexts and so explain divergent findings in data sets. For example, Germany has vocational training and apprenticeship systems that facilitate the emergence of strong occupational identities, whereas in Sweden big classes or aggregate classes have become stronger political operators.

Other Durkheimian Fields

This chapter so far has had a focus on cultural sociology in the United States, as this has been the place where the coherent, new, general paradigms and tools for social explanation have emerged since the mid-1980s. But it is important to inject a note of caution. Cultural sociology in the United States is by no means the only place where Durkheimian agendas have been pushed forward. We conclude by observing several other domains where Durkheim seems more relevant than ever.

Most obviously, Durkheim remains pivotal in the field of Durkheim studies. The comment is non-banal when we realize that this field was in a rapid growth phase during the period covered by this chapter. In 1975 there were arguably only a handful of Durkheim experts in the world who had done the hard yards – Steven Lukes, for example. By 2005 there were perhaps a dozen people who could debate the nuances of translation, or trade references to obscure letters and footnotes. Although there were some eminent exceptions globally, most such scholars were in Europe, and certainly the center of gravity was there at the interpersonal level. We noted at the start of this chapter that the *Durkheimian Studies/Études Durkheimiennes* group was embryonic in the 1980s. By the 1990s it was well populated and about to enter a highly productive period, supported somewhat by having a low-budget institutional home in the Oxford Center for Durkheimian Studies. Noted scholars in the circle included Philippe Besnard, Massimo Borlandi, Mark Cladis, Marcel Fournier, Mike Gane, Alexander Gofman, Robert Alun Jones, Susan Steadman Jones, Josep Llobera, Steven Lukes, Hans-Peter Müller, Frank Pearce, William S. F. Pickering, Alexander Riley, Kenneth Thompson, Edward Tiryakian, Stephen Turner, and William Watts Miller, among many others.

Output proliferated from this unusually intellectual, cosmopolitan, solidaristic, and international group starting around 1990 (see, for example, publication dates for items below). The scholarship tended to be concerned with biography, intellectual history, and interpretative reconstruction. It often engaged in the mode of social and political theory that is toward the philosophical end of the spectrum. A shared mission was to validate Durkheim as a first-rank intellectual. This last point is of note. Notwithstanding rigorous scholarship there is often a modestly boosterish subtext. Books often argue not just that Durkheim wrote about this or that but also that he had profound or unparalleled insights. This perspective perhaps inevitably accompanies the huge investments that are needed to get on top of a body of difficult work. Who will devote their life to studying someone and then decide they are second rate? The enthusiasm was a good thing as it offset the occasionally realist and critical tone of the previously dominant resource, which was the biography by Lukes (1973). That substantial analysis had given a good deal of attention to documenting confusions and imprecisions in Durkheim's work. Such moments could occlude those where Lukes celebrated Durkheim's achievements.

Evidence of a collective mission for this group can be found in the many edited volumes or collections of essays as well as in the *Durkheimian Studies/Études Durkheimiennes* journal itself. Often the books consisted of assembled papers considering one or more themes that were in dispute or in need of clarification. Yet some collections were highly eclectic. For example, *Debating Durkheim* (Pickering and Martins 1994) contains essays variously considering Durkheim's Jewishness, his views of method, sociological facts, the nation, and modernity. Other edited books revolved around a theme. Hence *Emile Durkheim: Sociologist and Moralist* (Turner 1993) contained essays that drew attention to the conjunction of the normative and analytic in Durkheim's work. We find this second pattern is the one generally repeated in the single-authored volumes from group affiliates. Even when they spanned the entirety of Durkheim's life and works, these tended to have a leitmotif that offered a lens for the activity of selection and interpretation. So in *Durkheim, Morals and Modernity*, Watts Miller (1996) offers an overview of Durkheim that has a loose focus on his views on morality, law, the division of labor, ethics, and virtue (i.e., as the title says, "morals and modernity"). Likewise Frank Pearce (1989) identified *The Radical Durkheim*, rubbing him up against Marx, speaking of a critical intellectual, and highlighting possibilities for a more comprehensive theory of social justice.

As already mentioned, by and large the work of this group was about "Durkheim" rather than about "society." It works to clarify his thinking, correct erroneous interpretations, demonstrate how his work was connected to his biographical context or other thinkers of his era, and illustrate the evolution of his ideas. This was a deeply scholarly milieu. Perhaps for that reason it was somewhat inward looking. Would that it was otherwise, but the scholars were largely talking to a small audience of social theorists and intellectual historians like themselves. Of course the work was important, but at least when measured in terms of citations, disciplinary impacts were higher for the kind of Durkheim scholarship that came to him from the outside and attempted to connect him to theory in major subfields (e.g. Garland 1990 in the case of punishment and criminology); that reworked his theory with an eye to improved general explanatory models (e.g. Alexander and Collins above), or that used his ideas as a source of inspiration for empirical inquiry wherein the *explicans* in the real world was the focus of attention (Grusky, Lamont, Zelizer above). The most important contribution for a wider social science legacy might not have been this or that specific interpretation or debate on a point of detail. It was arguably that these scholars reminded the community that Durkheim was not just the author of four books. In mining particular themes and topics, they inevitably came to display the fact that he had completed many medium-sized book projects in lecture series, innumerable extended essays, and multiple reviews. Durkheim's status as a prolific and multi-faceted intellectual was at last coming to the fore.

More recently, the generational wheel has seen the *Durkheimian Studies/Études Durkheimiennes* group lose some of its momentum. By 2018 a series of deaths and retirements had reduced the flow of published work. Younger scholars such as Alexander Riley are also involved with the wider field of cultural sociology, publishing not only on Durkheim and his group but also on popular culture and wider cultural theory. It is perhaps indicative that one of the later volumes attributable to the collectivity, *Durkheim, Durkheimians and the Arts* (Riley, Pickering, and Miller 2013) moved somewhat in this direction. As well as explicating, mining, and reconstructing texts by Durkheim and his followers, there are moves made in the book toward the analysis of art worlds and artistic traditions, and thence the scholars begin to engage with cultural sociology as a whole.

Arguably the center of gravity for work in the tradition of *Durkheimian Studies/Études Durkheimiennes* shifted toward German-speaking areas as momentum ebbed in France and the United Kingdom. Some two decades after the death of René König, a concentration of researchers emerged fascinated by the history of

Durkheim and the *Année*, by their work and its reception. Evidence of a newfound critical mass can be seen in the growing number of edited volumes after 2010. These featured intellectually dense, theoretical, and historically informed essays (e.g. Bogusz and Delitz 2013; Gephart and Witte 2017). To be sure, the contributors were generally theory all-rounders rather than Durkheim specialists in the manner of the *Durkheimian Studies/Études Durkheimiennes* group. Still, these efforts demonstrated there was at last a coterie of thinkers in Germany, Austria, and Switzerland interested in seriously engaging with the ideas of Durkheim and his students.

The most important figure in the German academic culture area trying to do something really ambitious was **Hans Joas** (2000; 2013). A truly international scholar associated not only with German sociology but very much with the University of Chicago, Joas had (arguably) been slowly migrating toward Durkheim for years. As a theorist with a normative agenda he had a longstanding interest in ethical action, coming to believe that the primary human experience of transcendence rather than abstract morality or social rules could form the basis for community and solidarity. Joas looked to William James and Charles Taylor, but it was Durkheim who was perhaps the most important contributor to his ideas. He built somewhat on René König's vision of Durkheim as a theorist of moral innovation (see Joas 1993) and found the *Elementary Forms* provided him with a tractable theory of emotion, belonging, and, crucially, the interpretation of powerful emotions via cultural frames. As Stephan Moebius (2020) points out, this emphasis on immediate experiential or existential aspects of the sacred as the foundation for society make Joas an unlikely heir to the line of thinking pushed by Bataille and the *Collège de sociologie* some seventy years before. Other figures in a leadership role in the German area since the 1980s were Bernhard Giesen and Hans-Peter Müller. During the 1990s and 2000s, Giesen and his group at Konstanz engaged in wide-ranging efforts at cultural sociology that were very much influenced by the Strong Program. Topics included classification, memory, iconicity, cultural trauma, and narrative. Müller was probably for many years the leading Durkheim specialist scholar in Germany. Indeed he had organized the conference in 1983 on the late Durkheim that had facilitated Jeffrey Alexander's transition out of neofunctionalism.

Another body of scholarship that continued to evolve was the Mary Douglas grid/group paradigm. This remained active in Britain and the United States. Although we considered Douglas's work in the prior chapter so as to keep it together in one place, it should

211

be remembered that *How Institutions Think* appeared in 1985 and that she continued to be an active scholar until her death in 2007. Douglas became more and more interested in theology and Biblical scholarship in her final years. She was also intrigued by something many would see as completely opposite from these seemingly humanist concerns – the material dimensions of brain function. Regardless, somehow sociological inquiry started to play second fiddle. The grid/group torch was passed in this period from cultural anthropology to political science and organizational studies. Perri 6 and Paul Richards (2017) report that the study of risk perception in North America and Europe was in large part responsible for this shift. A notable trend was toward psychometric approaches that attempted to map public attitudes concerning environmental or political issues using survey research, pushing the model in a more positivistic, quantitative, individualistic, demographic and less social-morphological, Durkheimian direction (see Kahan, Jenkins-Smith, and Braman 2011).

During the 1990s Michael Thompson and Aaron Wildavsky were more visible enthusiasts and advocates of grid/group than Douglas herself and published the key texts of the decade. The book *Cultural Theory* (Thompson, Ellis, and Wildavsky 1990; see also Wildavsky 1998) was particularly influential in translating a model based on esoteric anthropology and the sociology of knowledge for a less theoretically skilled/interested audience of political science and management professors. The main focus was on describing variation among the four forms of social organization defined by grid/group and asking what happened in each when challenging, anomalous, or disruptive events occurred. There was an emphasis on instabilities and the process of social learning through which organizations adapted (or didn't). The book was successful in part, as it presented a somewhat stylized vision of social or social-psychological types: hierarchy, individualism, fatalism, egalitarianism, etc. Whereas Douglas's own books were characterized by nuance and combination almost to a fault (they can be hard work), *Cultural Theory* was an easy, somewhat catchy read that seemed to offer a silver bullet for organizational diagnosis and reform. During the 1990s and 2000s, it was repeatedly shown that the model in one form or another could be applied to policy, attitudes, beliefs, dispute resolution, risk sensitivities, and thought styles.

Although still highly visible, the pathway coming out of the book *Cultural Theory* is just one in the Mary Douglas tradition. As noted in the last chapter, common complaints about Mary Douglas's paradigm have included reference to a static vision of locked-in cosmologies, confusion as to what "grid" referred to, and worries about the low-group/high-grid cell. Advocates have pushed back, suggesting critics do not fully understand the subtlety of the model and its potential (e.g. 6 2014: 95–9; 6 and Richards 2017). Notwithstanding such denials, much recent work has in fact responded to such critique. Indeed supporters of Douglas like 6 and Richards have been at the forefront of a theoretical spring-cleaning. This attempts to recover the potentials and identify the complexities in Douglas's work that have not been noticed by critics and enthusiasts alike. Applications have generally speaking become less dogmatic. Scholars have avoided deifying Douglas and her original formulation and locking this in as a source of oracular truth (see 6 and Richards 2017). For example, there has been more attention paid to what happens when several Douglasian elementary forms must coexist within a larger context (e.g. different branches of an organization); avoidance of simple, one-word summaries of the value orientations of each cell ("market," "hierarchy"); attention given to layered cell complexity; attempts to revive the high-grid/low-group cell with reference to levels of social regulation; and a subtle shift from talking about the content of cell beliefs to talking about "styles" of thought, judgment, justification, or policy. The idea is increasingly to highlight that this is a model not of ideology or beliefs but rather of how people handle their beliefs, for example with zealotry, with diffidence, instrumentally, or flexibly. Some parsimony and ambition are arguably lost through these accommodations, but by the same token the model starts to have a more nuanced fit with empirical realities. Perri 6 (2014; 2016) provides an example here. He shows how British government policy in the 1950s through to the 1970s shifted around. He uses neo-Durkheimian Douglasian theory, and explains that policy oscillates in its ambition and shifts in its intellectual coherence according to the grid/group location of the Prime Minister with regard to informal elite and party support during the term of an administration. The analysis is intriguing and detailed, but traditionalists might wonder whether it has moved too far from the Africanist origins of the paradigm and its interest in enduring social groups, interaction densities, baked-in cosmologies, and so forth. Now fleeting alliances, contexts, and political opportunity structures, not "groups" or the dynamogenic density of social contact, seem to be doing the lifting as an external environment of action.

Moving on from the grid/group paradigm, we can briefly note Durkheim's growing relevance for a comparative social psychology that is concerned with brain function, cognition, judgment, deliberation, and human evolution. Durkheim's focus on group beliefs, morality, and the sacred has been taken as ancestral to recent efforts to explain and identify divergent but seemingly entrenched value clusters in modern society, such as those separating liberals and conservatives. In this context, Durkheim's sociology is seen as an antidote to overly individualistic and rational explanations for moral orientations, and as compatible with themes in evolutionary biology regarding the primacy of group loyalty. Pivotal here has been the figure of Jonathan Haidt (2012). He sees Durkheim as a conservative who first mapped out the interplay, social origins, and clustering of authority, tradition, hierarchy, and sacrality that we find empirically today in attitudinal survey responses and experimental results. According to Haidt, this "Planet Durkheim" (his term) mentality is endorsed by large proportions of the United States population and sits behind their conservative beliefs about fairness, care, and economic redistribution. These shape in turn attitudes to specifics like gun control, welfare, or civic duty. Planet Durkheim is deeply wired into the brain and predates modernity. It is "the form of structure in which human evolution took place and the context in which intuitive ethics became part of the human mind" (Haidt and Graham 2009: 383). By contrast, liberal ideas about individual choice and freedom are cultural products arising from the recent transition to modernity. This saw a weakening of customary constraints upon action and a growing trend toward reflexivity that has been only partially institutionalized in moral systems.

The simplistic representation of Durkheim as an advocate rather than analyst of traditional conservative thought is a perhaps misleading aspect of the work of Haidt. For example, we should remember that Durkheim defended modern individualism as a sacred value. He also advocated for the state and occupational associations to take over from traditional sources of solidarity. We might add that most contemporary sociologists influenced by neuro-cognitive social psychology, including those citing Haidt, associate Durkheim not with their own camp but with the semiotic, discursive, deliberative, and representational forms of cultural explanation that they openly argue against. However, a glance at Haidt's general direction of travel can be useful. It helps indicate often forgotten potentials in the Durkheimian legacy; for example, that divergent moralities and worldviews are extremely amenable to quantification and attitudinal survey research methods. This is a quality that has also been exploited by some work adapting the Douglas grid/group model (see above). And for all the dominance of humanistic cultural theory today among Durkheim's devotees, connections can still be made through to more materialist evolutionary and biological paradigms. After all, Durkheim wrote a lot about the mind, the body, human activity, culture, and how these are shaped by collective life. Moreover, his texts are full of organic analogies and evolutionary narratives. Perhaps it should not be surprising that even a "cultural" scholar like Robert Bellah (2005) has explicitly drawn on evolutionary thinking to explain how ritual works via the body. Likewise in our first two chapters we noted that Durkheim had somewhat essentialist understandings of sex and gender. From the perspective of constructivist sociology and contemporary feminism these thoughts are deeply problematic. Yet ideas about hard-wired sexual differences in thought, judgment, emotion, and behavior are a stock-in-trade for many other disciplines, such as experimental psychology and evolutionary biology (for a compendium of such claims see Geary 2010). Durkheimian thought arguably offers pathways and opportunities in this direction even if they are unlikely to be a popular choice for many anthropologists and sociologists.

We conclude this chapter at the opposite end of the intellectual spectrum from biology, psychology, statistics, and science, and consider the attention Durkheimian scholars continue to give to philosophical and normative issues related to social theory and social repair. Back in its day Durkheim's work, of course, was centrally concerned with saving, or more modestly strengthening, the Third Republic. His own interpretation of the world around him saw anomie everywhere. This was instantiated in things like strikes and suicide rates. He argued the problem was associated with a transition to modernity that had been too rapid to permit corresponding and necessary cultural and institutional changes. Durkheim also proposed solutions that would bring solidarity to society and moral purpose to life. These would be things like reforms in education, an end to inherited wealth, and the emergence of guild-like industrial associations. After his death, such concerns had been reduced to tedious mantras in the French philosophy curriculum and then pushed aside for most of the twentieth century (we covered all this in chapters 1 and 2).

In more recent years, theorists have revisited Durkheim as a source of wisdom or insight concerning what is wrong with the world today. Normative Durkheimian theory, commentary, and humanist reflection have returned. The cumulative thrust of the work has been to push back against Paul Nizan and to suggest that Durkheim can be styled as a liberal, critical (even radical) thinker (Fournier 2005: 48; Pearce 1989) who was ahead of the game in thinking about the problems of modernity, morality, freedom, difference, and political organization. As Mike Gane (1992: 1) put it, "conventional commentary on Durkheim and Mauss in English" had not understood "just how radical the Durkheimian project attempted to be." It was regrettably treated as "simple-minded" and introductory sociology texts were misleading when they continued to "present a contrast between Marx and the revolutionary tradition and Durkheim in a conservative tradition."

Gane may well be right, but it is of course not immediately evident to everyone that Durkheim has this potential. Durkheim can still be seen as problematic or as in need of extremely complex theoretical redemptions. For example, in her effort to recover whatever normative and critical potentials Durkheim might have, Jennifer Lehmann (1993: 1) had to engage in a strategy of "close, textual/subtextual/ countertextual, symptomatic, 'writerly' reading ... which works against the grain of Durkheim's writing ... [This] looks for contradictions, ambiguities, and *aporia* rather than coherence, clarity, and plenitude." Although she judges that Durkheim falls short on most criteria, such as having worthwhile views on gender, class, or the radical reform of capitalism, Lehmann finds some hope in his "ontological and epistemological anti-subjectivism of social determinism and material rationalism" (1993: 8). It is a reading that curiously mirrors and flips Durkheim's own points of grudging praise for Marxism, seeing in it the elements of a structural understanding of society that moved beyond common sense (see chapter 2).

Going further than Lehmann, Zygmunt Bauman (2005) sees the case as quite straightforward and as beyond salvage. As he is less concerned than she is with recovering anything positive, he can launch into a scathing polemic. Informed by his wider postmodern social constructivism, Bauman suggests Durkheim's thinking about society was actively dangerous. It reified "society" into something hard and material, compelling duty, rather than seeing it as something socially constructed or imagined. Behind this, of course, was Durkheim's political ambition for his new discipline. It was all part of a "managerial posture" (2005: 365) with which modernity tried to "manage the world of humans and to make it manageable" (2005: 366). This involved efforts to eliminate "anything impenetrable, ambiguous, ambivalent, accidental and contingent" (2005: 366). In his other work Bauman sees this task of regulating, measuring, and controlling as leading to the Holocaust. So Durkheim was on the wrong side of history, much as he had been for Paul Nizan. Fortunately, Bauman asserted, times had changed and modernity was becoming more liquid. Old hierarchies, rules, and systems were breaking down in economic life, and grand designs no longer ruled the world of politics.

> Life-challenges, life-tasks, and life-pursuits tend to assume today colors and shapes quite different from those they bore in Durkheim's time ... They used to be, essentially, outcomes of and responses to the order-design-and-order-built concerns and actions of societal power. They are today, essentially, outcomes of and responses to the fading, phasing-out, and demise of such concerns. (2005: 379)

So Bauman can turn off the alarm bells and we can relax: Durkheim, no longer particularly dangerous, is becoming more irrelevant. As might be expected, Bauman says that what is needed instead of Durkheim is a more open, dialogical, ethical, reflexive kind of social theory and social vision. We might push back, perhaps, against this reading in several ways – for example, by pointing to the cult of the individual and the way that this has helped generate discourses on rights (Joas 2013) or to Durkheim's own suspicion of wealth, religion, and socialism. However, the strongest response might be through jujitsu and to point to the unexpected paths through which the Durkheimian tradition came to inform the very postmodern, existential, critical theory that Bauman endorses (e.g. Riley 2013; see end of chapter 4).

In fact Bauman is today something of an outlier with his negative normative reading of Durkheim. Most scholars see the French master in a positive light. Noted early efforts toward identifying a radical potential in Durkheim were made by Mike Gane (1992) and by Frank Pearce (1989). These authors fully acknowledged that Durkheim was opposed to communism and violent social change. However, the argument was made that Durkheim's structural orientation toward social explanation, his complex critique of social dysfunctions, his belief that modernity was tethered to growing egalitarianism, and his advocacy of collective life are at the root of a radical agenda that is in no way complacent or easily written off as an apologia for the status quo. Around the same time Stjepan Meštrović (1992) made an eclectic but also positive reading in which he sees in Durkheim a kind of proto-postmodernist, with his vision of communication and collective representation at the heart of social life, and his concern to diagnose and interpret *fin de siècle* anxieties. Likewise Mark Cladis (1992) made a particularly detailed, careful reading to show that Durkheim has been misunderstood as a conservative: "Not preserving the status quo, but working to transform it so that it better realizes and extends liberal democratic institutions and the normative

217

social conditions that sustain them – this describes Durkheim's vocation" (1992: 255).

For Cladis, Durkheim's project was not foundationalist (as Bauman would later style it) but rather attempted to show how meaning and morality were historically conditioned. The task of scholars and citizens in Durkheim's vision was to reflect upon this social morality. Cladis cites Durkheim's essay "Individualism and the Intellectuals" as Durkheim's best effort to reconstruct a common liberal faith and to hold his compatriots accountable to their own higher standard. It marks a way to move beyond the duality of communitarian and liberal theory by indicating that the group value was for increased individual rights, dignity, and self-expression.

Reflections on Durkheim's political and moral relevance for our age can be driven not just by such efforts at comprehensive theoretical reconstruction. Scholars have also been responding to the perplexing, the good, and the bad in the world around them in an *ad hoc* way. In recent work Durkheim has repeatedly proven to offer excellent resources for analyzing troubling current events (Alexander and Jaworsky 2014; Smith 2005; Strenski 2006). From such understandings it is often but a small step to the explicit normative move to endorse, disapprove, or recommend. Tiryakian (1995) was an early adopter of this intellectual possibility. For example, he interpreted the unpredicted "velvet revolutions" associated with the fall of communism in 1989 with ideas of contagious collective effervescence, this being engendered in spontaneous and courageous demonstrations in public space. Mark Cladis (2005) wrote in the wake of the 2001 terrorist attacks in the United States and observed the solidarity that emerged in the nation. He asks what it would take for this sense of solidarity to become more general and to be found outside of such exceptional times. Durkheim provides resources, as he can "help us think critically about the obstacles we face in achieving a genuinely multiracial, multicultural democracy" (2005: 383). For Cladis, Durkheim is significant because he understood that we could have both moral pluralism and common projects. For example, Durkheim's ideas about moral education could be used to build awareness of difference in the United States. Hence "schools are to foster in students the capacity to evaluate contemporary practices in light of alternatives found in foreign or past cultures, in new developments taking place within contemporary society, and in the long-standing ideals that need to be more fully realized in social practices" (2005: 394). Moreover, Durkheim's ideas about the state suggested that it should not be identical with the political community and that there should be intermediary groups. The state itself should support moral individualism and mitigate the corrosive impacts of capitalist globalization, sustain civic life, and so forth. The argument from Cladis, like many others in this genre, sees Durkheim as setting out a model of good society and suggesting ways to get there. Jeffrey Alexander's "performance theory" (2004, discussed above) was also illustrated with reference to the events of September 11, 2001. When terrorists attacked the United States it responded with defiance and spirit. It "performed" resilience. The choice of case study was hardly neutral. There is a sense behind the text that in the very act of investigating and understanding civil responses to terror (with a Durkheimian lens) we can come to a reflexive awareness of our solidarity and shared humanity. For all the analytic contribution, the example and theory packed a subtle normative subtext, much as Shils and Young's (1953) paper had done some fifty years before when discussing the coronation of the Queen as a celebration of democracy.

The economic crisis that started in 2008 offers yet another example of how a Durkheim who fuses aspirational, normative, analytic, and critical potential tends to pop up during times of trouble as a resource for thinking. Here we might look, for example, to contributors to a *Durkheimian Studies/Études Durkheimiennes* special edition. The financial crisis had origins in excessive speculation and poor oversight of financial institutions. Steven Lukes (2009) drew on Durkheim to argue that we needed more moral regulation and a stronger connection between capitalism and wider social solidarity. Mike Gane (2009) made use of Durkheim's analysis of the project of socialism. Socialism had demanded what Durkheim saw as an excessive connection, or lack of adequate differentiation, between economy and society. Gane argues that the logic of market capitalism in the neoliberal economy was similarly problematic. It had invaded organizations of government. Managerial techniques like rankings and benchmarks were not appropriate to schools or hospitals. We needed more differentiation organizationally and in terms of regulative norms. Edward Tiryakian (2009) makes a broadly similar critique. There had been too much "moral deregulation." However, economic issues were not the only ones we should be thinking about. There was a wider need for new forms of solidarity to be thought through that were appropriate to our time and to our changing social structures, such as those in the family.

So we end our chapter in 2020 with the Durkheimian tradition of the *Elementary Forms* pivotal in many branches of the highly productive field of cultural sociology in the United States. He has some revived influence too in normative theory and an emergent following in evolutionary psychology. Organizational theory and political science seem interested in the Mary Douglas paradigm, which remains a minor but not insignificant force. The lesson from this book, however, is that time will change everything. We have been looking over a span of decades and with the benefit of hindsight. We have seen repeatedly that paradigms ride high for about twenty or thirty years before becoming stale or being replaced. Durkheim's own group had about twenty years (say, 1893–1913) in the sun; Parsons and his structural functionalism about twenty-five (1937–62); the British structural functionalist anthropologists around thirty (1927–57); and so forth. Cultural sociology has been the major carrier of the Durkheimian legacy since about 1990 and the clock may well be ticking down on it. Readers of this book one or two decades after its publication will almost certainly be looking at a different landscape from the one visible at the time of writing. Hopefully this account will give them some tools with which to trace the new lineages and scholars and to connect them to the ones that have passed, to see how the idea-sets are assembled and recombined.

As I write, it is a little over one hundred years since Durkheim's death. His legacy has proven adaptable in ways that perhaps even his huge intellect could not have foreseen, running through structural functionalism, systems theory, structuralism, poststructuralism, and the cultural turn, and traversing sociology, anthropology, and associated disciplines, moving between the normative and analytic, abstract and concrete, theoretical and empirical, crossing the Atlantic back and forth. This book has provided but a rudimentary sketch of this complexity, with a particular eye to empirically productive theory in anthropology and sociology. It is anything but the final word. Yet as Durkheim and Mauss put it at the end of *Primitive Classification*, at least we have made a start.

References

6, Perri. 2014. "Explaining Decision-Making in Government: The Neo-Durkheimian Institutional Framework," *Public Administration* 92, 1: 87–103.

6, Perri. 2016. "Exploring Style and Political Judgment in British Government: Comparing Isolation Dynamics 1959–1974," *Journal of Political Policy* 31, 2: 219–50.

6, Perri and Richards, Paul. 2017. *Mary Douglas: Understanding Social Thought and Conflict*. New York. Berghahn Books.

Adorno, Theodor. 1967. "Einleitung," pp. 7–44 in *Emile Durkheim: Soziologie und Philosophie*. Frankfurt. Suhrkamp.

Alexander, Jeffrey C. 1978. *Theoretical Logic in Sociology. Vol. 1: Marx and Durkheim*. Berkeley. University of California Press.

Alexander, Jeffrey C. 1984. "Three Models of Culture and Society Relations: Toward an Analysis of Watergate," *Sociological Theory* 2: 290–314.

Alexander, Jeffrey C. (Ed.). 1985. *Neofunctionalism*. Thousand Oaks. Sage.

Alexander, Jeffrey C. (Ed.). 1988a. *Durkheimian Sociology: Cultural Studies*. Cambridge. Cambridge University Press.

Alexander, Jeffrey C. 1988b. "Introduction: Durkheimian Sociology and Cultural Studies Today," pp. 1–21 in J. C. Alexander (Ed.), *Durkheimian Sociology: Cultural Studies*. Cambridge. Cambridge University Press.

Alexander, Jeffrey C. 1988c. "Culture and Political Crisis: Watergate and Durkheimian Sociology," pp. 187–224 in J. C. Alexander (Ed.), *Durkheimian Sociology: Cultural Studies*. Cambridge. Cambridge University Press.

Alexander, Jeffrey C. 1992. "The Promise of a Cultural Sociology: Technological Discourse and the Sacred and Profane Information Machine," pp. 293–323 in N. Smelser and R. Munch (Eds.), *Theory of Culture*. Berkeley. University of California Press.

Alexander, Jeffrey C. 2004. "From the Depths of Despair: Performance, Counter-Performance and 'September 11,'" *Sociological Theory* 22, 1: 88–105.

Alexander, Jeffrey C. 2005 "The Inner Development of Durkheim's Sociological Theory: From Early Writings to Maturity," pp. 136–59 in J. C. Alexander and P. Smith (Eds.), *The Cambridge Companion to Durkheim*. Cambridge. Cambridge University Press.

Alexander, Jeffrey C. 2006. *The Civil Sphere*. Oxford. Oxford University Press.

Alexander, Jeffrey C., Bartmanski, Dominik, and Giesen, Bernhard (Eds.). 2012. *Iconic Power: Materiality and Meanings in Social Life*. London. Palgrave.

Alexander, Jeffrey C. and Jacobs, Ronald N. 1998. "Mass Communication, Ritual and Civil Society," pp. 23–41 in T. Liebes and J. Curran (Eds.), *Media, Ritual and Identity*. New York. Routledge.

Alexander, Jeffrey C. and Jaworsky, Bernadette N. 2014. *Obama Power*. Cambridge. Polity.

Alexander, Jeffrey C. and Smith, Philip. 1993. "The Discourse of American Civil Society: A New Proposal for Cultural Studies," *Theory and Society* 22, 2: 151–207.

Alexander, Jeffrey C. and Smith, Philip. 1996. "Social Science and Salvation: Risk Society as Mythical Discourse," *Zeitschrift für Soziologie* 25, 4: 251–68.

Alexander, Jeffrey C. and Smith, Philip. 2001. "The Strong Program in Cultural Theory: Elements of a Structural Hermeneutics," pp. 135–50 in J. Turner (Ed.), *Handbook of Social Theory*. New York. Kluwer Academic.

Alexander, Jeffrey C. and Smith, Philip. 2005. "Introduction: The New Durkheim," pp. 1–37 in J. C. Alexander and P. Smith (Eds.), *The Cambridge Companion to Durkheim*. Cambridge. Cambridge University Press.

Alexander, Jeffrey C. and Smith, Philip. 2010. "The Strong Program: Origins, Achievements, and Prospects," pp. 13–24 in J. R. Hall, L. Grindstaff, and M.-C. Lo (Eds.), *Handbook of Cultural Sociology*. London. Routledge.

Alexander, Jeffrey C. and Smith, Philip. 2019. "The Strong Program: Meaning First," pp. 13–22 in L. Grindstaff, M.-C. M. Lo, and J. R. Hall (Eds.), *Handbook of Cultural Sociology*, 2nd edn. Abingdon. Routledge.

Alexander, Jeffrey C. and Tognato, Carlo (Eds.). 2018. *The Civil Sphere in Latin America*. Cambridge. Cambridge University Press.

Alpert, Harry. 1961. *Emile Durkheim and His Sociology*. New York. Russell and Russell.

Alpert, Harry. 1976. "Durkheim's Functional Theory of Ritual," pp. 137–41 in R. Nisbet (Ed.), *Emile Durkheim*. Westport. Greenwood Press.

Atkinson, J. Maxwell. 1978. *Discovering Suicide*. London. Palgrave Macmillan.

Austin, John L. 1962. *How to do Things with Words*. Oxford. Clarendon Press.

Baiocchi, Gianpaolo. 2006. "The Civilizing Force of Social Movements: Corporate and Liberal Codes in Brazil's Public Sphere," *Sociological Theory* 24, 4: 285–311.

Barth, Fredrik. 1954. *Political Leadership Among the Swat Pathan*. London. Athlone Press.

Bataille, Georges. 1985. *Visions of Excess: Selected Writings*. Ed. A. Stoekl. Minneapolis. University of Minnesota Press.

Bataille, Georges. 1988. *The Accursed Share: An Essay on General Economy*. New York. Zone Books.

Bauman, Zygmunt. 2005. "Durkheim's Society Revisited," pp. 360–82 in J. C. Alexander and P. Smith (Eds.), *The Cambridge Companion to Durkheim*. Cambridge. Cambridge University Press.

Beck, Ulrich. 1992. *Risk Society*. London. Sage.

Bell, Catherine. 1992. *Ritual Theory, Ritual Practice*. Cambridge. Cambridge University Press.

Bellah, Robert N. 1959. "Durkheim and History," *American Sociological Review* 24: 447–61.

Bellah, Robert N. 1970a. "Civil Religion in America," pp. 168–89 in *Beyond Belief*. New York. Harper and Row.

Bellah, Robert N. 1970b. "Between Religion and Social Science," pp. 237–57 in *Beyond Belief*. New York. Harper and Row.

Bellah, Robert N. 2005. "Durkheim and Ritual," pp. 183–210 in J. C. Alexander and P. Smith (Eds.), *The Cambridge Companion to Durkheim*. Cambridge. Cambridge University Press.

Bellah, Robert N., Madsen, Richard, Sullivan, William M., Swidler, Ann, and Tipton, Steven M. 1985. *Habits of the Heart*. Berkeley. University of California Press.

Benzecry, Claudio and Collins, Randall. 2014. "The High of Cultural Experience: Toward a Microsociology of Cultural Consumption," *Sociological Theory* 37, 4: 307–26.

Besnard, Philippe. 1983. "The *Année sociologique* Team," pp. 11–39 in P. Besnard (Ed.), *The Sociological Domain*. Cambridge. Cambridge University Press.

Besnard, Philippe. 1993. "Anomie and Fatalism in Durkheim's Theory of Regulation," pp. 163–84 in S. P. Turner (Ed.), *Emile Durkheim: Sociologist and Moralist*. London. Routledge.

Besnard, Philippe. 2005. "Durkheim's Squares: Types of Social Pathology and Types of Suicide," pp. 70–9 in J. C. Alexander and P. Smith (Eds.), *The Cambridge Companion to Durkheim*. Cambridge. Cambridge University Press.

Bogusz, Tanja and Delitz, Heike. 2013. *Émile Durkheim: Sociologie – Ethnologie – Philosophie*. Frankfurt. Campus.

Bouglé, Célestin. 1907. "Note sur le droit et le caste en Inde," *L'Année sociologique* 10: 138–68.

Bouglé, Célestin. 1971. *Essays on the Caste System*. Cambridge. Cambridge University Press.

Caillois, Roger. 1959. *Man and the Sacred*. Glencoe. Free Press.

Caillois, Roger. 1961. *Man, Play and Games*. New York. Free Press.

Cladis, Mark. 1992. *A Communitarian Defense of Liberalism: Emile Durkheim and Contemporary Social Theory*. Stanford. Stanford University Press.

Cladis, Mark. 2005. "Durkheim, Solidarity and Democracy," pp. 383–409 in J. C. Alexander and P. Smith (Eds.), *The Cambridge Companion to Durkheim*. Cambridge. Cambridge University Press.

Clifford, James. 1981. "On Ethnographic Surrealism," *Comparative Studies in Society and History* 28: 548–53.

Clifford, James and Marcus, George. 1986. *Writing Culture*. Berkeley. University of California Press.

Collins, Randall. 1975. *Conflict Sociology: Toward an Explanatory Science*. New York. Academic Press.

Collins, Randall. 1988. "The Durkheimian Tradition in Conflict Sociology," pp. 107–28 in J. C. Alexander (Ed.), *Durkheimian Sociology: Cultural Studies*. Cambridge. Cambridge University Press.

Collins, Randall. 2004. *Interaction Ritual Chains*. Princeton. Princeton University Press.

Collins, Randall. 2005. "The Durkheimian Movement in France and in World Sociology," pp. 101–35 in J. C. Alexander and P. Smith (Eds.), *The Cambridge Companion to Durkheim*. Cambridge. Cambridge University Press.

Cotterrell, Roger. 1999. *Emile Durkheim: Law in a Moral Domain*. Stanford. Stanford University Press.

Cowell, Andrew. 2002. "The Pleasures and Pains of the Gift," pp. 280–97 in M. Osteen (Ed.), *The Question of the Gift*. London. Routledge.

Cuvillier, Armand. 1953. *Où va la sociologie française?* Paris. Marcel Rivière.

Cuvillier, Armand. 1983. "Preface to the French Edition of 1955," pp. xi–xxii in E. Durkheim, *Pragmatism and Sociology*. New York. Cambridge University Press.

Davy, Georges. n.d. (*c*.1911). *Émile Durkheim: choix de textes avec étude du système sociologique*. Paris. Editions Louis-Michaud.

Debord, Guy. 1959. "The Role of Potlatch Then and Now," *Potlatch* 30. Retrieved at *Situationist International Online*, 26 January 2019. https://www.cddc.vt.edu/sionline/si/potlatch.html

Debray, Eva. 2017. "The Politics of the Individual: Luhmann Reading Durkheim," *Journal of Classical Sociology* 17, 4: 361–81.

Derrida, Jacques. 1978. "From Restricted to General Economy: A Hegelianism without Reserve," pp. 251–77 in *Writing and Difference*. Chicago. University of Chicago Press.

Derrida, Jacques. 1992. *Given Time*. Chicago. University of Chicago Press.

Doroszewski, Witold. 1933. *Quelques remarques sur les rapports de la sociologie et de la linguistique: Durkheim et F. de Saussure*. Paris. Alcan.

Douglas, Jack D. 1967. *The Social Meanings of Suicide*. Princeton. Princeton University Press.

Douglas, Mary. 1963. *The Lele of Kasai*. London. Oxford University Press.

Douglas, Mary. 1966. *Purity and Danger*. London. Routledge.

Douglas, Mary. 1970. *Natural Symbols: Explorations in Cosmology*. London. Barrie and Rockliff.

Douglas, Mary. 1978. *Cultural Bias*. London. Royal Anthropological Institute.

Douglas, Mary. 1980. *Evans-Pritchard*. Brighton. Harvester Press.

Douglas, Mary. 1985. *How Institutions Think*. Syracuse. Syracuse University Press.

Douglas, Mary and Isherwood, Baron. 1979. *The World of Goods: Towards an Anthropology of Consumption*. New York. Basic Books.

Douglas, Mary and Wildavsky, Aaron. 1982. *Risk and Culture: An Essay on the Selection of Technical and Environmental Dangers*. Berkeley. University of California Press.

Dumont, Louis. 1970. *Homo Hierarchicus*. Chicago. University of Chicago Press.

Durkheim, Émile. 1902. "Sur le totémisme," *L'Année sociologique* 5: 82–121.

Durkheim, Émile. 1905. "Sur l'organisation matrimoniale des sociétés australiennes," *L'Année sociologique* 8: 118–47.

Durkheim, Émile. 1906. "Review of Howitt: *The Native Tribes of South East Australia*," *L'Année sociologique* 9: 355–68.

Durkheim, Émile. 1911. "Jugements de valeur et jugements de réalité," *Revue de métaphysique et de morale* 3 July 1911: 99–114.

Durkheim, Émile. 1913. "Le Problème religieux et la dualité de la nature humaine," *Bulletin de la Société française de philosophie* 13: 63–75.

Durkheim, Émile. 1915. *L'Allemagne au-dessus de tout*. Paris. Librairie Armand Colin.

Durkheim, Émile. 1947. *The Division of Labor in Society*. Trans. George Simpson. Glencoe. Free Press.

Durkheim, Émile. 1952. *Suicide: A Study in Sociology*. Trans. J. Spalding and G. Simpson. London. Routledge and Kegan Paul.

Durkheim, Émile. 1956. *Education and Sociology*. Trans. S. D. Fox. Glencoe. Free Press.

Durkheim, Émile. 1957. *Professional Ethics and Civic Morals*. London. Routledge and Kegan Paul.

Durkheim, Émile. 1958. *Socialism and Saint-Simon*. Yellow Springs. Antioch Press.

Durkheim, Émile. 1964. *The Rules of Sociological Method*. New York. Free Press.

Durkheim, Émile. 1970. "L'Individualisme et les intellectuels," pp. 261–78 in *La science sociale et l'action*. Paris. Presses universitaires de France. (First published in *Revue bleue*.)

Durkheim, Émile. 1973. *Moral Education*. New York. Free Press.

Durkheim, Émile. 1974a. "The Determination of Moral Facts," pp. 35–62 in *Sociology and Philosophy*. Trans D. F. Pocock. New York. Routledge.

Durkheim, Émile. 1974b. "Value Judgments and Judgments of Reality," pp. 80–98 in *Sociology and Philosophy*. Trans D. F. Pocock. New York. Routledge.

Durkheim, Émile. 1977. *The Evolution of Educational Thought*. Trans. P. Collins. London. Routledge and Kegan Paul.

Durkheim, Émile. 1978. Review of A. Schaeffle "Bau und Leben des sozialen Korpers: Erster Band," pp. 93–114 in *Émile Durkheim on Institutional Analysis*. Trans. Mark Traugott. Chicago. University of Chicago Press.

Durkheim, Émile. 1983. *Pragmatism and Sociology*. Trans. J. C. Whitehouse. Ed. J. B. Allcock. New York. Cambridge University Press.

Durkheim, Émile. 1986a. "Review of A. Labriola: *Essais sur la conception matérialiste de l'histoire*," pp. 128–36 in *Durkheim on Politics and the State*. Ed. A. Giddens. Trans. W. D. Halls. Cambridge. Polity.

Durkheim, Émile. 1986b. "Review of Gaston Richard: *Le Socialisme et la science sociale*," pp. 121–8 in *Durkheim on Politics and the State*. Ed. A. Giddens. Trans. W. D. Halls. Cambridge. Polity.

Durkheim, Émile. 1986c. "Individualism and Freedom" [extract from "Individualism and the Intellectuals"], pp. 79–83 in *Durkheim on Politics and the State*. Ed. A. Giddens. Trans. W. D. Halls. Cambridge. Polity.

Durkheim, Émile. 1995. *The Elementary Forms of Religious Life*. Trans. Karen Fields. New York. Free Press.

Durkheim, Émile. 2009. "La Politique de demain," trans J. Mergy and W. Watts Miller, *Durkheimian Studies/Études Durkheimiennes* 5: 8–12.

Durkheim, Émile and Denis, Ernest. 1915. *Qui a voulu la guerre?* Paris. Librairie Armand Colin.

Durkheim, Émile and Mauss, Marcel. 1963. *Primitive Classification*. London. Cohen and West.

Eliot, T. S. 1916. "Durkheim," *The Westminster Gazette*, 9 August, p. 2.

Emirbayer, Mustafa. 1996. "Useful Durkheim," *Sociological Theory* 14, 2: 109–30.

Erikson, Kai. 1966. *Wayward Puritans*. New York. Macmillan.

Eulriet, I. 2010. "Durkheim and Approaches to the Study of War," *Durkheimian Studies/Études Durkheimiennes* 16: 59–76.

Evans-Pritchard, E. E. 1937. *Witchcraft, Oracles and Magic Among the Azande*. Oxford. Clarendon Press.

Evans-Pritchard, E. E. 1940. *The Nuer*. Oxford. Clarendon Press.

Evans-Pritchard, E. E. 1951a. *Social Anthropology*. London. Cohen and West.

Evans-Pritchard, E. E. 1951b. *Kinship and Marriage Among the Nuer.* Oxford. Clarendon Press.

Evans-Pritchard, E. E. 1954. "Introduction," pp. v–x in M. Mauss, *The Gift.* London. Cohen and West.

Evans-Pritchard, E. E. 1956. *Nuer Religion.* Oxford. Clarendon Press.

Evans-Pritchard, E. E. 1960. "Introduction," pp. 9–24 in R. Hertz, *Death and the Right Hand.* London. Cohen and West.

Evans-Pritchard, E. E. and Fortes, Meyer (Eds.). 1940. *African Political Systems.* London. African Institute.

Fardon, Richard. 1999. *Mary Douglas: An Intellectual Biography.* London. Routledge.

Fauconnet, Paul. 1920. *La Responsibilité: étude de sociologie.* Paris. Alcan.

Fauconnet, Paul and Mauss, Marcel. 1901. "La Sociologie: objet et méthod," pp. 165–75 in *Le Grande encyclopédie,* vol. 30. Paris. Société anonyme de la Grande Encyclopédie.

Fields, Karen. 2005. "What Difference Does Translation Make? *Les Formes élementaires de la vie religieuse* in French and English," pp. 160–82 in J. C. Alexander and P. Smith (Eds.), *The Cambridge Companion to Durkheim.* Cambridge. Cambridge University Press.

Fine, Gary Alan. 2005. "Interaction Ritual Chains: Review," *Social Forces* 83, 3: 1287–8.

Firth, Raymond. 1936. *We the Tikopia.* London. Allen and Unwin.

Firth, Raymond. 1957. "Introduction: Malinowski as Scientist and as Man," pp. 1–14 in Firth (Ed.), *Man and Culture: An Evaluation of the Work of Bronislaw Malinowski.* London. Routledge and Kegan Paul.

Fournier, Marcel. 2005. "Durkheim's Life and Context: Something New about Durkheim," pp. 41–69 in J. C. Alexander and P. Smith (Eds.), *The Cambridge Companion to Durkheim.* Cambridge. Cambridge University Press.

Fournier, Marcel. 2013. *Émile Durkheim: A Biography.* Cambridge. Polity.

Frazer, James. 1940. *The Golden Bough.* New York. Macmillan.

Fuchs Epstein, Cynthia. 2010. "The Contributions of Robert K. Merton to Culture Theory," pp. 79–93 in C. Calhoun (Ed.), *Robert K. Merton.* New York. Columbia University Press.

Gane, Mike. 1983. "Durkheim: Woman as Outsider," *Economy and Society* 12, 2: 227–70.

Gane, Mike. 1988. *On Durkheim's Rules of Sociological Method.* London. Routledge.

Gane, Mike (Ed.). 1992. *The Radical Sociology of Durkheim and Mauss.* London. Routledge.

Gane, Mike. 2009. "The Paradox of Neoliberalism," *Durkheimian Studies/ Études Durkheimiennes* 15: 2–25.

Garfinkel, Harold. 2002. *Ethnomethodology's Program: Working Out Durkheim's Aphorism.* Ed. A. Rawls. Lanham. Rowman and Littlefield.

Garland, David. 1990. *Punishment and Modern Society.* Chicago. University of Chicago Press.

Geary, David C. 2010. *Male, Female: The Evolution of Human Sex Differences,* 2nd edn. Washington, DC. American Psychological Association.

Geertz, Clifford. 1973. *The Interpretation of Cultures.* New York. Basic Books.

Gephart, Werner and Witte, David. 2017. *The Sacred and the Law.* Frankfurt. Klostermann.

Gerhardt, Uta. 2002. *Talcott Parsons: An Intellectual Biography*. Cambridge. Cambridge University Press.

Giddens, Anthony. 1978. *Durkheim*. London. Fontana/Collins.

Giddens, Anthony (Ed.). 1986. *Durkheim on Politics and the State*. Cambridge. Polity.

Girard, René. 2005. *Violence and the Sacred*. London. Continuum.

Gluckman, Max. 1954. *Rituals of Rebellion*. Manchester. Manchester University Press.

Gofman, Alexander. 2000. "The Reception of *Suicide* in Russia," pp. 126–32 in W. S. F. Pickering and G. Walford (Eds.), *Durkheim's Suicide: A Century of Research and Debate*. London. Routledge.

Goffman, Erving. 1967. *Interaction Ritual*. New York. Doubleday.

Gouldner, Alvin. 1970. *The Coming Crisis of Western Sociology*. New York. Basic Books.

Grusky, David and Galescu, Gabriela. 2005. "Is Durkheim a Class Analyst?" pp. 322–59 in J. C. Alexander and P. Smith (Eds.), *The Cambridge Companion to Durkheim*. Cambridge. Cambridge University Press.

Habermas, Jürgen. 1987. *The Theory of Communicative Action. Vol. 2: The Critique of Functionalist Reason*. Cambridge. Polity.

Haidt, Jonathan. 2012. *The Righteous Mind*. New York. Knopf.

Haidt, Jonathan and Graham, Jesse. 2009. "Planet of the Durkheimians: Where Community, Authority and Sacredness are the Foundations of Morality," pp. 371–401 in J. Jost, A. Kay, and H. Thorisdottir (Eds.), *Social and Psychological Bases of Ideology and System Justification*. Oxford. Oxford University Press.

Halbwachs, Maurice. 1980. *The Collective Memory*. New York. Harper and Row.

Healy, Kieran. 2017. "Foreword," pp. ix–xviii in V. Zelizer, *Morals and Markets*. New York. Columbia University Press.

Heilbron, Johan. 2015. *French Sociology*. Ithaca. Cornell University Press.

Heritage, John. 1984. *Garfinkel and Ethnomethodology*. Cambridge. Polity.

Hertz, Robert. 1960. *Death and the Right Hand*. Trans. R. and C. Needham. London. Cohen and West.

Hertz, Robert. 2002. *Un Ethnologue dans les tranchées*. Eds. A. Riley and P. Besnard. Paris. CNRS Éditions.

Hilbert, Richard. 1992. *The Classical Roots of Ethnomethodology: Durkheim, Weber and Garfinkel*. Chapel Hill. University of North Carolina Press.

Hubert, Henri and Mauss, Marcel. 1964. *Sacrifice: Its Nature and Functions*. Trans. W. D. Halls. Chicago. University of Chicago Press.

Hubert, Henri and Mauss, Marcel. 2001. *Toward a General Theory of Magic*. London. Routledge.

Huizinga, Johan. 1949. *Homo Ludens*. London. Routledge and Kegan Paul.

Huvelin, Paul. 1907. "La Magie et droit individual," *L'Année sociologique* 10: 1–47.

Jacobs, Ronald N. 2000. *Race, Media and the Crisis of Civil Society*. Cambridge. Cambridge University Press.

Joas, Hans. 1993. "Durkheim's Intellectual Development," pp. 223–38 in S. P. Turner (Ed.), *Emile Durkheim: Sociologist and Moralist*. London. Routledge.

Joas, Hans. 2000. *The Genesis of Values*. Chicago. University of Chicago Press.

Joas, Hans. 2013. *The Sacredness of the Person*. Washington, DC. Georgetown University Press.

Jones, Robert Alun. 1993. "Durkheim and *La Cité antique*," pp. 23–50 in S. P. Turner (Ed.), *Emile Durkheim: Sociologist and Moralist*. London. Routledge.

Jones, Robert Alun. 1999. *The Development of Durkheim's Social Realism*. Cambridge. Cambridge University Press.

Jones, Robert Alun. 2005. "Practices and Presuppositions: Some Questions about Durkheim and *Les Formes élementaries de la via religieuse*," pp. 80–100 in J. C. Alexander and P. Smith (Eds.), *The Cambridge Companion to Durkheim*. Cambridge. Cambridge University Press.

Kahan, Dan M., Jenkins-Smith, Hank, and Braman, Donald. 2011. "Cultural Cognition of Scientific Consensus," *Journal of Risk Research* 14, 2: 147–74.

Karady, Victor. 1981. "The Prehistory of French Sociology," pp. 3–47 in C. Lemert (Ed.), *French Sociology: Rupture and Renewal Since 1968*. New York: Columbia University Press.

Katz, Elihu and Dayan, Daniel. 1992. *Media Events*. Cambridge, MA. Harvard University Press.

Kertzer, David. 1988. *Ritual, Politics and Power*. New Haven. Yale University Press.

König, René. 1976. "Emile Durkheim: Der Soziologe als Moralist," pp. 312–64 in D. Käsler (Ed.), *Klassiker des Soziologischen Denkens*, vol. 1. Munich. Beck.

König, René. 2013. *Zur Bestimmung der französichen Soziologie in Deutschland*. Wiesbaden. Springer.

Kuper, Hilda. 1984. "Function, History, Biography: Reflections on Fifty Years in the British Anthropological Tradition," pp. 192–213 in G. W. Stocking (Ed.), *Functionalism Historicized: Essays on British Social Anthropology*. Madison. University of Wisconsin Press.

Kurakin, Dmitry. 2015. "Reassembling the Ambiguity of the Sacred," *Journal of Classical Sociology* 15, 4: 377–95.

Lamont, Michèle. 1992. *Money, Morals, and Manners: The Culture of the French and American Upper-Middle Class*. Chicago. University of Chicago Press.

Lamont, Michèle. 2000. *The Dignity of Working Men*. Cambridge, MA. Harvard University Press.

Lamont, Michèle and Fournier, Marcel (Eds.). 1992. *Cultivating Differences*. Chicago. University of Chicago Press.

Lapie, Paul. 1908. *La Femme dans la famille*. Paris. O. Doin.

Leach, Edmund. 1954. *Political Systems of Highland Burma*. Cambridge, MA. Harvard University Press.

Leach, Edmund. 1970. *Lévi-Strauss*. London. Fontana.

Leach, Edmund. 1983. *Structuralist Interpretation of Biblical Myth*. Cambridge. Cambridge University Press.

Lehmann, Jennifer M. 1993. *Deconstructing Durkheim*. London. Routledge.

Leiris, Michel. 1934. *L'Afrique fantôme*. Paris. Gallimard.

Leiris, Michel. 1988. "The Sacred in Everyday Life," pp. 24–31 in D. Hollier (Ed.), *The College of Sociology 1937–39*. Minneapolis. University of Minnesota Press.

Lemert, Charles. 1981. "Reading French Sociology," pp. 3–32 in C. Lemert (Ed.), *French Sociology: Rupture and Renewal Since 1968*. New York. Columbia University Press.

Lévi-Strauss, Claude. 1963a. *Totemism*. Boston. Beacon Books.

Lévi-Strauss, Claude. 1963b. *Structural Anthropology*. New York. Basic Books.

Lévi-Strauss, Claude. 1966a. "The Scope of Anthropology," *Current Anthropology* 7, 2: 112–23.

Lévi-Strauss, Claude. 1966b. *The Savage Mind.* Chicago. University of Chicago Press.

Lévi-Strauss, Claude. 1969a. *The Raw and the Cooked.* New York. Harper and Row.

Lévi-Strauss, Claude. 1969b. *The Elementary Structures of Kinship.* Boston. Beacon Press.

Lévi-Strauss, Claude. 1973. *Anthropologie structurale deux.* Paris. Plon.

Lévi-Strauss, Claude. 1985. *The View from Afar.* Oxford. Blackwell

Lévi-Strauss, Claude. 1987. *Introduction to the Work of Marcel Mauss.* London. Routledge.

Lévy-Bruhl, Lucien. 1925. "L'Institut d'ethnologie de l'université de Paris," *Revue d'ethnologie et des tribes populaires* 23, 4: 1–4.

Lienhardt, Godfrey. 1961. *Divinity and Experience: The Religion of the Dinka.* Oxford. Oxford University Press.

Lockwood, David. 1992. *Solidarity and Schism.* Oxford. Clarendon Press.

Luhmann, Niklas. 1982. "Durkheim on Morality and the Division of Labor," pp. 3–19 in *The Differentiation of Society.* New York. Columbia University Press.

Lukes, Steven. 1973. *Emile Durkheim: His Life and Work.* London. Allen Lane.

Lukes, Steven. 1975. "Political Ritual and Social Integration," *Sociology* 9, 2: 290–307.

Lukes, Steven. 2009. "The Current Crisis: Initial Reflections," *Durkheimian Studies/Études Durkheimiennes* 15: 15–19.

Malinowski, Bronisław. 1962. *The Sexual Lives of Savages.* New York. Harcourt Brace.

Malinowski, Bronisław. 1965. *Coral Gardens and Their Magic.* Bloomington. Indiana University Press.

Malinowski, Bronisław. 1966. *Argonauts of the Western Pacific.* London. Routledge and Kegan Paul.

Mallard, Grégoire. 2018. "The Gift as Colonial Ideology?" *Journal of International Political Theory* 14, 2: 183–202.

Marica, George E. 1932. *Emile Durkheim: Soziologie und Soziologismus.* Jena. Gustav Fischer.

Mast, Jason L. 2017. "Jeffrey C. Alexander," pp. 375–86 in R. Stones (Ed.), *Key Sociological Thinkers.* New York. Palgrave.

Mast, Jason L. 2018. *The Performative Presidency: Crisis and Resurrection During the Clinton Years.* Cambridge. Cambridge University Press.

Mauss, Marcel. 1950. *Sociologie et anthropologie.* Paris. Presses universitaires de France.

Mauss, Marcel. 1954. *The Gift.* Trans. I. Cunnison. London. Cohen and West.

Mauss, Marcel. 1973. "Techniques of the Body," *Economy and Society* 2, 1: 70–88.

Mauss, Marcel. 2013. *La Nation.* Paris. Presses universitaires de France.

Mauss, Marcel and Beuchat, Henri. 1979. *Seasonal Variations of the Eskimo: A Study in Social Morphology.* Trans. J. J. Fox. New York. Routledge.

McCormick, Lisa. 2015. *Performing Civility.* Cambridge. Cambridge University Press.

McNeil, William H. 1995. *Keeping Time Together*. Cambridge, MA. Harvard University Press.

Merton, Robert K. 1934. "Recent French Sociology," *Social Forces* 12: 537–45.

Merton, Robert K. 1957a. "Social Structure and Anomie," pp. 131–60 in *Social Theory and Social Structure*. Glencoe. Free Press.

Merton, Robert K. 1957b. "Continuities in the Theory of the Social Structure and Anomie," pp. 161–94 in *Social Theory and Social Structure*. Glencoe. Free Press.

Merton, Robert K. 1957c. *Social Theory and Social Structure*. Glencoe. Free Press.

Merton, Robert K. 1976. "Durkheim's Division of Labor in Society," pp. 105–12 in R. A. Nisbet (Ed.), *Emile Durkheim*. Westport. Greenwood Press.

Meštrović, Stjepan. 1992. *Durkheim and Postmodern Culture*. New York. Routledge.

Miller, Daniel. 1999. *A Theory of Shopping*. Cambridge. Polity.

Moebius, Stephan. 2006. *Die Zauberlehrlinge: Soziologiegeschichte des Collège de Sociologie*. Konstanz. Konstanz Universitätsverlag.

Moebius, Stephan. 2020. "Sociology of the Sacred," in H. Joas and A. Pettenhofer (Eds.), *The Oxford Handbook of Durkheim*. Oxford. Oxford University Press.

Moebius, Stephan and Nungesser, Frithjof. 2013. "'La Filiation est direct': Der Einfluss von Marcel Mauss auf das Werk von Claud Lévi-Strauss," *European Journal of Sociology* 54, 2: 231–63.

Needham, Rodney. 1963. "Introduction," pp. vii–xlviii in E. Durkheim and M. Mauss, *Primitive Classification*. London. Cohen and West.

Needham, Rodney (Ed.). 1973. *Right and Left: Essays on Dual Symbolic Classification*. Chicago. University of Chicago Press.

Nisbet, Robert. 1952. "Conservatism and Sociology," *American Journal of Sociology* 58, 2: 167–75.

Nisbet, Robert. 1975. *The Sociology of Emile Durkheim*. London. Heinemann.

Nisbet, Robert (Ed.). 1976. *Emile Durkheim*. Westport. Greenwood Press.

Nizan, Paul. 1981. *Les Chiens de garde*. Paris. François Maspero.

Norton, Matthew. 2014. "Classification and Coercion: The Destruction of Piracy in the English Maritime System," *American Journal of Sociology* 119, 6: 1537–75.

Osteen, Mark (Ed.). 2002. *The Question of the Gift*. London. Routledge.

Parkin, Frank. 1992. *Emile Durkheim*. Oxford. Oxford University Press.

Parsons, Talcott. 1949. *The Structure of Social Action*. New York. Free Press.

Parsons, Talcott. 1952. *The Social System*. London. Tavistock.

Parsons, Talcott. 1968. "Emile Durkheim," p. 314 in *International Encyclopedia of the Social Sciences*, vol 4. New York. Macmillan and Free Press.

Parsons, Talcott and Shils, Edward (Eds.). 1962. *Toward a General Theory of Action*. New York. Harper and Row.

Parsons, Talcott and Smelser, Neil J. 1956. *Economy and Society*. London. Routledge and Kegan Paul.

Pearce, Frank. 1989. *The Radical Durkheim*. London. Unwin Hyman.

Pickering, William S. F. and Martins, Herminio (Eds.). 1994. *Debating Durkheim*. London. Routledge.

Pollner, Melvin. 1987. *Mundane Reason*. New York. Cambridge University Press.

Price, Sally and Jamin, Jean. 1988. "A Conversation with Michel Leiris," *Current Anthropology* 29, 1: 157–74.

Radcliffe-Brown, Alfred R. 1952. *Structure and Function in Primitive Society.* London. Cohen and West.

Rawls, Anne Warfield. 2001. "Durkheim's Treatment of Practice: Concrete Practice vs. Representation as the Foundation of Reason," *Journal of Classical Sociology* 1: 33–68.

Reed, Isaac A. 2013. "Charismatic Performance: A Study of Bacon's Rebellion," *American Journal of Cultural Sociology* 1, 2: 254–87.

Richard, Gaston. 1897. *Le Socialisme et la science sociale.* Paris. Alcan.

Richard, Gaston. 1898. Review of Emile Durkheim, *Le Suicide, L'Annee sociologique* 1: 404–5.

Riley, Alexander T. 2005. "Durkheim, the Sacred and Transgression," pp. 274–301 in J. C. Alexander and P. Smith (Eds.), *The Cambridge Companion to Durkheim.* Cambridge. Cambridge University Press.

Riley, Alexander T. 2013. *Godless Intellectuals.* New York. Berghahn Books.

Riley, Alexander T. 2015. *The Social Thought of Emile Durkheim.* London. Sage.

Riley, Alexander T., Pickering, W. S. F., and Watts Miller, William. 2013. *Durkheim, Durkheimians and the Arts.* New York. Berghahn Books.

Schwartz, Barry. 1967. "The Social Psychology of the Gift," *American Journal of Sociology* 73, 1: 1–11.

Schwartz, Barry. 1981. *Vertical Classification: A Study in Structuralism and the Sociology of Knowledge.* Chicago. University of Chicago Press.

Schwartz, Barry. 1983. "George Washington and the Whig Conception of Heroic Leadership," *American Sociological Review* 48, 1: 18–33.

Schwartz, Barry. 1991. "Social Change and Collective Memory: The Democratization of George Washington," *American Sociological Review* 56, 2: 221–36.

Schwartz, Barry. 2000. *Abraham Lincoln and the Forge of National Memory.* Chicago. University of Chicago Press.

Selvin, Hanan C. 1958. "Durkheim's *Suicide* and Problems of Empirical Research," *American Journal of Sociology* 63, 6: 607–19.

Shilling, Chris. 2005. "Embodiment, Emotions and the Foundations of Social Order: Durkheim's Enduring Contribution," pp. 211–38 in J. C. Alexander and P. Smith (Eds.), *The Cambridge Companion to Durkheim.* Cambridge. Cambridge University Press.

Shilling, Chris and Mellor, Philip A. 1998. "Durkheim, Morality and Modernity: Collective Effervescence, *Homo Duplex* and the Sources of Moral Action," *British Journal of Sociology* 49, 2: 193–209.

Shils, Edward. 1975. *Center and Periphery.* Chicago. University of Chicago Press.

Shils, Edward and Young, Michael. 1953. "The Meaning of the Coronation," *The Sociological Review* 1, 2: 63–81.

Simiand, François. 1902. "Essai sur le prix du charbon en France au XIXe siècle," *L'Année sociologique* 5: 1–81.

Simiand, François. 1903. "Methode historique et science social," *Revue de synthèse historique* 6: 1–22 and 129–57.

Smelser, Neil. 1959. *Social Change in the Industrial Revolution.* Chicago. University of Chicago Press.

Smith, Philip. 1998a. "Barbarism and Civility in the Discourses of Fascism,

231

Communism and Democracy: Variations on a Set of Themes," pp. 115–37 in J. C. Alexander (Ed.), *Real Civil Societies*. London: Sage.

Smith, Philip (Ed.). 1998b. *The New American Cultural Sociology*. Cambridge. Cambridge University Press.

Smith, Philip. 2005. *Why War?* Chicago. University of Chicago Press.

Smith, Philip. 2008a. *Punishment and Culture*. Chicago. University of Chicago Press.

Smith, Philip. 2008b. "Durkheim and Criminology: Reconstructing the Legacy," *Australia and New Zealand Journal of Criminology* 41, 3: 333–44.

Smith, Philip. 2014a. "Of Near Pollution and Non-Linear Cultural Effects: Reflections on Masahiro Mori and the Uncanny Valley," *American Journal of Cultural Sociology* 2: 329–47.

Smith, Philip. 2014b. "The Cost of Collaboration," *Anthropological Quarterly* 87, 1: 245–54.

Smith, William Robertson. 2002. *Religion of the Semites*. New Brunswick. Transaction Books.

Sorel, Georges. 1895. "Les Théories de M. Durkheim," *Le Devenir* 1: 1–15, 148–80.

Spencer, Baldwin and Gillen, F. J. 1899. *The Native Tribes of Central Australia*. London. Macmillan.

Sperber, Dan. 1975. *Rethinking Symbolism*. Cambridge. Cambridge University Press.

Spickard, James. 1989. "A Guide to Mary Douglas's Three Versions of Grid/ Group Theory," *Sociological Analysis* 50, 2: 151–70.

Spillman, Lyn. 1991. *Nation and Commemoration*. Cambridge. Cambridge University Press.

Spillman, Lyn. 2012. *Solidarity in Strategy: Making Business Meaningful in American Trade Associations*. Chicago. University of Chicago Press.

Srinivas, M. N. 1952. *Religion and Society Among the Coorgs*. Oxford. Clarendon Press.

Srinivas, M. N. 1962. *Caste in Modern India and Other Essays*. London. JK.

Steiner, Philippe. 2011. *Durkheim and the Birth of Economic Sociology*. Princeton. Princeton University Press.

Stocking, George W. 1984. "Radcliffe-Brown and British Social Anthropology," pp. 131–91 in G. W. Stocking (Ed.), *Functionalism Historicized: Essays on British Social Anthropology*. Madison. University of Wisconsin Press.

Strenski, Ivan. 2006. *The New Durkheim*. New Brunswick. Rutgers University Press.

Swidler, Ann. 1986. "Culture in Action: Symbols and Strategies," *American Sociological Review* 51, 2: 273–86.

Thompson, Kenneth. 2002. *Emile Durkheim*. London. Routledge.

Thompson, Michael, Ellis, Richard, and Wildavsky, Aaron. 1990. *Cultural Theory*. Boulder. Westview Press.

Tilly, Charles. 1981. "Useless Durkheim," pp. 95–108 in *As Sociology Meets History*. New York. Academic Press.

Tiryakian, Edward. 1979. "L'École Durkheimienne à la recherche de la société perdue: la sociologie naissante et son milieu culturel," *Cahiers internationaux de sociologie* 66: 97–114.

Tiryakian, Edward. 1995. "Collective Effervescence, Social Change and Charisma: Durkheim, Weber and 1989," *International Sociology* 10: 269–81.

Tiryakian, Edward. 2009. "Durkheim's Reflections on the Crisis: But Which One?" *Durkheimian Studies/Études Durkheimiennes* 15: 26–38.

Turner, Jonathan and Maryanski, Alexandra R. 1988. "Is Neofunctionalism Really Functional?" *Sociological Theory* 6, 1: 110–21.

Turner, Stephen. 1986. *The Search for a Methodology of Social Science.* Dordrecht. Reidel.

Turner, Stephen (Ed.). 1993. *Emile Durkheim: Sociologist and Moralist.* London. Routledge.

Turner, Victor. 1969. *The Ritual Process.* Chicago. Aldine.

Vierkandt, Alfred (Ed.). 1931. *Handwörterbuch der Soziologie.* Stuttgart. Enke.

Wagner-Pacifici, Robin. 1986. *The Moro Morality Play: Terrorism as Social Drama.* Chicago. University of Chicago Press.

Wagner-Pacifici, Robin and Schwartz, Barry. 1991. "The Vietnam Veterans Memorial: Commemorating a Difficult Past," *American Journal of Sociology* 97, 2: 376–420.

Wallwork, Ernest. 1972. *Durkheim: Morality and Milieu.* Cambridge, MA. Harvard University Press.

Warner, W. Lloyd. 1959. *The Living and the Dead.* New Haven. Yale University Press.

Warner, W. Lloyd. 1963. *Yankee City.* New Haven. Yale University Press.

Warner, W. Lloyd and Lunt, Paul S. 1941. *The Social Life of a Modern Community.* New Haven. Yale University Press.

Watts Miller, William. 1996. *Durkheim, Morals and Modernity.* London. UCL Press.

Watts Miller, William. 2012. *A Durkheimian Quest.* New York. Berghahn Books.

Weiss, Raquel. 2019. "Between the Spirit and the Letter: Durkheimian Theory in the Cultural Sociology of Jeffrey Alexander," *Sociologia et Antropologia* 9, 1: 85–109.

Wherry, Frederick F. 2012. *The Culture of Markets.* Cambridge. Polity.

Wildavsky, Aaron. 1998. *Cultural Social Theory.* New Brunswick. Transaction Press.

Wilson, Bryan R. (Ed.) 1979. *Rationality.* Oxford. Blackwell.

Woodward, Ian. 2007. *Understanding Material Culture.* London. Sage.

Zelizer, Viviana. 1985. *Pricing the Priceless Child.* Princeton. Princeton University Press.

Zelizer, Viviana. 1994. *The Social Meanings of Money.* New York. Basic Books.

Zelizer, Viviana. 2017. *Morals and Markets.* New York. Columbia University Press.

Zúquete, José Pedro. 2007. *Missionary Politics in Contemporary Europe.* Syracuse. Syracuse University Press.

Index

Page numbers in **bold** indicate where a key idea, thinker, or text is introduced or given extended treatment. Often there is a basic explanation or definition nearby.